Maurice F. Villeré is the author of *Successful Personal Selling Through TA* (Prentice-Hall, 1980). He has an extensive academic and professional training in organizational behavior and has written numerous articles and papers in the field of organizational management. He has also conducted numerous training programs and workshops in the organizational behavior area. A former N.D.E.A. Title IV Fellow, Maurice F. Villeré has a Ph.D. in labor and industrial relations from the University of Illinois.

Maurice F. Villeré

A Guide for Business
and Professional People

Transactional Analysis at Work

A SPECTRUM BOOK

PRENTICE-HALL, INC. Englewood Cliffs, N.J. 07632

Library of Congress Cataloging in Publication Data

Villeré, Maurice F.
Transactional analysis at work.

(A Spectrum Book)
Bibliography: p.
Includes index.
1. Organizational behavior.   2. Organizational effectiveness.   3. Transactional
analysis.   I. Title.
HD58.7.V54   658.3'001'9   81–11905
                                      AACR2

ISBN 0-13-928150-9
ISBN 0-13-928143-6 [PBK.]

Material from Villeré/Duet, *Successful Personal Selling Through* TA, © 1980 is reprinted by permission of Prentice-Hall, Inc., Englewood Cliffs, New Jersey.

This Spectrum Book is available to businesses and organizations
at a special discount when ordered in large quantities. For
information, contact Prentice-Hall, Inc., General Book Marketing,
Special Sales Division, Englewood Cliffs, N.J. 07632.

Prentice-Hall International, Inc., *London*
Prentice-Hall of Australia Pty. Limited, *Sydney*
Prentice-Hall of Canada, Ltd., *Toronto*
Prentice-Hall of India Private Limited, *New Delhi*
Prentice-Hall of Japan, Inc., *Tokyo*
Prentice-Hall of Southeast Asia Pte. Ltd., *Singapore*
Whitehall Books Limited, *Wellington, New Zealand*

CONTENTS

PREFACE

Transactional Analysis at Work: A Guide for Business and Professional People is a unique and exciting book for anyone interested in learning more about how organizations function at all levels and what specific steps can be taken to improve conditions on the personal, departmental, or corporate level.

The purpose of this book is to provide a comprehensive and practical approach to organizational behavior through transactional analysis. Through reading this book, the reader (whether college student, corporate executive, office clerk, or government administrator) will be in a better position to understand and to adjust to the inner workings of organizational life at the individual, interpersonal, group, or organizational level.

Organizations are complex behavioral entities involving a multiplicity of considerations, from individual differences in personality and needs to group problem-solving methods, ways of communication, and leadership modes. In addition, there are such organizational level factors as rules and regulations, politics, behavioral climate, and general "red tape." *Transactional Analysis at Work: A Guide for Business and Professional People* will help you successfully cope with these problems and many more.

It is written in a style and format everyone can understand and benefit from. Concepts and theories are generously blended with down-to-earth, practical examples and exercises that can be done by oneself or with friends. Traditionally, the field of organizational behavior has been burdened with academic rhetoric and material that is sometimes difficult for even a Ph.D. to understand. This book is not designed as an academic exercise. It is designed to give you, the practicing organizational member—whether you are a top level executive or a first line supervisor—tools you can apply tomorrow, the next day, and on and on whenever there are problems to be solved or conflicts to be dealt with.

Concepts and exercises have been successfully tested through numerous workshops with a great variety of organizational types from maintenance foremen to high-level executives. At last, here is the practical, no-nonsense book on organizational behavior so many have asked for. It will be of great benefit to you.

ACKNOWLEDGMENTS

To Marilyn, for her patience, friendship, and love.
To John Hunger, Dean Karrel, Lou-Ann Leahy, and all the
    Prentice-Hall family for their support and help.
To Kathy Ackermann for another great typing job.
To my parents, my family, and my in-laws.
To Patsy Maloney, Michael Giroir, and Richard Arellano
    for their consultation and advice.

TRANSACTIONAL ANALYSIS
History, Popularity, and Relevance to Organizational Behavior

1

Although it has only recently come into use as an organizational and business tool, Transactional Analysis (TA) has long enjoyed a tremendous amount of popularity and success. Research indicates that the first planned application of Transactional Analysis in a business organization took place in 1969 (1).

TA continues to gain in popularity (2). Blue chip companies and organizations that have employed TA include J. Ray McDermott & Co., Inc., Bank of America, Westinghouse Electric Corporation, United Gas, Inc., American Airlines, Questor Corp., Sears, Roebuck and Company, the American Express Company, IBM, the American Heart Association, Pan American World Airways, and the New York Telephone Company (3).

Participants in TA training programs have included all organizational levels from top management to rank-and-file employees (4). They have covered a wide variety of job disciplines from marketing managers and engineers to flight service personnel and credit interviewers (5).

The interest in TA as a viable and productive organizational tool is budding, rather than waning, on both pragmatic and theoretical fronts. On the front page of the January 9, 1979 *Wall Street Journal*, it was indicated that more firms were turning to Transactional Analysis as a training technique (6). Recent editions of textbooks on organizational behavior are beginning to include readings, chapters, or chapter sections on TA for the first time. Transactional Analysis is currently taught in more than 1,000 colleges and universities in a variety of departments including business administration, psychology, and law (7).

Like many business and organizational tools, TA has its origins in psychotherapy. The founder of TA, the late Eric Berne (1910–1970), was a psychiatrist who practiced in the San Francisco area until his death. Berne began developing TA theory in 1949 and wrote a number of articles on TA that were published in psychology journals in the late 1950s. In 1961 he wrote the first textbook on the subject, *Transactional Analysis in Psychotherapy: A Systematic Individual and Social Psychiatry* (8), and in 1964 he wrote the very popular text, *Games People Play: The Psychology of Human Relationships* (9). In 1967 another psychiatrist, Thomas Harris, popularized TA with his book, *I'm Okay— You're Okay: A Practical Guide to Transactional Analysis* (10). Probably the best basic book on the subject, however, was written by two women, Muriel James and Dorothy Jongeward. The name of their book is *Born to Win: Transactional Analysis with Gestalt Experiments* (1971) (11). This book is comprehensive and easy to read. It also gives a lot of practical self-help examples. For those who want to follow up further on the general field of Transactional Analysis, the author also heartily recommends *The Total Handbook of Transactional Analysis* (1979) by Stan Woollams and Michael Brown (12).

An early student of Eric Berne, Muriel James reminisces about the founder of TA:

> I saw Eric as responsible, brilliant, shy, fun to be with, and very clever, both personally and professionally. . . .
> Eric loved children including the Child in his clients and colleagues. Although his Adult was clearly the executive, his own Child was often active, especially when he danced or banged away on his son's drums. Furthermore, when leading the TA seminars he often used some of his hard-working Parent (13).

Eric Berne developed Transactional Analysis for a number of reasons. He felt that traditional psychotherapy, particularly Freudian therapy, which was popular at the time he began writing in TA, was too slow a process. As research indicates today, people overcome their emotional ills as quickly through the normal process of maturing as they do if they undergo traditional psychoanalysis. Additionally, Berne was concerned about the academic rhetoric of earlier psychological theories. He felt that if we are going to use these concepts with everyday, ordinary people; why not use an everyday, ordinary language?

Basically, Transactional Analysis is a communication-based theory. Berne developed it by watching people interact. He noticed that sometimes people act like children, sometimes like adults, and sometimes like parents. He noticed that sometimes people play communications games with each other and don't come off straight; they often have ulterior reasons and messages for their behavior. There are transactions in which people further communications through complementary behaviors. At other times they cross each other up in their communications by working against each other. Berne became aware of a life script that each person begins to write at an early age, one that determines destiny and accomplishments. The great writers are very sensitive to such life scripts and portray vividly how some scripts are tragic, leading to the downfall of the individual. Some are even suicidal. Others lead to the fulfillment and development of the individual, as they give the person options to grow and develop as he or she would wish.

In TA there are four fields of study and practice: (1) Personality Analysis, the study of ego states; (2) Transactional Analysis (which is the namesake for this practical science), the study of communication lines between people; (3) Time Structuring, the study of time utilization (which includes game playing); and (4) Script Analysis, the study of role development.

In order to professionally perpetuate its theory and philosophy, Eric Berne began the first TA Seminar in 1958 at his Washington Street apartment in San Francisco. Only six people attended his first professional exchange of ideas and documentation on the subject. By 1964 practitioners and followers of TA had grown extensively, with members in many of the fifty states as well as England, Canada, and Costa Rica. In this same year the International Transactional Analysis Association (ITAA) was formed. Headquartered in San Francisco (1772 Vallejo Street), the ITAA is the official organ of educational and training data on TA. It publishes an international journal, the *Transactional Analysis*

Journal, conducts two annual conferences, and can answer any questions on educational and training opportunities and standards.

The four areas of study are discussed in detail in chapter two. For now I explore the relevance of TA to organizational behavior. This exploration will help explain TA's immense success, popularity, and suitability as a behavioral tool for organizations.

1. *TA provides a unifying and concrete language that cuts across all the levels of analysis or concern in organizations: the individual, interpersonal, group, and organizational.*

One of the biggest stumbling blocks to understanding behavior in organizations is due to semantics, mainly as a result of the levels of analysis issue. Except for very small operations, like one- or two-man firms, organizations are very complex entities from a behavioral viewpoint. To fully appreciate how they function, one has to be somewhat fluent in the vernacular of each organizational entity or collectivity of individuals involved, whether the collectivity consists of a single person (the individual level), a handful of people to a few dozen in a given department (the group level), or hundreds and thousands of people forming many departments in combination (the organizational level).*

Each level has problems and issues peculiar to itself. Individual level issues might include such factors as differences in personality, perception, ability, self-esteem, motivation, etc. Individual level concerns such as these often fall under the discipline of psychology.

"Why does he or she behave this way on the job? Why is her morale so low? What can I do to increase individual performance? How can I get him or her to respect authority?" These are the kinds of questions that particularly puzzle and challenge the industrial psychologist and his or her business counterpart—the manager or supervisor.

Once an individual is placed in a group setting—once he or she must work with other individuals in order to achieve certain objectives or goals—other behavioral phenomena begin to play a significant role. Individuals acting alone function very differently from those acting in concert. Factors such as group norms or standards of conduct, the size of the group, group sanctions or ways and means of keeping mem-

---

* A more complete definition of each level of analysis will follow at the beginning of chapters introducing a given level.

bers in line, communication patterns between members (or who frequently talks to whom), and group problem-solving methods all play an important role at this level of analysis. Those with a social-psychological bent would classify such variables as a part of their umbrella of study.

The organizational level, the largest collectivity of all, deals with the broadest perspective of all. Areas of concern here often involve organizational level issues like organizational structures (who reports to whom and how many authority levels are involved), goals, technology, power relationships and politics, and economics and competitive relationships between and among departments. The sociologist, as well as top management, has a prime interest in these broad level variables.

To fully bridge the language problem that necessarily results when many types of variables and disciplines are involved requires either an enormous vocabulary or a rhetoric common to all levels.

In the March 1976 issue of the *Academy of Management Journal,* Dr. Villeré and Dr. Stearns make the following observation:

> The core course in organizational behavior is some students' first exposure to a multidisciplinary, social science approach to business. Yet, by being a relatively new field of study and by dealing with organizational problems at all levels of analysis—the individual (psychological), the group (social psychological), organizational behavior and society (anthropological and sociological)—organizational behavior invites semantic problems. Each discipline has its own definition of organizational phenomena. The psychologist may define an organization at the individual level as a decision making entity. The sociologist, who approaches the problem from a broader level, views the organization on the basis of power and the structure of relationships among people (14).

Even if an individual is gifted with an amazingly great facility for language, it still makes little sense for him or her to be constantly chasing a language "tail" that appears to grow in leaps and bounds every year as each discipline (from psychology to economics) adds more and more definitions and more and more contradictory jargon.

Unless you are a devout believer in the life complication theory (why make difficult things understandable when you can confuse them with jargon and unnecessary analysis) or a rhetorical masochist, the logical solution to the semantics problem in organizational behavior is to find a unifying language that can adequately deal with behavioral problems or issues on all levels.

Although the systems language, with broad concepts like input, thruput, and output, is frequently used to analyze any behavioral problem at any level of analysis, its terminology is too broad and too vague to serve as anything more than a framework for analysis. Granted— individuals, groups, and organizations can all be discussed in terms of inputs (data, materials, and resources) coming into them, thruputs (the processes used to convert inputs into outputs, such as machinery, chemical processes, labor, etc.) and outputs (what goes out of the system, such as finished products, services, and money). However, systems terminology is very vague and very broad.

TA, on the other hand, provides a *concrete* language tool that cuts across all levels of analysis: the individual, the interpersonal, the group, and the organizational. As you will observe, concepts such as parent, adult, or child, games, and scripts can be easily and specifically related to personal, interpersonal, group, or organizational problems. TA accomplishes no minor rhetorical feat. Here, almost miraculously, is a language vehicle that makes it possible for psychologists to speak sensibly to sociologists and economists to boot—not to mention all the other experts and job types that exist in organizations—from engineers to marketing managers.

2. *TA improves awareness of self and others with specific, concrete "handles."*

As one wise father, Polonius, counseled his son, Laertes:

> This above all,—to thine own self be true; and it must follow, as the night the day, thou canst not then be false to any man (15).

One of the biggest problem areas faced by anyone, on any level, in any type of organization—public or private—is that of communications. Atlhough inadequate or poor communication may spring from a number of causes, one of the prime sources is inaccurate perceptions. We cannot communicate any more accurately than we perceive in the first place. If our perceptions of reality are biased and shaded with distortions of what we conceive of ourselves as well as others, we start off on the wrong foot in conveying clear and accurate information to others.

The image we hold of ourselves colors our perceptions of others and is a key to our perceptual world. People with a negative self-image (in terms of their abilities, potential, etc.) tend to see others more negatively and vice versa for those with a positive self-image. Therapy demonstrates that as one gets better, he or she begins to view life more favorably. When you have an accurate and balanced image of yourself, you can more accurately perceive others. To paraphrase Polonius, being true to self means being true to others.

Transactional Analysis has clear, observable, and concrete definitions or "handles" for describing ourselves as well as others. The parent, the adult, and the child (defined in detail in chapter two) are real and observable measures of what we, as well as others, are like. When someone comes out of his or her parent, we can easily observe this. If his or her child is activated, we know this also. The adult in all of us is also readily perceived. TA concepts provide us with what some researchers term operational definitions—definitions that are concrete, observable, and measurable. Due to these specific definitions—these specific handles on our personalities as well as the personalities of others—we are in a much better position to accurately perceive ourselves as well as others.

Although other psychological approaches, such as so-called sensitivity training, have aimed at improving personal and interpersonal sensitivity of organizational members, none have brought us such concrete and measurable concepts as TA. As you begin to explore further with me in this book, you will readily see how TA can better equip you to understand yourself as well as those working with you. As a result, you cannot help but become a more accurate and more proficient communicator.

To use Freudian concepts, I might not know an "Id" or a "Superego" if it came up and said hello, but I would damn well know an adult or an angry child if I met one. The latter two are life and blood parts of ourselves and others that we can readily comprehend and observe. The previous concepts are somewhat vague and broad academic terms.*

3. *TA relates to the whole person—thinking as well as feelings.*

* The Id and Superego are parts of Freud's definition of personality structure. The Id is vaguely defined as a mixed-up or chaotic mass of instincts seeking gratification or release of tension or energy. The Superego is viewed broadly as a moral censoring type of mechanism representing the conscience. For a view of Freudian concepts and how they relate to organizational behavior, see Joe Kelly, *Organizational Behavior* (Homewood, Ill.: Richard D. Irwin, Inc. and Dorsey Press, 1969), pp. 167–174 and 200–201.

Although it makes little sense, behavioral theories and techniques in the past have assumed that only half of man's nature existed.

Many traditional management and organizational development approaches have viewed the work setting as a purely rational phenomenon. The assumption being: organizations are rational decision-making entities. If you know how the decision process takes place—how decisions are made and who makes them—then you know everything there is to know about what goes on in an organization.

Of the approximately 175 hours of college course work I took in obtaining my BBA (bachelor of business administration) and MBA (master of business administration) degrees, what I learned dealt almost exclusively with analyzing rational decision-making models and factual case situations. We spent reams of time identifying problems, suggesting alternative solutions, figuring out ways of implementing these, and then setting up one or more logical feedback mechanisms to see if we were solving issues properly. The analyzation of a typical business case went something like this:

> Now, let's see. The primary problem appears to be a lack of coordination between sales and production. The organization is losing customers to competitors because sales personnel are pushing new products far ahead of possible delivery dates (problem identification). We need better coordination and communication between sales and production. Through mutual agreement between the departments, we set a reasonable sales lead time so as to get new products launched but so as not to frustrate good customers by whetting their appetite prematurely (solution). Sales and production have agreed with no more than a month lead time on new products, which appears reasonable from the nature of our product and customer's normal delay time (implementation). A coordinator of sales and production will monitor the progress of the new plan to see how smoothly things are going (feedback).

I am not knocking the decision-making process in organizations. I am definitely not opposed to sound planning, organizing, controlling, implementing, and whatever else is involved in reaching sound logical decisions. Any solidly run organization—private or public—that expects to survive with any degree of effectiveness or efficiency needs to set up mechanisms and policies for dealing rationally with problems. I very heavily endorse good rational sense in any organization.

What I am saying, though, is that a lot of the activities that occur in an organization are *not* rational. Some people spend a lot of their time playing "spin-the-wheel" games in order to avoid work. Some critical decisions are made out of spite, jealousy, impulse, or the sheer, explosive desire to "nail" some s.o.b. Sometimes employees are corrected for things they did not do because the boss was upset at the time. Some organizations resist healthy change, creativity, or achievement like the plague so as to avoid "rocking the boat." Sometimes, what does not appear to make a bit of well-thought-out, rational (even computer-assisted) sense turns out to be one of the best decisions possible. The decision was made just because a manager felt good about it. He or she was playing a hunch.

Anyone with only a very brief encounter with any type of organization knows that a lot of what goes on is irrational. Things are often done with little, if any, logic and occasionally with only a tiny appreciation for profits, expenses, or any other organizational measuring stick.

To deal with the irrationalities, emotional upsets, and impulses—so much a part of organizational behavior—we need a comprehensive theory. TA's concepts of the child ego state (the emotional part of a person) and irrational game playing do a great deal to help us understand and deal with the illogical side of all of our natures.

My purpose is not to just help you deal with the emotional side of man, but to help you enjoy it. We all live at the feelings level. Whether we make a decision to hire or fire, to buy a new computer, to change the organizational chart, or to institute a new incentive system, we must all live with the decision. If we feel miserable about our work most of the time, it is best for us to change jobs. If we feel comfortable with our feelings and glad about what we do, no amount of material wealth—or lack of it—can say we are not a success. We'll probably be more productive to boot. As demonstrated throughout this book, the better we can deal with our feelings and our irrational tendencies, the better thinkers we'll be in the bargain.

Other behavioral approaches, such as so-called sensitivity or T-group training, have dealt almost exclusively with the other half of man's nature—feelings. As a result, what is learned is not transferred very well to the organizational setting in many cases.

When it is all over, the members of the group have to make it back to the real world and this can be a significant problem. Most people experience difficulty making the transition. Transferring the learning of the T group is a tricky problem. One member of a group, after completing his T group, walked into his house and said to his wife, "Don't speak to me, I'll tell you when I'm ready to talk." (16).

There is no concrete evidence to demonstrate that T-group experiences have resulted in improved organizational results—for example, increased productivity or output (17).

T-groups are unstructured groups with no special agenda, where here-and-now behavior is focused upon in order to make members more aware of and more sensitive to one another's feelings and methods of expression. Group members are often encouraged to let all their feelings hang out—to bluntly and spontaneously confront other members—positively or negatively. A thoughtful or discreet discussion about something is viewed as intellectualizing and is shunned.

A former group member tells his story:

> My first and only brief experience with a so-called sensitivity group ended after the leader encouraged us to confront each other about some negative aspect of another member. I referred to this one particular female member as being "rather domineering." When my comment was discounted as being an intellectualization, I referred to her as a pushy bitch. Some of the members applauded me for what I guess was supposed to mean my newly found level of emotional expression. Though frankly, vulgarity was a part of my vocabulary for many years prior to this group experience. In short order, this particular female returned my expression in kind and a guy, who I later learned was her husband, came close to engaging me in a fist fight.

My purpose here is not to discount T-group training in general. For many participants and for many organizations, the results have been beneficial. However, the T-group's emphasis on "letting-it-all-hang-out," without discretion, can be damaging in the organizational setting. Research demonstrates that the open discussion about feelings, with discretion, is associated with higher performance, while the spontaneous and emotional expression of feelings, without rational reflection, is not correlated with higher productivity (18).

Timing, alert and mature sensitivity to other's predicaments, tact, and concern—along with honesty—are all important qualities for any job holder who wishes to enjoy organizational relationships and to climb the promotional ladder. Indiscreet, emotional confrontations with bosses or co-workers will often lead to dead-end jobs or to a quick exit. It takes a little logic to realize that the boss you call an s.o.b. today may have you removed from your job tomorrow. Additionally, individuals who are subject to spontaneous, emotional outcrys do not inspire the confidence shown by calmer heads.

Strauss and Sayles, two eminent authorities in the personnel field, comment:

> It is charged that whatever changes occur in the T-group tend to fade out once the trainee returns to an unsympathetic environment where company policy and the boss's attitude may inhibit the exercise of newly-learned skills. . . .
> . . . The answer may be to provide T-group training for everyone, but this may be prohibitively expensive. Even if it were possible to send everyone through T-groups, the kinds of "dirt" aired in such sessions and the intense feelings often engendered by them may in fact make it harder for managers to work together after the session is over. T-group training may improve the interpersonal relations for some managers, but may be harmful for others (19).

A psychologist friend of mine told me of the case of a number of psychiatrists who attended a T-group a number of years ago. After "letting-it-all-hang-out" in the T-group sessions, it took some six months to get relations back to normal. The hurtful attacks expressed during the sessions lingered even among those who were supposed to be experts in handling emotional outbursts.

The honest and open expression of feelings is important to any human encounter in any type of organization or group. However, without discretion, the exchange can be much more harmful than productive for all parties. (How to level appropriately and constructively when giving negative feedback is discussed in detail in chapter nine.) To be a truly happy and productive organizational participant, your mind and your heart must be a part of your work and your relationships. TA—better than any other behavioral approach I know of—does an excellent job of dealing with the total nature of man or woman.

4. *TA is a great aid in dealing with authority problems common to any type of organization.*

There are basically two problem children with whom managers or supervisors in any type of organization have to contend: the overly submissive or dependent worker and the overly rebellious one.

The overly submissive or dependent worker refuses to stand on his or her own two feet. This is the type of worker who must constantly check with the boss to see if he or she is doing things correctly. Even minor, trivial matters are hashed and rehashed with the boss. Such subordinates are heard to ask questions like:

How much margin should I leave in preliminary reports?

Should I deal with this customer's complaint first or that one?

Is it okay for me to bring a note pad to the meeting?

I've read it over a couple of times and I know it is supposed to be simple, but why don't you check it and give me your interpretation first?

I know you have explained it over and over to me, but do I fill out this part of the shipping order first or not?

All of us need guidance to a certain extent, particularly when we are starting a new job. However, the overly submissive or dependent worker needs *excessive* guidance and—even over time—still fails to cut the umbilical cord. As a result, supervisors find themselves in positions where they have to do the subordinate's work as well as their own.

The overly rebellious worker feels compelled to constantly work against a given authority figure, even for no logical reason. This is the kind of subordinate who does "A" when the supervisor says "B" or "walks" when the supervisor suggests "running." Authority is an issue for this adolescent type of subordinate. The overly rebellious worker seems to transfer resentments against parents to supervisors. In this situation the supervisor has to unnecessarily tussle with subordinates as well as with everyday problems.

Maturity Stage	Infancy	Adolescence	Adulthood
Mode of Relating to Authority	Dependence	Counter-dependence	Inter-dependence
Style of Behaving on the Job	"I can't do it myself."	"To hell with your way of doing things."	"I can stand on my own two feet, but I am willing to cooperate as required."

On a continuum measuring maturity, the overly submissive or dependent worker might be viewed at the helpless, infancy stage; the overly rebellious at the adolescent stage. The ideal worker to cultivate for any type of job in an organization, particularly at the higher levels where more maturity is required, is the worker who predominately operates out of the adulthood stage. He or she is capable of independent judgment and will actually embrace responsibility rather than shy away from it. Additionally, this type of worker realizes that much can be learned from others and that cooperation is necessary for the proper functioning of any organization.

As you will see, appropriate applications of TA's concepts of the adapted child (adapted in terms of authority figures) and symbiotic relationships can do a great deal to resolve these authority nightmares of supervisors.

5. *TA is a good tool for understanding and facilitating various managerial philosophies and leadership styles like Theory X (autocratic), Theory Y (democratic), or Theory Z (contingency).*

Although concepts relating managerial styles and TA are explored in detail in chapter ten, I would now like to give you a "feel" for how, naturally and pragmatically, the two blend. The following Management-Life Position Chart will help pave the way.

I'm OK

Managerial Style: Management by Commitment and Self-Direction	*Managerial Style:* Management by Edict
Relationship to Subordinates: Adult to Adult	*Relationship to Subordinates:* Parent to Child
1	**3**
2	**4**
Managerial Style: Management by Abdication	*Managerial Style:* Management by Chaos
Relationship to Subordinates: Child to Parent	*Relationship to Subordinates:* Child to Child

You're OK ———————————————— You're Not OK

I'm Not OK

In quadrant one the subordinate is treated as a mature worker. His or her suggestions are not only appreciated but are often solicited. By being directly involved in important decisions concerning his or her own job, the worker is in the best possible position to grow and to develop in terms of self-confidence and competence.

In quadrant two the subordinate is viewed the way a parent might view a child—as lacking the competence and maturity to assume any reasonable amount of independent judgment. In this top-down managerial style, dictums and edicts are carefully spelled out from above, with little or no permission for feedback or change. This type of management style, as we shall see, often tends to breed what it wishes to avoid— irresponsible, overly dependent workers or apathy. Treat workers like children and you often get childlike responses in turn.

Quadrant three epitomizes the style of the manager who, either through insecurity or lack of motivation or both, refuses to take responsible command of his or her unit or department. Wishy-washy and overly submissive, this manager frequently abdicates his leadership role to an informal leader who really runs the show. Easily pressured by subordinates into compromising decisions, this manager often creates a lot of unnecessary conflict. As time passes, the popularity he consciously or unconsciously seeks by being an "easy touch" for worker demands dwindles into a lack of respect for him and for his position.

Quadrant four is truly the loser's position for any manager. The superior who predominantly comes out of the dual not-OK position runs his or her department into chaos. Lacking respect for his or her own abilities and for those of the subordinates, he or she haphazardly frustrates everyone involved. Luckily, the incompetence of this type of manager is easily detected and is usually short-lived.

6. *TA uses a down-to-earth language that any supervisor or worker can easily relate to, regardless of authority level or type of job.*

Too often, professionals in the behavioral areas—psychology, sociology, etc.—become so impressed with their rhetoric and jargon that nobody can understand what they are talking about but themselves. Even they have problems at times. As a result, the very people who should benefit from their research findings—the ordinary, everyday worker, businessman, or public servant—find the material unintelligible and confusing. Although one may be impressed by the sophistication of the rhetoric used by such professionals, little is gained in meaningful ideas that can be practically used. Many professional journals read like the tax code and insurance policies—very poorly.

Here is the type of phraseology you are likely to find in a typical behavioral journal:

> Having controlled for variances pertaining to demographic characteristics, it was found that the satisfaction quotient of seasonal part-time workers and permanent part-time types demonstrated no appreciable difference.*

The above material, in clearer and down-to-earth English, simply says:

> Demographic data like sex will affect the satisfaction level of part-time workers. For example, *female* seasonal part-time workers are found to be just as happy with their jobs as steady *male* part-time employees.

Traditionally, the field of organizational behavior has been burdened with academic rhetoric that is sometimes difficult for even a Ph.D. to understand. Russell and Black, Jr., in their book, *Human Behavior in Business,* comment on how many behavioral authors make understanding people in organizations an even more difficult problem:

> Of the three factors of any business enterprise—money, materials, and people—it is the people-factor which seems to confuse, confound, and perplex. It is least possible to predict what people will do within an organization. The behavioral sciences of psychology, sociology, and anthropology have produced a wealth of information which could be useful in achieving success individually in a group, but much of this information is unavailable to the employee or manager in business.
>
> It would make you angry to discover that information had been withheld which would save you money and stress. . . . Yet, unwittingly, this is precisely what is happening. If a behavioral scientist publishes a book or article which is unreadable because it is too technical or too boring, he is accidentally keeping that information from the public (20).

TA uses a down-to-earth and practical language that can be easily understood and applied by anyone, even those with a limited education.

---

* In order not to pick on any particular behavioral journal, I have rephrased this material and I will decline to cite the source of the data. However, despite the paraphrasing, the language I used is very typical journal rhetoric.

A first-line foreman with an eight-grade education will have no more difficulty in understanding concepts such as parent, adult, and child than would a college student majoring in organizational psychology. In TA the stress is on practical ideas, backed up by solid rationale—*not* on sophisticated rhetoric. Eric Berne deliberately wanted his theory to be as useful and as practical as possible. His aim was not to impress colleagues with a sophisticated rhetoric* that the layman would have a difficult time using. Muriel James, a TA author and student of Eric Berne, states that Eric encouraged his followers to write very simply (21).

7. *As a management development tool, TA does not produce the negative psychological side effects that have resulted from other behavioral methods such as T-group training.*

Sensitivity training has come under criticism as a cause of psychological damage:

> Criticisms of sensitivity training revolve around several issues. The principal problem is the casualty rate, meaning those who are psychologically harmed by the experience. . . .
> One research study of encounter groups and sensitivity training reported a casualty rate of about 10 percent. Casualties were defined as those who showed evidence of serious psychological harm six to eight months after the groups ended, and this harm could reasonably be attributed to the group experience. . . . The casualty rate and negative changes show that sensitivity training is a high-risk training method that organizations should use with great caution (22).

Although it is conceded that two major factors leading to these harmful side effects are poor screening of participants who may have emotional problems to begin with and poorly trained leaders (23), part of the harmful effects are inherent to the T-group process itself. When individuals are required to reveal feelings unwillingly or without discretion, as in some sensitivity groups** (in TA terminology, without the use of the adult), even the most well-adjusted individuals might suffer at

---

* I feel some behavioral scientists use complex rhetoric as a defense mechanism. If you cannot understand what they are saying, their ideas cannot be challenged.
** I am not condemning all T-groups. Many have been very helpful to participants. Casualties are high among leaders who stimulate intensive emotional reactions (24).

least some temporary psychological problems, if not work adjustment problems, as in the case of the group of psychiatrists mentioned earlier. I have conducted numerous TA workshops with hundreds of participants—from first-line supervisors to top managers—over the past six years. I have yet to hear of a single casualty. Research literature in TA books and journals and organizational behavior books have also revealed no psychologically harmful effects directly attributable to TA.

Besides the fact that TA offers excellent training programs for leaders,* the process, as already mentioned, deals with the whole person—feelings and thinking together. As a result, unnecessary and potentially damaging and hurtful interpersonal exchanges either are eliminated or, at least, are tempered with discretion.

CONCLUSION AND SUMMARY

In conclusion, let me say that TA is one of the greatest organizational behavioral tools to ever enter the world of work. It is ideally suited—practically and theoretically—to deal with many types of behavioral problems that exist in any type of organization—small or large, public or private. It is a theory that has worked well with personality conflicts and interpersonal communications problems. As you will also see, it works expertly with group level problems and organizational snafus.

Let me caution the reader. Like any other behavioral theory or concept, TA is no panacea. It works best when applied by well-trained leaders who are well grounded not only in basic TA theory but in other behavioral and management theories as well. As pointed out, TA complements other organizational theories and approaches very well (for example, leadership theories). Even champions of the TA approach acknowledge its limitations.

They present the theory to potential users as something that can be helpful to most people, but not as a cure-all for an organization's ills. In fact, most company training and development specialists stress that special care must be taken to avoid a panacea approach (25).

* For those further interested in TA training programs, contact the International Transactional Association, 1772 Vallejo Street, San Francisco, California 94123.

When implemented properly, TA has had fantastic results. In one case it reduced turnover rates by 400 percent (26).

The American Airlines' director of training and development states that their investment in TA training was well worth it:

> I'm convinced that TA can create greater sensitivity to one's own behavior and to the behavior of others much more quickly and with much more permanence than any other training tool that I'm aware of. Certainly it is more easily carried over from seminar to the job than laboratory training (27).

Of the 8,000 employees who have gone through the TA training program at American Airlines, 99 percent reacted favorably and 86 percent feel more confident and positive in their jobs (28).

The Bank of New York has trained approximately 250 first-line managers and about 50 middle and senior divisional managers in Transactional Analysis and is expanding TA training to include senior vice-presidents as well as customer-contact personnel (29).

A personnel officer of the bank also endorses TA as an effective behavioral tool for organizations:

> Transactional analysis is clearly not the salvation of the organization, so we've never introduced it as such. But we are convinced after nearly three years of experience with TA that it can be a useful tool for both personal and organizational growth.
>
> Most importantly, TA is something that people can grasp easily within a short time of exposure and relate it to their everyday lives, on the job and off (30).

Now that I have whetted your appetite with the benefits that TA can bring to your organization and to you as an organizational member, let's get into the theory and the practice of it. If you diligently apply the concepts as developed in the rest of this book, you cannot help but become a more productive and happier individual and organizational member.

NOTES

1. Harold M. F. Rush and Phyllis S. McGrath, "Transactional Analysis Moves into Corporate Training: A New Theory of Interpersonal Relations Becomes

a Tool for Personnel Development," *The Conference Board Record,* vol. 10, no. 7 (July 1973), p. 38. This article is also cited in *Organizational Development: Theory, Practice, and Research* by Wendell L. French, Cecil H. Bell, Jr., and Robert A. Zawacki (Dallas, Tex.: Business Publications, Inc., 1978), pp. 223–230.

2. Rush and McGrath, "Transactional Analysis Moves into Corporate Training," p. 38.

3. Maurice F. Villeré, "Transactional Analysis: An Effective Management Tool," *Louisiana Business Survey,* vol. 7, no. 2 (April 1976), p. 2; "Business Tries Out Transactional Analysis," *Business Week* (12 January 1974), pp. 74–75; Eileen Milling, "A New Way to Improve Effectiveness on the Job," *Nation's Business* (July 1975), pp. 65–68.

4. Rush and McGrath, "Transactional Analysis Moves into Corporate Training," p. 38.

5. "Business Tries Out Transactional Analysis," p. 74; Rush and McGrath, "Transactional Analysis Moves into Corporate Training," pp. 42–43.

6. "Labor Letter," *The Wall Street Journal,* vol. 63, no. 6 (9 January 1979), p. 1.

7. Muriel James et al., *Techniques in Transactional Analysis: For Psychotherapists and Counselors* (Reading, Mass.: Addison-Wesley Publishing Co., Inc., 1977), p. 28.

8. Eric Berne, *Transactional Analysis in Psychotherapy: A Systematic Individual and Social Psychiatry* (New York: Grove Press, Inc., 1961).

9. Eric Berne, *Games People Play: The Psychology of Human Relationships* (New York: Grove Press, Inc., 1964).

10. Thomas A. Harris, *I'm OK—You're OK: A Practical Guide to Transactional Analysis* (New York: Harper & Row, Publishers, Inc., 1969).

11. Muriel James and Dorothy Jongeward, *Born to Win: Transactional Analysis with Gestalt Experiments* (Reading, Mass.: Addison-Wesley Publishing Co., Inc., 1971).

12. Stan Woollams and Michael Brown, *The Total Handbook of Transactional Analysis* (Englewood Cliffs, N.J.: Prentice-Hall, Inc., 1979).

13. Muriel James et al., *Techniques in Transactional Analysis for Psychotherapists and Counselors,* © 1977 by Addison-Wesley Publishing Co., Inc., pp. 23 and 25. Reprinted with permission.

14. Maurice F. Villeré and G. Kent Stearns, "The Readability of Organizational Behavior Textbooks," *Academy of Management Journal,* vol. 19, no. 1 (March 1976), p. 133.

15. William Shakespeare, *Hamlet Prince of Denmark,* act 1, scene 4.

16. Joe Kelly, *Organizational Behaviour: An Existential-Systems Approach,* rev. ed. (Homewood, Ill.: Richard D. Irwin, Inc., 1974), p. 664. © 1974 by Richard D. Irwin, Inc.

17. David R. Hampton, Charles E. Summer, and Ross A. Webber, *Organizational Behavior and the Practice of Management*, 3d ed. (Glenview, Ill.: Scott, Foresman & Company, 1978), p. 779.

18. Robin D. Willits, "Company Performance and Interpersonal Relations," *Industrial Management Review*, vol. 8, no. 2 (Spring 1967), pp. 91–107.

19. George Strauss and Leonard R. Sayles, *Personnel: The Human Problems of Management*, © 1972, pp. 539–540. Reprinted by permission of Prentice-Hall, Inc., Englewood Cliffs, N.J.

20. G. Hugh Russell and Kenneth Black, Jr., *Human Behavior in Business*, © 1972, pp. vii–viii. Reprinted by permission of Prentice-Hall, Inc., Englewood Cliffs, N.J.

21. Muriel James et al., *Techniques in Transactional Analysis for Psychotherapists and Counselors*, p. 25.

22. Keith Davis, *Human Behavior at Work: Organizational Behavior*, 5th ed. (New York: McGraw-Hill Book Company, 1977), p. 184.

23. James B. Lau, *Behavior in Organizations: An Experiential Approach*, rev. ed. (Homewood, Ill.: Richard D. Irwin, Inc., 1979), p. 284.

24. Morton A. Lieberman, Irvin D. Yalom, and Matthew B. Miles, "Encounter: The Leader Makes the Difference," *Psychology Today*, vol. 6, no. 10 (March 1973), p. 74.

25. Harold M. F. Rush and Phyllis S. McGrath, "Transactional Analysis Moves into Corporate Training: A New Theory of Interpersonal Relations Becomes a Tool for Personnel Development," *The Conference Board Record*, vol. 10, no. 7 (July 1973), p. 42.

26. Donald D. Ely and John T. Morse, "TA and Reinforcement Theory," *Personnel*, vol. 51, no. 2 (March–April 1974), pp. 40–51.

27. Harold M. F. Rush and Phyllis S. McGrath, "Transactional Analysis Moves into Corporate Training: A New Theory of Interpersonal Relations Becomes a Tool for Personnel Development," *The Conference Board Record*, vol. 10, no. 7 (July 1973), p. 42.

28. Rush and McGrath, "Transactional Analysis Moves into Corporate Training," p. 43.

29. Rush and McGrath, "Transactional Analysis Moves into Corporate Training," p. 42.

30. Rush and McGrath, "Transactional Analysis Moves into Corporate Training," p. 42.

AN OVERVIEW OF TRANSACTIONAL ANALYSIS

2

As mentioned at the beginning of chapter one, TA is divided into four areas of study and practice: (1) Personality Analysis, the study of ego states; (2) Transactional Analysis, the study of communication lines between people; (3) Time Structuring, the study of time utilization (which includes game playing); and (4) Script Analysis, the study of role development. Although all of the four areas of concentration can be used and have been used to dea' with any level of analysis, applications have been concentrated as follows:

TA Area of Study	Primary Applications
(1) Ego State Analysis	Individual, organizational
(2) Transactional	Interpersonal, group
(3) Game Playing	Interpersonal, group, organizational
(4) Script	Individual, organizational

Each TA area or field of study builds upon the other. An understanding of ego states is a prerequisite for understanding communication lines between people. Game playing involves somewhat complex communication strategies. Scripts contain various games as part of the plot, personality types, and characteristic ways of transacting.

A crucial concept to Transactional Analysis is the "stroke." A stroke is an act of recognition. Whether we wish to admit it or not, everyone has a need for recognition of some kind or other. Some psychologists consider strokes basic to survival. Few people, regardless of how interesting or challenging the work, would choose to work in a social vacuum. Occasionally, the story of the hermit explorer is recounted in some TV biography, but few people live like hermits. More importantly, few people would choose to do so.

Anyone who has worked for any international corporation is aware of the salary premium paid to those who are sent to jobs located abroad. The premium is, in a TA sense, pay for stroke deprivation. People whose jobs isolate them from friends and family ties and all the good strokes that go with these relationships—love, affection, good times— are being paid 50 percent and 100 percent salary premiums for temporarily doing without them. For many people, permanent separation could not be replaced with money, regardless of amount.

There are two kinds of strokes: positive and negative. A positive stroke is a form of positive recognition that may take the form of verbal praise, money, additional responsibilities, or whatever is successful in reinforcing someone positively. A negative stroke is a form of negative reinforcement—for example, a verbal put-down, a cut in salary, or a reduction in status and responsibilities. Managers can use strokes for increasing productive behavior or for extinguishing unproductive behavior. As the cliché goes in TA, you get what you stroke. Stroking the proper ego states will bring out the desired behaviors. Stroking a clear-thinking approach to solving a problem will help bring out an employee's adult. On the other hand, stroking a supervisor for his or her concern for their employees will bring out the nurturing parent. More on keeping strokes on target and the types of strokes to give is discussed later.

EGO STATES (OR WHAT IS THAT OTHER PERSON REALLY LIKE?)

According to Transactional Analysis, an individual's personality is divided into three parts or ego states: the parent ego state, the adult ego state, and the child ego state. An ego state is defined as a consistent pattern of feeling, thinking, and behaving. Ego states are consistent in the sense that each ego state uniformly acts differently than the others. TA's concept of personality is observable. It is not a theoretical concept that is hard to understand. It is easy to see when someone is acting like an adult, a parent, or a child.

Even though we may not agree with what our parents said or did, we can never forget them. In essence, according to TA, we carry our parents around in our heads—all their "do's and don'ts," "how to" statements, and other data obtained from our parents when we were children. Idiosyncracies and habitual ways of dealing with money, friends, things, and even our morals are borrowed from our parents— borrowed for a lifetime. Some of the parent "tapes" or recordings they have left with us are beneficial and practical. Some have even saved our lives, such as "don't play with fire" and "don't run in front of a passing car." However, other "tapes" have restricted our creativity and our abilities to function effectively and appropriately in the present. Messages such as "you can never be too careful" or "most people can't be trusted" can lead an individual to a stereotyped and lonely existence.

One of the purposes of TA, as well as one of the purposes of this book, is to identify and to deal with some of the past messages so that the functional ones are used and the destructive ones are shelved. In any given situation, at any given time, any of the ego states can be useful and productive. At other times they can be destructive. TA assists its practitioners in gaining flexibility and in learning how to appropriately deal with themselves as well as with others.

The Parent Ego State

The parent ego state is divided into two parts: the critical parent and the nurturing parent. The critical parent expresses itself exactly as the term implies: very critically. It has a conditional regard for people and things. This means that it will like you if you do it its way, and if you don't—you will get a negative stroke. In terms of rewards, the critical parent is the main dispenser of negative strokes or put-downs.

A critical parent employee might express himself or herself like this:

What do you mean you don't like my work!

You're a real dummy.

Why do I get all the jackasses? You could have at least checked with me first before placing that order.

Joe won't cooperate. That's the last time I work on a project with that s.o.b.

That no good . . . I'll fix her good next time. When she asks for a report early she can do it herself.

You know what they can do with this crummy outfit. They can take and shove it _____.

I hate to be critical, but they don't give us the tools to work with. Over at BBX, everyone gets a new top of the line electric typewriter each year. Not only that . . . (bitch, bitch, bitch).

The bitchy, irritable, and critical parent employee is a part of any organization. Each one of us—to a certain extent, and periodically— exhibits this punitive side of our personality. No less familiar to the organizational setting is the grumpy or overdemanding critical parent boss.

What's the matter? You can't read the instructions?

I give you a simple job to do and what do you do—you don't do it the right way. (Critical parents often feel they have the one best way of doing things.)

How about this triple put-down to each ego state which I refer to as the triple corkscrew:

You don't understand what is going on (a discount to the thinking part of the person or the adult); you don't give a damn (a discount to the feelings and needs part of the person or the child); and you never do what you ought to (a general discount to the rules and authority figure part of the person or the parent).

For some employees, the most infuriating critical parent supervisor is the one who acts in a condescending or patronizing manner:

Gee, if I had known you couldn't handle the work, I would have given it to someone else.

(With a little pat on top of the head): For a woman, Mary, you are doing a fine job.

The critical parent expresses itself very critically, and this criticism may take a number of forms. Besides being patronizing and condescending, the critical parent may act in an arrogant or just plain obnoxious way. Fundamentally, the critical parent expresses negative emotions.

The nurturing parent, on the other hand, expresses itself with an "unconditional positive regard." This is a $2,000 expression meaning acceptance. The nurturing parent is the main dispenser of positive strokes or positive recognition. While the critical parent tends to put people down, the nurturing parent tends to build them up. Even if you don't do things the way the nurturing parent wants, it still has a high regard for you and still likes you. Nurturing parent sales managers treat a salesman's mistake as a learning experience for the salesman, not as an opportunity to get even with him or to "nail" him. The critical parent, on the other hand, views mistakes as an opportunity to punish. The nurturing parent nurtures, supports, and stresses building up the individual through self-confidence. It is essentially the positive part of the personality and, thus, a very attractive part. People are repelled by vinegar, which would be the critical parent, but they are attracted by honey, which would be the nurturing parent. If you are an employee in any type of organization, a nurturing parent supervisor is the kind to have, because he or she is understanding and is willing to listen.

Don't believe that the nurturing parent boss doesn't push for progress. The nurturing parent has a genuine interest in the individual, and helping the subordinate progress is one way of demonstrating that interest. While the critical parent boss often uses people, the nurturing parent boss is trying to develop them. He or she genuinely cares. The nurturing parent boss would express himself or herself as follows:

Bob, you're doing an excellent job in that area. That client is particularly hard to deal with. You are doing a great job.

When correcting someone, he or she might say:

Overall, your report is excellent. You have given me the background material and figures I need to convince my superiors to move ahead. But you have given me a little too much data in the charts. Why don't we work on arranging these so that we can better emphasize your key selling points.

Unlike the critical parent, the nurturing parent manager is *not* trying to "nail" subordinates. His or her approach is very constructive. Rather than just pointing out a problem or getting involved in name calling, he or she is saying:

Okay, here's the problem. How can I help you correct it?

The nurturing parent is in the business of finding solutions rather than finding faults.

Nurturing parent employees are gems to have working for you also. With their genuine concern for the organization and for their co-workers, they help foster a climate of cooperation and dedication. When required by the job, they are top-notch team players. Rather than trying to figure out ways to exploit the organization (for example, by extra long lunch breaks or coffee breaks or by hedging on projects), the truly committed, nurturing parent employees are figuring out ways to be more productive. They feel that self-growth and organizational growth go hand-in-hand. Their emphasis on giving of themselves, rather than taking, helps not only to develop their own work skills but usually reaps for them reciprocal rewards from the organization in terms of raises, promotions, and other organizational benefits.

A comment from a typical nurturing parent employee would be:

Sure, boss, no problem. I'll update that report for you right now. Is there anything else you wish changed?

His or her response to a co-worker for help is patently cooperative:

> Look, Joe, no problem at all. I should be finished what I am doing here in an hour. How about meeting at eleven o'clock? I've worked on those designs before. I might be able to help you cut your work in half.

In many organizations the nurturing parent employee is a rare phenomenon. Where he or she is present, organizational life is made much more pleasant and productive. This type of employee even helps compensate for the employees who seem to enjoy making the boss's life miserable.

The Adult Ego State

The adult ego state is the nonfeeling part of the personality. The adult state might be thought of as a computer bringing in and analyzing information before generating and selecting alternatives. The adult is the thinking, rational part of the personality. When making a decision, the adult should definitely be involved. This is the most alert and analytical part of the personality. If an individual around you is very emotional, go into the adult. This is one good way to cool down emotions. The individual who is cool under fire has easy and frequent access to his or her adult ego state. At least you won't get upset if you are in the adult. If you are in the critical parent and somebody gets critical to you, you are probably going to explode. The adult manager is looking at rationale:

> Why can't you make more sales? How is it that you aren't able to order this product? What can we order in the future? What can we do to alleviate the problem?

Basically, adults will be asking questions like who, what, where, when, why, and how. The adult's prime concerns are problem identification, analyzation, and the generating of solutions. To function competently in any organization, a certain amount of adult reasoning is necessary.

For example, an adult salesperson would approach a prospect and size him or her up something like this:

> Now let's see, how old is the prospect? What would this person be interested in buying, given his or her present economic situation? What would be a feasible purchase? What are the customer's needs? What would be the best product to meet these needs?

A supervisor can readily delegate to the adult employee. Talking down to or trying to "spoon feed" such an intelligent worker is the perfect wrong way to treat him or her. The adult employee has the computer to correctly identify problems, determine alternative solutions, select the best solution, and implement it. When seeking advice or guidance, the adult employee is very hard to bluff. He or she relates to solid, "meat and potatoes" information. Although the adult employee can take a load off the mind of his or her boss by expertly discharging his or her duties and responsibilities, the supervisor better be on his or her "toes" also. He or she better be in a position to answer challenging adult employee questions like:

> Specifically, in terms of corrosive and physical characteristics, how durable is it?

> Given our current fat liquidity (or cash) position, our low P/E ratio,* and the fact that our stock is selling below book value,** we better buy up some of our own shares or risk acquisition. What are your thoughts on this?

> Given assumptions A, B, and C, would you suggest alternative D or E? Here is my rationale. I would like your suggestions on this.

---

* The market price of a stock divided by the earnings per share. A low P/E ratio in the current market is often indicative of a cheaply priced stock.
** The book value is the net worth of a company (assets minus liabilities) divided by the number of shares outstanding. A company whose assets are readily salable and are selling below net worth can be liquidated by an acquiring company for a sizeable profit.

I have developed the new employment application form as you suggested. However, I am uncertain as to whether these two questions are consistent with EEOC* requirements. We need this information to adequately fulfill our job requirements. How about if we word it like this . . . ?

The Child Ego State

As the song goes, we are all children at heart, and this "kid" in us won't be denied. We all live at the feelings level. Whether the decision is to hire or fire, buy a new computer, incorporate a new sales pitch into a training program, or just to buy a cup of coffee, we *feel* the consequences of these decisions. People who do not like what they feel about their jobs long enough will change jobs. Feeling miserable about work much of the time is no way to live, even if the adult ego state tells us it makes sense financially to work in that type of job.

The child ego state, according to TA, is the feelings part of the personality. Living without sensitivity to the child ego state could make one nothing more than an automaton. Effective managers and effective employees are not impassionate computers. Enthusiasm, coupled with intelligence, makes for a productive and satisfied work force in any organization.

The child ego state, like the parent ego state, is divided into two parts: the adapted child and the free child. The adapted child is best understood in relation to the critical parent. The adapted child tries to adapt to the dictums or messages of the critical parent in one of two ways: through rebellion or submission. For example, a critical parent might say,

Hey, you are an awful person.

and the adapted child would say,

Yes, I am awful.

* The Equal Employment Opportunity Commission is charged with the duty of enforcing the Civil Rights Act of 1964. Though the federal government has published no specific guidelines on pre-employment inquiries, questions that appear to be discriminatory in terms of the spirit of the law must be proven not to be so.

Or, the critical parent would say,

> You are an awful person

and the adapted child would say,

> To hell with you, you're the one who is awful.

These two problem children become authority problems for managers and are perfect manifestations of the adapted child ego state. These problems are observed in the overly submissive worker who won't make his or her own decisions and in the overly rebellious worker who does "A" when the manager tells him or her to do "B."

The critical parent and the adapted child often go together. In fact, depression or feeling bad is expressed by an internal dialogue—that is, a dialogue inside an individual's head between the critical parent and the adapted child. The critical parent puts out the criticisms and the adapted child buys into them. For example, let's say a salesman goes out to crack a new account and he doesn't get it. In fact, he doesn't even get in to see the prospect. He may leave that situation and inside his head a dialogue between his critical parent and adapted child may go on in the following manner:

> Adapted child: Maybe I didn't try hard enough to get by the secretary.
>
> Critical parent: Yes, you didn't try hard enough.
>
> Adapted child: Yes, I guess I didn't.
>
> Critical parent: You'll never amount to anything.
>
> Adapted child: Yes, I guess I never will. I guess I just can't make it as a salesman.
>
> Critical parent: You are right, you can't.

Between these two ego states has been established a negative, vicious cycle that can destroy any employee's morale.

The worker who would be primarily an adapted child employee would be one who does everything the supervisor, customer, or co-worker wants him or her to do. When the boss tells him or her to jump, he or she would ask,

How high?

and often is so intimidated as to be unable to operate effectively on some of his or her own initiative. The overly adapted employee also creates unnecessary burdens for his or her superiors. Often, the boss ends up doing the employee's work as well as his own.

The adapted child manager would be the kind of manager who, in many cases, wouldn't be able to make his or her own decisions. He or she would tend to be the wishy-washy manager, unable to demand the factory or home office support and services so necessary for his or her department. Such managers might neglect to pass on negative feedback necessary for solving problems for fear of offending top management personnel. When not meeting department goals or quotas, they will accept criticism or blame that is passed on to their unit without attempting to objectively analyze and address the real reasons for lack of success if they are beyond their control. Such managers, in their attempts to please their superiors, fail to stand up for their department or employees in the face of limited economic resources. As a result, their people go "hungry" in terms of proper tools (such as typewriters, calculators, computers, and other work materials) and salaries, while competing departments grow fat and greedy. Everyone loses under the command of these "gutless wonders."

As a rebellious adapted child, he or she is equally ineffective, because his or her actions are frequently in conflict with management plans and his or her actions can lead to incongruity between company policy and his or her department's activities. As a result, organizational productivity suffers, as healthy interdepartmental competition degenerates into territorial fights, "witch hunting," and demoralizing political games. Despite his or her apparent tough, rebellious stand on most issues, such a manager is often easy prey for those who are wise enough to manipulate him or her through negative psychology. The division head of a large organization comments on dealing with an overly rebellious department head:

> I never have much problem with George. If I want to get his backing on a departmental policy, I take a stand contrary to my own policy. He takes the opposite stand and my policy gets implemented in his department with flying colors. But, to tell you the truth, I hate using negative psychology. Sooner or later my tactics are going to backfire on a critical issue. Damn it, I hate manipulating people. I'd rather simply come off straight with George. In fact, I would have fired him a long time ago if he wasn't so technically competent.

The free child is very different from the adapted child. The free child expresses itself with straightforward feelings. The term "straightforward feelings" indicates that the free child does not express himself or herself in an attempt to adapt to the wishes of the authority figure of the critical parent. The free child is free to express itself the way it wants to. This freedom is made possible by the unconditional regard of the nurturing parent. The nurturing parent feels OK with the expression of all feelings. Whether feelings are bad, sad, glad, mad, scared, or whatever, the free child is able to express feelings the way they really are, not adapted or contorted to meet the wishes of the critical parent. In other words, the adapted child would respond to what it feels the critical parent wants to hear, while the free child couldn't care less. Thus, authority figures are not an issue for the free child. The free child is much more in touch with his or her feelings and is freer to express these feelings. The free child can be further explained by two ego states: the natural child and the "little professor." While the natural child relates to the straightforward expression of feelings, the "little professor" ego state embodies creativity and intuition. The "little professor" is like a little adult in the child ego state, making decisions and coming to conclusions without the benefit of rational thinking. Intuition is easier to define by example. It may appear that it wouldn't be wise for the purchasing department to buy certain products, but the manager—from his or her other vast experiences—just gets an overall feeling that the products will do well. Often his or her intuition is right and everyone benefits.

Examples of free child employee expressions are:

Gosh, it's a beautiful day to be working outside.

I don't know any other way to put it. I just feel great about our new proposal.

Wow! I think I've solved the problem.

Mary, you're a neat gal to work with.

A free child supervisor might say:

I just plain love having you guys and gals work for me.

Hey, Joe, you're looking good. I am as excited about your design for the new plant as you are.

Wow, guys, we're licking all competition for April!

For a handy reference on ego states, you might wish to periodically refer to the following Fundamentals of TA chart.

TRANSACTIONS (OR HOW PEOPLE COMMUNICATE IN ORGANIZATIONS)

There are numerous variables that contribute to the success of an organization: geographical location, competition, economic conditions, available products, physical plant, etc. However, with most other conditions and variables being equal, the prosperity of an organization is most dependent upon the activities of its personnel. An organization can be defined in terms of an *event structure,* "event" meaning the activities of an organization and "structure" referring to the coordination of these activities to determine the character and productivity of the organization.

The activities of a hospital staff are distinctly different from the activities of the sales force at IBM. *How* the activities are coordinated

FUNDAMENTALS OF TRANSACTIONAL ANALYSIS (1)

TA divides the individual's personality into *three* ego states. An ego state is defined as a consistent pattern of thinking, feeling, or behaving. The three ego states are:

Parent

That part of the personality dealing mainly with values, opinions, and how-to prescriptions. It may be expressed through: (a) *critical parent*—only accepts the individual if he follows the parent's instructions very closely, (b) *nurturing parent*—the supportive type of authority that accepts the individual unconditionally.

Adult

The rational part of the personality. Rather than being concerned with outdated parental dictums, the adult part of us acts as a computer by digesting current factual data for problem-solving purposes. The adult often plays the role of executive of the personality, utilizing parent and child data for decision making and permitting the activation of the other ego states where appropriate.

Child

The emotional part of the personality. It may be expressed through: (a) *free child*—the source of straightforward feelings, creativity, and spontaneity, (b) *adapted child*—expresses itself as rebellious or overly submissive, the "yes man" in all of us.

Parent Cues

Verbal: "shoulds"
"oughts"
"do's"
"don'ts"
"Be like me."

Visual: Pointing finger critically; crossed arms; impatient sighs

Adult Cues

Verbal: "who?"
"what?"
"how?"
"why?"
"Let's consider this."

Visual: Attentive listening; good eye contact; reflective posture—i.e., hand on chin

Child Cues

Verbal: "I need"
"I feel"
"wow"
"gee"
"I want it my way."

Visual: Expressive eyes; overt emotions—i.e., laughing, crying, whining; enthusiastic or depressive gestures in a hospital is also, in many cases, very different from *how* activities are coordinated in a sales group at IBM. In both instances, however, there are transactions that must occur between and among personnel, and the nature of these transactions reflects upon the quality of the working life in the organization.

If the exchanges and transactions—the fundamental activities between and among personnel—are pleasant and productive, then the organization and the individuals become closer and are likely to prosper. If these exchanges leave personnel feeling offended and defensive, productivity and morale suffer.

A transaction is made up of a stimulus and a response and can take a verbal or nonverbal form. The stimulus is that which initiates the transaction, and the response is the reaction to the stimulus or, in some instances, stimuli. In most verbal transactions the spoken part of the transaction is often only half the message. The *way* the words are spoken and the accompanying *body language* are often far more important in eliciting a response than are the spoken words. Equally effective for communication purposes are transactions that are entirely nonverbal. A shake of the hand in greeting or a wave in recognition will result in a corresponding gesture. In Transactional Analysis, transactions are not complete without there being communication between two or more people, and these communications are either complementary, crossed, or ulterior.

Complementary Transactions

The demeanor of the complementary transaction is one of mutuality. It is a communications situation in which people are trying to pull in harness and work together. The complementary transaction is evident when the person who initiates the communications gets what he or she expects to get. For example, if we ask a person what time it is and we are told the time, the transaction is complementary. We asked for certain information and it was given back to us. The majority of transactions that occur in the business or organizational setting are adult-to-adult complementary. Any of the ego states—parent-to-parent, adult-to-adult, or child-to-child—may be involved in a complementary transaction. Also, complementary transactions between parent and child or even adult and child or adult and parent are possible, although the latter two are more infrequent. Usually, complementary transactions are between adults, parents, children, or parents and children ego states. You will notice in the following exhibit that the communication lines between co-worker A and co-worker B are parallel. Parallel lines are indicative of the demeanor of mutuality. The people communicating are working in concert. Complementary transactions can usually be identified by the rule of thumb that the ego state addressed is the one that will respond. If we ask for information from an adult, the adult comes back to us.

A Complementary Transaction

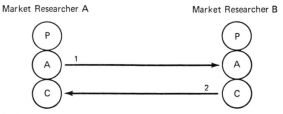

Dialogue

1. *Co-worker A: Is it agreeable with you that we hold the staff meeting tomorrow at 11:00 A.M.?*

2. *Co-worker B: Sounds fine. I have nothing on my calendar for that time.*

3. *Co-worker A: Remember to bring your costs estimates on the new product.*

4. *Co-worker B: Thanks for reminding me. They should help defend our proposal.*

Dialogue

1. *Market Researcher A: Here is the information provided by the factory on total costs for the new X-170.*

2. *Market Researcher B: Why don't we get a drink. I'm tired of discussing this stuff.*

Although rare exceptions, there are instances when the communication lines are parallel but the transaction is not complementary. In this instance, market researcher A has addressed market researcher B in an adult manner, providing information that would be of interest to researcher B's adult. Researcher B responds as a child attempting to "hook" his co-worker's child. Hook is the TA term for engaging a given ego state. The communication lines are parallel, but notice that researcher B responded from an ego state other than the ego state addressed.

During a complementary transaction, communication will continue to some logical conclusion, because people are working with each other. However, complementary transactions do not necessarily mean that people are telling us what we want to hear. We could ask someone what time it is, and we could be hoping in our hearts that it's going to be 2 P.M., but they tell us it is 3 P.M., which means to us that we are not going to have enough time. Now, the response is a complementary one. The spirit is one of cooperation. However, the respondent is not telling us just what we want to hear. Complementary transactions can also be vehicles for negative feedback. Sometimes the objective of cooperation that complementary transactions embody involves giving negative feedback. Without this negative feedback, the respondent may be omitting information necessary for continuing the relationship in a constructive vein. Such feedback is sometimes referred to as constructive criticism.

Crossed Transactions

A crossed transaction is the opposite of a complementary transaction. In the crossed transaction, the person receiving an initial communication is not responding as expected. If a boss asks a secretary to type a letter and the secretary tells the boss to type it himself, a crossed transaction has occurred. The situation is one that calls for an adult to adult response, instead of the critical parent response received. Another example might be the following response to a request for the time:

Who do you think I am? Do you think I am your mother? Can't you tell time?

In the crossed transaction the atmosphere is one of hostility—not mutuality—and the lines cross. In other words, during crossed transactions people are operating at crossed purposes. The respondent is working against the initial communication. Rather than giving what is expected, an unexpected reaction occurs. As a result, crossed transactions often terminate communications. If you feel like you are not getting anywhere, if you feel like you are being put down, or if somebody seems to be coming to you out of "left field," you are probably in a crossed transaction.

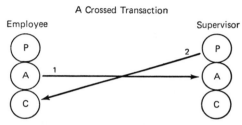

A Crossed Transaction

Dialogue

1. *Employee: Is it okay if I take my coffee break at 3:00 P.M. instead of 3:30 P.M.?*

2. *Supervisor: You're always watching the clock. If you did some work for a change, you wouldn't have time to worry about coffee breaks.*

Although they should generally be avoided because of their disruptive impact, there are a few situations in which crossed transactions can be beneficial. In some cases a person may want a certain type of communications or relationship to end. A manager may have an employee who won't make any of his or her own decisions. The employee continues to set up complementary transactions in which the supervisor acts as a parent and makes all the decisions for him or her as he would for a child. It may be good to cross the employee as an adult and say:

> Hey, I think you ought to make this decision yourself. What are *your* opinions on the new contract?

Ulterior Transactions

Ulterior transactions are transactions that consist of an on-the-surface message and an ulterior message. An ulterior transaction is a complex one in the sense that often there are four ego states involved rather than two. There is the overt message between two ego states and the implicit message between two other ego states. The problem with the ulterior transaction is that it can be very confusing. Which does one relate to: the dialogue message on the surface or the implied message? Sometimes the ulterior transaction can be useful. At times there is a need to conceal something in front of a third party, and the ulterior message is the way to do this. Generally, however, ulterior transactions should be avoided because of their confusion and lack of straightforward demeanor.

An Ulterior Transaction

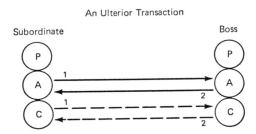

Dialogue

1. *Subordinate: Mary, that is a beautiful dress you have on.*
2. *Boss: Thanks, I thought you might wish to look over the plans for the new committee room.*

Hidden Meaning

1. *Subordinate: I want her in a good mood before discussing my six month raise.*
2. *Boss: If I can keep his mind on something else, maybe I can postpone discussing his raise until I get approval from my boss.*

As you will notice in the exhibit, the ulterior message is drawn with broken lines in order to distinguish it from the overt message. According to many TA practitioners, many people will choose to respond to the ulterior message before the overt message. The intent of a facetious or sarcastic comment is picked up quickest.

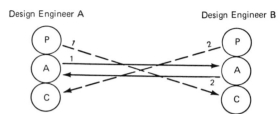

Design Engineer A   Design Engineer B

Dialogue

1. *Design Engineer A: Sure, I welcome your feedback on the new design.*
2. *Design Engineer B: Being the senior design engineer in the department, I thought you would.*

Hidden or Implied Sarcastic Message

1. *Design Engineer A: Just because he has a little seniority on me, he thinks he's the top designer in the world. The poor fool is obsolete.*
2. *Design Engineer B: These fresh kids out of school never listen. They think they know it all. Without my help, they couldn't design their way out of a paper bag.*

GAMES WITHOUT WINNERS

Some say that life is a game—some win and some lose. No doubt, to a certain extent this is true. Much of our entertainment is centered around some sort of game or other. Whether these games are football, tennis, golf, horse racing, or badminton, they all have two basic elements: rules that define how the game is played and a pay off. Both rules and pay off vary a great deal among sports. Pay offs, for example, may be points, money, or sets won. In most cases, someone wins and someone loses.

Games, as TA defines them, are basically the same as other games in terms of having rules and a pay off. The primary difference between TA games and other games is that nobody wins in TA games. The TA game is an irrational activity.

A game, according to Transactional Analysis, consists of on-the-surface complementary transactions, an ulterior transaction, and a negative stroke or put-down that is delivered in the ulterior transaction.

40

The "gameyness' of the game is the ulterior transaction, the rules are characterized by the transactions, and the pay off is the negative stroke. Games are played out of three possible roles: persecutor, rescuer, and victim. These are concepts developed by Dr. Stephen B. Karpman and are called the roles of the Karpman Triangle (2). The critical parent plays the roles of the persecutor and the rescuer. In the rescuer role, the critical parent is often disguised as the nurturing parent and the victim is the adapted child. (The reason for the critical parent's disguise will be discussed shortly.)

In a given game, usually two of the three Karpman roles are played. Most games involve the persecutor and victim roles, with the critical parent assuming the persecutor role. This may happen when the manager demands of an employee objectives that can't possibly be accomplished. In this fashion, the manager can always come in and say,

Hey, what is the matter? You didn't finish the project.

On the surface it appears that the manager is trying to set meaningful objectives, but underneath the motive is really to "pop" the employee by catching him or her deficient in meeting impossible quotas or demands.

A person will often set himself or herself up as victim in a very common game called "Kick me." A personnel assistant might come to a meeting with his boss without reviewing the necessary background information requested by the meeting notice.

1. *Personnel Assistant: Well, gee, I forgot to read the material on contemporary performance appraisal methods.*
1. *Ulterior: Hey, kick me. I've been a bad boy. I deliberately didn't read the material on appraisal methods.*

On the surface it looks like the transaction is simply a complementary adult to adult one. It appears the personnel assistant is simply giving feedback to his supervisor. Underneath, though, the subordinate is really acting like a child to a parent. The personnel supervisor is liable to respond with the appropriate "kick."

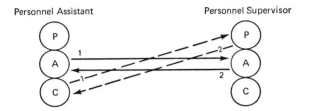

Personnel Assistant   Personnel Supervisor

2. *Personnel Supervisor: I'm sorry to hear that. I was going to let you head up the program to design our new appraisal form. Apparently, you aren't interested in this important project.*
2. *Ulterior: Here's your kick for not coming prepared.*

As mentioned earlier, the rescuer role is played by a critical parent disguised as a nurturing parent. The nurturing parent has a genuine interest in whoever it is dealing with, and the rescuer in the Karpman Triangle is not a real rescuer. The rescuer in the Karpman Triangle is an exploiter, not a nurturer. It's like a finance manager telling the marketing manager:

> We'll be glad to take that rotten computer off your hands. It's too much of a burden for you to fool with.

In reality he's trying to take perfectly effective computer facilities for himself. The finance manager pretends to be helping others but, in actuality, he is helping himself. Another common example of the rescuer is the manager who wants to keep a subordinate dependent on him or her by carefully screening available information, fearing that maybe the subordinate will take the manager's job if he or she knows too much. The rescue is staged as trying to keep irrelevant information out of the subordinate's hair, but it is a false rescue.

The free child, the nurturing parent, and the adult are not game players. The free child does not play games because the free child comes off straight, and games are not straight. The nurturing parent doesn't play games because games are designed to hurt someone, and the nurturing parent is in the supportive business. The adult does not play games because it can see that games are a waste of time. The game player gets nowhere; the game is a kind of "spin the wheel" activity. Games are often played to get out of work, to hurt the company, or to frustrate the customer. There is nothing redeeming about the kind of games discussed in TA. They should be avoided.

Since the consequence of a TA game is lack of progress, games are the least productive way organizational members can spend their time. In instances where you feel you are making no progress or are being put down, you are probably involved in a game.

SCRIPTS (OR THE WORLD'S A STAGE)

"All the world's a stage, and all the men and women merely players; they have their exits and their entrances." . . . (3)

A script is the life program or life drama of an individual. As in a theatrical play, a script dictates the action and the speech of the character. According to Transactional Analysis, each individual is his own playwright, director, producer, and certainly the central character. Tragedy, comedy, boredom, and excitement are usually parts of each script and are present to varying degrees. An individual's organizational career can contain measures of these script elements. The extent to which these are present will be reflected in the success or failure of the organizational member. Work histories are a synopsis of each individual's script up to a certain point in time.

Like individuals, organizations (and groups as well) have scripts. Organizational scripts are often determined by the scripts of the founders or by the scripts of those currently in top managerial positions. Reflected in the rules, regulations, and administrative practices of the organization, some organizational scripts are healthy in the sense that they stress the growth and development of organizational members and the achievement of appropriate organizational goals. Other organizational scripts stifle the potential of members and, in some cases, lead to the ultimate collapse of the organization.

At early ages children begin developing scripts under the influence of the authority figures close to them. Activities of an authority figure are more important than verbal messages in influencing the child's script.

The probability of becoming an alcoholic is higher for children whose parents are alcoholics. Children will model their parents' behavior, and after several years they are programmed in a fairly permanent fashion. Scripts can be changed later in life, but once learned it is a difficult matter to replace an old script with a new one.

Scripts are primarily based around injunctions and life positions. Injunctions, which are called the negative cornerstones of scripts, are "don't messages" received in a lifetime. Common injunctions would include "don't feel," don't be you," "don't succeed," "don't be close," "don't grow up," "don't belong," "don't be important." All of these injunctions are developed by the relationship of the child to his parents and peer groups. The "don't be you" injunction might evolve through constant pressure on the child to be like Uncle Charlie or his sister or somebody else, but "don't be who *you* want to be." The "don't make it" or "don't succeed" injunctions might come across because what the child does is never good enough. The "don't grow up" injunction might come about because the child is discounted when he thinks for himself. The parents prefer to think for the child, which stunts the growth of the adult ego state.

Life positions concern one's personal worth as well as the personal worth of others. Most are familiar with the following four life positions.

I'm Okay, You're Okay

This life position indicates an acceptance of one's own self-worth and the worth of others. A supervisor holding this life position will employ management by self-direction. It is the life position of the person who is a good problem solver. He or she can stand on his or her own two feet and yet be able to cooperate with others. This is a beautiful position to have in a supervisor or employee.

I'm Okay, You're Not Okay

This life position indicates a valuing of self but not of others. This type of supervisor tends to manage by edict. Such a person feels that his or her ideas are okay but those of everybody else are poor. Such a personality tends to be aggressive, as the one holding the first life position tends to be assertive. This individual gets his or her needs met, but at the expense of others.

I'm Not Okay, You're Okay

This position indicates an acceptance of others but not of oneself. It is the feeling of some psychologists that most individuals begin with this life position. As children, we have to get our needs met through others, and we are totally dependent on them. In management, this life position might be expressed through management by abdication, the wishy-washy manager who cannot make his or her own decisions. Such an employee would shrink away from additional responsibilities. He or she feels that he or she is not okay. Thus, this individual's organizational career is short-lived or limited.

I'm Not Okay, You're Not Okay

This is truly the life position of the loser. It indicates rejection of self as well as others. This is the person who chooses not to stand on his or her own two feet; the person who chooses not to cooperate with others. Management by chaos would be a common product of this life position. It is reflected in the type of manager who can't make his or her own decisions and, additionally, doesn't trust subordinates. It is a position that gets people nowhere fast and is the perfect wrong position for anyone wishing to obtain any reasonable degree of organizational success.

As we can see from injunctions, one of the basic problems with acting out a script is that it limits the individual's options. These are things that he or she doesn't think they can do. Negative script messages are things we all need to work on. Such internal script messages can be compounded by the organization. Passed down the chain of command, the "don't messages" lead to hang-ups, preventing employees from reaching the goals they should be reaching. Different types of individual and organizational scripts are examined in detail in chapters four and eleven respectively.

NOTES

1. M. Michael LeBoeuf and Maurice F. Villeré, "Tambo—Applying TA to MBO," *Atlanta Economic Review,* vol. 25, no. 2 (March–April 1975), pp. 30 and 33. Reprinted by permission of the publisher.

2. Stephen B. Karpman, "Fairy Tales and Script Drama Analysis," *Transactional Analysis Bulletin,* 7, no. 26 (April 1968), pp. 39–43.

3. William Shakespeare, *As You Like It,* act 2, scene 7.

THE INDIVIDUAL LEVEL
Increasing Productivity
and Morale by Overcoming
Motivational Myths

3

Two of the biggest problems encountered in any type of organization—
large or small, private or public—are motivation and communications.
I concentrate on motivation in this chapter, appropriately saving my
main remarks on communications for the section of this book dealing
with the interpersonal level.

In spite of the thousands of articles and hundreds of books that
have been written on the subject of motivation, stimulating employees
to be more productive is still a key problem for any organization. I
feel and think that one of the primary difficulties here is the number
of myths that individuals assume are fact when trying to motivate others.
Regardless of the abundance of research and practical experience to
the contrary, some supervisors cling to these "old wives' tales" on how
to motivate employees, even in spite of decreasing productivity and
morale. This chapter is an exercise on decontaminating supervisors'
adults from motivational myths.

SATISFIED WORKERS ARE
THE TOP PERFORMERS

Probably the most heavily cherished myth of organizational personnel
involves the notion that satisfaction leads to performance, or that happy

workers are productive workers. In fact, to the average reader, the proposition that happy workers are productive ones is unquestioned fact. To many, it would be organizational heresy to question such a myth. The responses of some readers would be typical:

> Don't tell me that. Anybody knows that happy workers are more productive. When they are happy, they are willing to get more involved in their work.

> I can tell you about me. If I don't like what I am doing, I only give a half-hearted effort.

> Look at sports. If you have a player who isn't satisfied with the position he or she is playing, they won't put out one hundred percent.

All these arguments appear to make a lot of common sense, but they do not mesh with the tremendous amount of research data on the subject. There have been hundreds upon hundreds of excellent studies in all types of organizational settings with bottom level employees to top managers trying to link satisfaction to performance with no success (1).

The reasons for not being able to link satisfaction directly to performance are multiple, but they mainly come down to what researchers and experts on the topic term moderator variables. "Moderator variables" is fancy terminology for saying that other factors moderate or influence the relationship between satisfaction and performance. In other words, the relationship between satisfaction and performance is too complex to understand without considering the effects of other factors.

Satisfaction————Moderating Factors————Performance

Ability

One big determinant of individual productivity is the innate capacity to do the job. An individual's child ego state may be overflowing with joy at the prospect of being a professional athlete, but the individual may not have the size, speed, or agility to get the job done. One primary example that almost everyone can relate to, the case of the irritating singer, demonstrate clearly that satisfaction on a task does not automatically lead to quality performance. Every family or organization always seems to have at least one individual who bursts into song without any provocation, but who cannot carry a tune. Although it is obvious that he or she is a happy singer, it is also obvious to listeners that the performance leaves a lot to be desired.

Responsibility

Some individuals constantly come out of their child ego state, particularly the rebellious child. Regardless of how much they enjoy the task at hand, they do not have the adult and parent control to responsibly complete the task.* Many organizations have members who would be great at what they do and who enjoy doing it, but who lack the discipline to keep reasonable office hours or appointments. Who has not heard the laments of managers:

> Joe could be one of our best account executives. He knows the product well and he is happy in what he does. Clients comment on the enthusiasm he radiates. But my guess is as good as another as to whether he will show up for an appointment or not.

> Mary excels in training supervisors on how to use our new performance appraisal form. She is good in front of a group and I know she likes her job. But often she will forget to bring basic training materials and we have to go through the ordeal of rescheduling the training class.

Too Much Contentment

Work does not have to be drudgery. In fact, it can be fun and stimulating. However, as the cliché goes, "all things in moderation." Too much contentment can stifle free child enthusiasm to produce. Without some even negative impetus—such as a little anxiety—learning tapers off. For example, if I gave students all A grades before the semester began, many would not even "crack" a book all year.

There was the case of a large, prominent, southern university that hired some well-established professors from the north. They were

---

* Information on how to deal with irresponsible workers is discussed in detail in chapter four.

all tenured, given full professor ranks (the top academic rank a university can bestow), and paid large salaries as conditions of employment. After a brief stay at the southern school, it was evident that these esteemed professionals were too contented to produce. Their needs in terms of recognition (they had acquired prominence through past publications), security, and advancement had been met. Their child ego states were so contented with past glories and security that these professors coasted to retirement at the southern school with little further productive effort. Usually, decadence—*not* achievement—comes from too much contentment.

Let me make it crystal clear in closing this section on the first work myth: Having a happy or satisfied work force is an asset to any organization. By saying that satisfaction does not directly or automatically lead to productivity does not mean that satisfaction is not a worthy goal in itself. In fact, the two primary objectives of any type of organization are productivity and morale. Without productivity, the needs of the organization are not met and the ultimate outcome is bankruptcy. On the other hand, poor morale—or a low satisfaction level on the part of subordinates—leads to higher turnover and absentee rates (2). Unsatisfied workers either quit or show up for work less often. Depending on training costs for new employees and the competition for labor in a given industry, poor morale can be costly in its own right. Additionally, severe long-term dissatisfaction with work or working conditions can lead to strikes, union formation, or even industrial sabotage. From the standpoint of the manager's free child as well, there is little joy in directing and in working day-in and day-out with a disgruntled work force.

Even though morale and productivity are primary and important organizational goals in and of themselves, the linkage between the two is definitely questionable. Satisfaction to a certain level is only one ingredient necessary for increased productivity. Other factors, such as ability, responsibility, and the amount of satisfaction involved also play critical roles in determining productive effort.

Supervisors and managers at any level in the organization do not achieve organizational or even individual objectives by turning their company, governmental department, or school system into a play yard or a country club. Work and fun do and can mix. The free child needs good strokes and feelings to keep the worker stimulated and committed to the organization. However, all play and no work leads to organizational suicide for everyone. Without development of the worker's adult ego state in the form of technical competence and the parent ego state in the form of responsible work habits, the country club manager is doing favors for no one. Employees who do not additionally receive adult and parent ego state nurturing and development soon lose their jobs and don't develop the skills and requirements to acquire new ones.

If you are truly interested in the welfare of your subordinates, stimulate growth to all ego states. Concentrate on productivity as well as satisfaction. In fact, productivity does lead to satisfaction to a certain extent. Without a certain level of productivity, how can a worker derive some of the most fulfilling rewards any job can offer—a sense of achievement, recognition, and competence (3).

WORKERS ARE MIND READERS

Although few managers would consciously admit they believe workers can read their minds, many treat employees as if they were devoutly devoted to this myth. Rather than specifically correct difficulties or praise specific accomplishments, they relate to workers in a vague way when appraising them.

I recall one foreman in a manufacturing plant who was chastised by his boss for being sloppy during the annual appraisal session. Until a later session with his boss two weeks later, he thought "sloppy" meant sloppy dress or an unkempt work area. It turned out his boss meant sloppy in meeting safety requirements.

In correcting or praising employees, target your strokes and comments to specific, concrete goals or behaviors. Individuals can only get a handle on specifics. If a news editor tells a reporter her "feel" for the news is okay, good, or not so good, the feedback is about as useless as the hot air surrounding it. However, if the editor gives specifics, like the following, the reporter has concrete feedback to learn from:

> You do a great job interviewing witnesses. Your quotes are right on target to the central theme of your stories. However, you 'beat around the bush' too much in your lead-in. Try working on a more complete approach that gives the reader the who, what, when, where, why, and how of the situation in the first two paragraphs. Here, let me give you a few sample stories on what I am talking about.

Target your strokes to specific ego states. Remember, you get what you stroke or reinforce. If you want to develop a certain part of the employee's personality, then specifically stroke that ego state. Examples of specific strokes targeted to ego states are:

Parent	Adult	Child
"Your work is always in on time."	"I could have never solved that equation without your help."	"You literally 'beam' when you smile. If you're that glowing over the prospectus, let's move ahead on the project."
"I can always count on you. If I give you a job to do, I know you'll be there with a top effort."	"Thanks for saving the company those extra tax dollars. I would have never thought of deduction. . . ."	
"Thanks for listening. Most people couldn't care less about issue XXX."	"You have a way of presenting reports that makes the complicated so clear and to the point that everybody on the staff can grasp the material."	"Without your sense of humor, this title work would be sheer dullsville."
"You put him in his place with your comment about . . ."		"I'm sorry you're feeling so down about the Doe Account. Believe me, even the best sales reps lose customers to competitors."
"Gosh, I never expected to get the day off. You're a great boss. You helped me when I needed it."	"That is one of the clearest, yet most concise explanations of Policy A I have ever heard."	"Hey, how about a big fat steak dinner and some cold beers to celebrate? We earned it!"

MONEY IS THE ONLY MOTIVATOR (OR MONEY STROKES ARE THE ONLY KINDS TO GIVE)

Frank McKinney Hubbard (1868–1930), the American humorist, once said:

> When a fellow says, "It ain't the money but the principle of the thing," it's the money.

If you talk to a number of supervisors, they apparently take Hubbard's words seriously in the work situation. Haven't we all heard critical parent remarks similar to these?

You can't take recognition to the grocery store.

Employees are like machines. Put in the money and out comes productivity.

You can't b.s. me. The bottom line is money.

All right. If you don't work, no pay.

Look, if you guys and gals put in a little extra during this rush order, there'll be a sweetener in your paychecks.

You want to know what motivates workers? Take away all the baloney rhetoric and you come down to what it's all about—money.

I am not trying to discount money as a motivator. Obviously, it is a necessity in meeting basic needs such as food and shelter. With money strokes, individuals may even be free to buy the time off and materials needed to fulfill personal growth needs. For example, with the aid of money, an individual can obtain the equipment and skills necessary to explore a personally fulfilling hobby or avocation.

However, money is just one among many sources of motivation. If used exclusively, money can turn an organization into an army of mercenaries. These types of workers will do whatever they are paid for—but not a bit more. Because their commitment is to money and not to people or organizational ideals, goals, or spirit, such workers will be quickly off to peddle their wares elsewhere when the next highest bidder comes along. Used as a sole method of motivating employees, money fosters a climate of flat productivity and high turnover.

Additionally, as some say in TA, there are different strokes for different folks. People differ in terms of what motivates them. Some people are motivated by social needs. Their enjoyment comes from the people with whom they work. Others are motivated by self-actualization or the need to realize their full potential. They seek work that offers them a challenge. Others work almost exclusively for monetary rewards. According to two management consultants, Russell and Black, Jr.: "There are three principles of motivation: people are different; people are different; people are different." (4)

Abraham Maslow, the late prominent psychologist, classified the needs of individuals into five types: physiological, security and safety, social, ego, and self-fulfillment (5). Rewards that might satisfy these needs and the ego states they relate to are as follows.

Physiological Needs

These needs are met by basics such as food, rest, drink, and the physical comforts. Through adequate compensation, the individual is able to purchase the basics that will meet his physiological needs. *These are the basic needs of the free child.*

Security and Safety Needs

These needs deal with concerns over physical or psychological danger. Protective rules, insurance policies, retirement programs, adequate salary, good pension programs, burglar alarm systems, and safety features are obvious ways of meeting this need. *The insecure adapted child needs strokes targeted to meet this need.*

Social Needs

This is the need to be accepted, to be loved, and to belong. Jobs can be structured to meet these needs by affording personnel various opportunities to socialize and to talk to each other. For example, friendly and helpful support personnel such as secretaries and trainers can make the job of the salesperson or professional a much more enjoyable experience. Extracurricular activities and social functions can help meet social needs and build team work to boot. Many large insurance companies find that their most effective sales training workshops are conducted in resort areas that afford an excellent opportunity for social interaction among sales personnel. *The child in all of us needs good social strokes.*

Ego Needs

This is the need to be somebody by gaining status, prestige, and respect. Jobs providing for advancement and adequate recognition are on target to meet ego needs. Performance charts displayed on bulletin boards is a common technique used by sales staffs for increasing sales effort via ego needs. Recognizing outstanding producers in organizational newsletters or house organs is another excellent way of stroking ego needs. *The child and the parent particularly crave this need for importance.*

Self-Fulfillment Needs

Reputed by Maslow to be the ultimate of all needs, self-fulfillment deals with the individual's drive to realize his or her full potential in whatever he or she does. Giving an individual challenging work or work that offers autonomy can help meet the self-fulfillment need. Some organizations have gone to management by objective (MBO) approaches in order to stimulate productivity by tapping the self-fulfillment need (6). During MBO, employees are given the autonomy to set their own specific goals, timetables, and strategies. Managers deal with personnel more like coaches than bosses. By permitting personnel freedom to set their own goals and strategies, the manager is, in effect, stroking the self-fulfillment need. *Stroking the adult, the individual's ability to think for himself, is a good way to develop this need in anyone.*

Some managers have used questionnaires for exploring ways of motivating subordinates. This approach lacks the personal touch of face-to-face contact, but might be useful particularly as an overall measure of job motivating factors or rewards.

One of the best self-report instruments around for measuring motivation factors is the Job Orientation (JOI) Scales. These scales divide motivation rewards or strokes into ten categories. For comparison purposes I have linked Maslow's needs to each category.

Strokes for *self-fulfillment* needs	1. Achievement or sense of accomplishment
	2. Responsibility or control
	3. Opportunity for personal growth.
Ego needs strokes	4. Recognition from the community and from friends
	5. Job or company status
Social needs strokes	6. Interpersonal relationships or friendships

Can really stroke almost any needs	7. Pay or monetary reward
Security needs strokes	8. Job security
Physiological needs strokes	9. Provision for family
Strokes for *self-fulfillment* needs	10. Support for hobbies or avocational activities (7)

In order to avoid a ranking bias, the ten different stroke categories could be placed on separate index cards so that all appear to carry equal weight. Then you could ask the individual involved to number each in order of preference. If some appear to carry equal weight in terms of their goals or needs, then score these as a tie. Although the above factors were generated from a large sample of different types of workers, if they do not seem complete for your particular work situation, add more factors. The best measuring instruments are those tailored to a particular situation.

WORKERS NEED TO BE FRUSTRATED TO BE MOTIVATED

Some managers subscribe to the philosophy that if workers are not "kept on their toes" through constant badgering, conflicts, or hurdles that they won't put forth a top effort. These types of supervisors say: "Keep your workers constantly off guard and they will have to work doubly hard to keep up."

As mentioned earlier, too much contentment can lead to complacency and poor performance. On the other hand, the opposite is also true. Put an individual or a group of individuals in a very frustrating situation for a long period of time and a number of things are likely to happen. Almost all of these are bad.

From an individual standpoint, we know that too much frustration can lead to emotional ills if turned inward or to violence if turned outward toward others. The adult ego state functions best under the relaxed and confidence building climate generated by the nurturing parent, not the turmoil created by the critical parent. Symbolically, this is why the nurturing parent ego state is drawn closest to the adult.

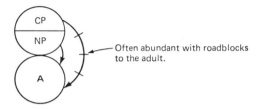

Often abundant with roadblocks to the adult.

It is easier to think clearly and logically when one is relaxed rather than when one is frustrated. Although a moderate amount of anxiety is necessary to stimulate learning (as already indicated, one whose needs are totally satiated has no desire to perform), too much anxiety incapacitates the adult with an overload of confusion or conflict.

Responses of employees in a very frustrating climate are very obvious.

> Son of a gun. I do not know what to do anymore. My superior, Mr. Jones, keeps piling the work on so fast I don't know which end is up.

> First, she tells me to do A, then to do B, then to do C, and then back to A again. . . . She's driving me up the wall.

> Screw him. If he gives me one more last minute problem to handle today, I quit.

> All right! Let her shove all this stuff at me all at once. I'll fix her little wagon! I'll slow my production down to a halt.

From the above comments, it can be seen that it is typically the counterproductive adapted child that the superior engages—not a keyed-up adult—in the "keep them frustrated" environment. Pile on the aggravations and you often activate the rebellious adapted child in terms of procrastination or slowdown: "You push me too far, critical parent boss, and I'll show you by coming to a standstill." Or, quite frequently, the end result is the helpless adapted child, too confused to do much of anything except to pass time exclaiming: "Ain't it awful what's happening to me."

At the group level, too much frustration can lead to organized rebellion in such forms as deliberately damaging equipment, striking, union organizing, clique forming, and damaging power struggles.

I recall a university situation in which associate professors were repeatedly denied promotion to the rank of full professor. For six years not one associate professor was recommended to the rank of full professor, in spite of the fact that most of the associates had outpublished the fulls three to one in journal output and were considered overall, according to student evaluations, to be superior teachers. Claiming to be vanguards of academic excellence, the fulls would constantly up promotion standards, change promotion criteria halfway through the year, and harass associates with time-consuming committee assignments.

Although in the short run the fulls' harassment approach to motivation may have stimulated extra research effort on the part of some associates, in the long run the results proved clearly counterproductive and disastrous. Two of the top associates left for better paying positions at more prestigious universities. The remaining six associates joined the newly-affiliated teacher's union. With the aid of the union faculty representatives and union lawyers, they immediately filed a grievance suit. Though the matter is still in litigation, it appears that the associates will win hands down, with costly repercussions to the university. At a minimum, the rift in the department between fulls and associates has widened and has become more solidified.

Once launched on a full-scale basis, the ill effects of the harassment approach are hard to remedy without serious repercussions to all parties involved. Here is some wise preventive maintenance for any administrator or supervisor.

First of all, give your subordinates challenges, not hurdles. Design the work environment so that there are healthy challenges for both the workers' adult and free child. In a straightforward fashion, challenge subordinates with demands that are consistent with the subordinates' adult data and background at that point in time. Working with the employees, help them set realistic goals for themselves. Act more like a coach or a guide than a boss in helping employees set goals. In this fashion you will boost morale by demonstrating a respect and trust in the subordinates who will reciprocate in kind. Additionally, by treating subordinates as origins of motivation, and not as pawns to be manipulated, you will help them expand their own adult capacities to produce. With a solid organizational climate based on trust and expanding technical adult competence, your work unit will pay dividends in morale and productivity in the long run that trickery and manipulation could never reap.

> You know, I love working in this department. It's a challenge. It's never dull or boring. I actually feel no one is out to use me. As inconceivable as it is in some work situations, here they actually try to help you develop your own talents. Having pride in your own abilities is something no one can ever take from you.

What might amaze you is that when left with an opportunity to pace themselves, employees will often set higher goals than a fair boss would. You will find, in many cases, that your guidance role will involve tempering employees' goals down to more realistic levels.

Goals should be moderately stretching. Goals set too low lead to boredom for the employee's adult. Goals set too high can be even more costly, as already indicated. In setting goals with employees, let them clearly know that they are not locked into any unrealistic demands they may have placed on themselves. Inform them that the goal-setting process, like any other meaningful human process, is a dynamic one. Though certain minimum standards and deadlines must be met, adjustments can always be made to bring demands into line with realistic expectations and circumstances. Only critical parent game-playing bosses lock subordinates into no-win goals.

Foster the subordinate's free child by making creativity and innovation something to be lauded, not discounted. Too often managers hinder worker ingenuity by critical parent injunctions, expressed verbally or nonverbally, such as:

> Don't make waves. Just do your job and be quiet about it.

> Sure it's okay to alter our procedure on X process. But don't do it without filling out forms A, B, C, D, E, amended forms J & K, and appended forms Y to Z.

Yes, indeed, we encourage new ideas. Don't forget to put them in the suggestion box. We'll get to them in a couple of years at least.

I don't object to new and novel approaches to anything around here provided they don't disagree with mine.

Secondly, when practical, temper your lead by example. The truly great leaders do not put demands on others that they have not or would not place on themselves. Management by hypocrisy, or measuring employees by standards alien to your own, is fated to doom. The full professors discussed previously never would have reaped disaster on their department if they had placed the same research demands on themselves that they placed on the associate professors. If the standards are constantly rising, they should rise for everyone.

Individuals who, through experience, know what it takes to publish so many articles per year, close so many sales, design so many structures, establish so many personnel policies, set up so many computer programs, file so many briefs, write up so many reports, or retool so much machinery are not very likely to harass others by excessive or frustrating demands. Experience is a teacher rooted in adult sobriety and practicality if it is rooted in anything. By and large, I have found that supervisors who make excessive demands on others have the least productive output themselves. There is no job too big for the person who doesn't do it.

THE MANAGER'S JOB IS TO CONVERT WORKERS OVER TO NEW MOTIVES

Some individuals confuse motivation with brainwashing or some form of intensive psychotherapy. Consciously or unconsciously, they relate to employees by trying to change their whole value and motivational systems. If an individual detests solitary work, they put him or her in a clerical or research job far away from others, telling them—in effect—that they are missing the joys of privacy that come from working alone. To those who want challenging self-actualizing work, the manager tries to convince that routine, ordinary work tempers the soul with needed discipline. Individuals who prefer not to speak in front of groups are lectured on the joys of public speaking.

I know what I am saying sounds a lot like claims made about

the military where, supposedly, individuals were placed in jobs in direct conflict to their needs and qualifications. You have heard the stories of drafted engineers who were made medical assistants and drafted accountants who were placed in engineering jobs. However, even if these claims were true in the past, the military no doubt now refrains from such poor use of manpower since we no longer have a military draft.

This mistaken way of motivating workers—by trying to convert them over to needs other than their own—takes place day-in and day-out in all types of organizations—large or small, public or private. I recall the case of a large law firm that tried to convince a shy new female recruit to get in the litigation section. Litigation, for those not familiar with legal work, involves the handling of cases in court. However, much legal work—approximately 90 percent of it—involves non-litigation duties like research, drafting contracts, closing loan transactions, etc.

The new recruit became so "worked-up" over the prospect of trying her first court case that she made herself ill. Finally, after another agonizing week prior to the trial, she quit the firm and later joined another. She is now doing very well in a nonlitigation section of an equally prominent firm.

Another case involved an honors MBA graduate who was in an executive training program with a large oil company. Despite his protestations concerning accounting work, particularly cost accounting, he was placed in a cost accounting section for an extended period of his training. The end result was that he left for a competing concern that offered him a job in the business field most interesting to him, personnel.

In the case of both the law firm and the oil company, there was a shortage of personnel in the areas to which management tried to push the new recruits. Other reasons for trying to convince employees to want what they do not need are: insensitivity to others, a misguided view of one's persuasive abilities, and the parental injunction, which probably overrides all other rationale—don't be you. In essence, be what I want you to be.*

Basic needs and desires are developed at an early age. For example, individuals who are reared in a environment in which most of their needs are met through others tend to develop a large social need. Individ-

* A detailed discussion on injunctions and life scripts follows in chapter four.

uals who receive little assistance in getting earlier needs met tend to have larger ego needs. Though fundamental needs may change over time, it is unlikely that this will happen without a great deal of time, insight, and hard work on the part of an individual who is strongly motivated to make such a change.

The proper and appropriate role of a supervisor or manager is to tap or work with the needs structure that the employee brings with him or her to the work situation. In this fashion you will be doing what is practical and effective, both morale wise and productivity wise. One able and experienced personnel director put it this way:

> It is much easier to work with individuals than against them. Anyway, individual needs are as much a part of the individual as fruit is to a tree. You can't any more induce an individual to do or not to do something if such a need does not exist than you can pick fruit from a tree that is barren.

The effective manager or supervisor might find it useful to do a little exploratory history when hiring a new employee in order to get a "feel" for his or her stroke needs. After hiring, strokegrams might be constructed, based on personnel histories, and then updated periodically. As pointed out earlier, you get what you stroke. Stroke an individual for clear thinking and you bring out the adult. Stroke him or her for being fun to be around and you bring out the free child. The strokegram will help you target your strokes toward the ego states that best meet the productivity needs of your organization, as well as the needs of the individual worker.

The strokegram for employee X would read as follows.

STROKEGRAM

Ego States	History	Types of Strokes to Give
Nurturing parent	Does part-time work at the cripple children's hospital. Loves to nurture others.	Keep on stroking his nurturing parent for taking on responsibility and caring functions when dealing with clients. A little extra nurturing can mean a lot of repeat business and good strokes for everyone.

Ego States	History	Types of Strokes to Give
Critical parent	Likes to be punctual and is critical of those who aren't, but does not have a critical nature otherwise.	Being punctual is an okay thing to stroke. But I don't want him getting upset with co-workers who are late. It could cause friction. I'll let him know it is my job to give constructive criticism to tardy co-workers.
Adult	Prefers to have full responsibility for his own projects and opted for doing a lot of his college term projects alone. Get's a "kick" out of thinking through things on his own. He grew up in a family where the parents encouraged self-responsibility early on. But he can work with others agreeably when needed.	I'll stroke his adult need for autonomy by self-management. I'll give him a lot more discretion early on in setting his own goals and in completeing work projects
Free child	Loves to tell jokes, but these don't interfere with getting the job done.	I love a good sense of humor—makes the serious stuff go down easier. A good laugh is the best way to stroke this free child need.
Adapted child	Despite his great abilities and individual initiative, he tends to be somewhat insecure when starting up a new project.	In dealing with this need I have to be careful. Trying to take on too much responsibility myself will turn off his adult and parent needs for autonomy. A few general guidelines and some solid reminders of his talents in accomplishing projects in the past seems to work well. This one stroke approach I may want to monitor carefully to avoid conflicting with his strong need for autonomy.

THE "SINK-OR-SWIM" PHILOSOPHY
IN DEALING WITH NEW EMPLOYEES

Some employers view new recruits as one swimming instructor viewed new swimmers: "Throw them in the water and they'll learn how to swim quickly. They have no choice." As one manager stated:

> The employee's probationary period is a testing ground for the survival of the fittest theory. Those who naturally learn the technical and interpersonal ropes the quickest will survive and become great assets to the organization. Those who go by the wayside were of no use to the organization anyway.

In actuality, the "sink-or-swim"—no orientation and no training approach—is a very costly way to run an organization and is based on a number of fallacious assumptions. First of all, the individuals who survive the "throw them to the wolves" approach may be excellent short-term adapters, like the athletic kid who physically matures quickly in grade school. However, over the long haul, he or she might not continue to grow in expertise and interpersonal competence. Late bloomers often easily surpass the physically precocious kid in high school or college athletics.

Secondly, the "sink-or-swim" approach ignores the established fact that with proper guidance and coaching morale and productivity can be increased significantly for late or early bloomers at a great savings in start-up costs. Start-up costs are costs involved in getting any new employee launched in a new career from machine maintenance to top management.

> The new employee does not know the job, how the organization works, or whom to see to get the job done. This means that for a while the new employee is less efficient than the experienced employee, and additional costs are involved in getting the new employee started. These start-up costs have been estimated for various positions as follows: top manager, to $2,000; middle manager, $1,000; supervisor, $1,000; senior engineer, $900; accountant, $750; and secretary, $400. Effective orientation reduces

these start-up costs and enables the new employee to reach standards sooner.

Additionally, good orientation programs mean good time management:

> Improperly oriented employees must still get the job done, and to do so they need help. The most likely people to provide this help are the co-workers and supervisors, who will have to spend time breaking in new employees. Good orientation programs save everyone time (8).

Concerned over morale, productivity, and turnover problems with new female assemblers, Texas Instruments developed an experiment to see if an orientation program designed to reduce new worker anxiety would help alleviate some of the above problems. The results were dramatic. The group subjected to the orientation program were absent or tardy 50 percent less. In addition, waste was cut by 80 percent, product costs were down 15 to 30 percent, training time was cut by 50 percent, and training costs were reduced an amazing 66⅔ percent (9).

Improper orientation programs lead to higher turnover and, thus, the additional costs involved in recruiting still other new employees. The initial working period for any employee is difficult enough. Just learning the new technology for the job can be a significant adult challenge. To hinder the employee's adult learning curve with additional anxiety in the form of an indifferent "sink-or-swim" critical parent management approach adds nothing to morale or productivity. Employees who leave in droves from what appears at first glance to be a hostile work environment won't make additional recruiting any easier. Having worked for an engineering search company has made me well aware of how disgruntled employees can effectively do a negative public relations number on their previous employer. In a tight labor market, where employees are in short supply, the p.r. effects can be extremely costly.

In closing this chapter I would like to give you a tested stroking formula that should serve you well not only in helping newcomers over the hump but that should also work well with experienced employees learning a new job (10). However, an expansion on the TA concept of stroking is necessary for a complete understanding of the formula.

According to TA, there are actually four strokes: two types of positive strokes and two types of negative ones. These are conditional and unconditional positive and conditional and unconditional negative. Graphically, these might be viewed as follows:

Positive		Negative
Conditional Strokes for doing things right.		*Conditional* Strokes for doing things wrong.
Outcome: You win under certain conditions.	**1** | **3**	*Outcome:* You lose under certain conditions.
	2 | **4**	
Unconditional Good strokes whether you do something wrong, right, or nothing at all.		*Unconditional* Negative strokes regardless of what you do.
Outcome: You can't lose for winning.		*Outcome:* You can't win for losing.

In a business situation, generally the conditional strokes are best because they are tied to specific performances or behavior. Conditional strokes are conditioned upon or are consequences of certain behavior. The name of the game is to reinforce effective behavior and to extinguish what is unproductive. Work behaviors, such as selling techniques and methods, for example, are a function of their consequences. If you perform well, you get a sale. The reward, which is a conditional positive stroke, then induces you to sell well again. Similarly, if you fail to close a lot of sales, you either receive no strokes or no reward or negative strokes on terms of criticism from the boss that should help to extinguish this type of unproductive behavior. The boss's criticism following unproductive sales behavior would be a conditional negative stroke.

An effective sales manager, like any good manager, then appropriately ties types of sales performance (good, bad, or indifferent) to the appropriate consequences or strokes. It might be said that the essence of management is the management of consequences or strokes. For how you connect strokes or consequences to work behaviors determines how you get work done through your personnel. If there is little or no connection or instrumentality between work behavior and rewards or strokes, then mediocrity will be the order of the day (11). Why push hard if you get paid the same? This principle explains why some type of sales commission is necessary for most selling jobs. Salespersons on straight salaries receive unconditional positive strokes (money whether they sell or not) and as a result may often be seen sitting on their hands. This might be why it is hard for customers to find salaried salespersons in department stores.

In order to get a reading of how well you are managing your personnel, a behavior instrumentality stroke questionnaire such as the following might be helpful.*

Work Behavior   Stroke

As a result of:

1. Having problems with my equipment, I _____

_____.

2. Doing a superior job, I _____

_____.

3. Making suggestions to the boss, I _____

_____.

5. Getting my quota in on time, I _____

_____.

---

* Although the one given here is designed to be filled out by employees, it can very easily be changed to be filled out by managers as raters of the employees by changing the "I" to a third person personal pronoun like "he" or "she."

6. Saving the organization and the client money, I _____

   _____ .

7. _____

   , I will receive adult strokes from my supervisor._____

8. Doing an excellent job servicing clients, I _____

   _____ .

9. Having a free child sense of humor, I _____

   _____ .

10. Playing games, I _____

    _____ .

11. _____

    _____ , I will be given added responsibilities.

Feel free to add other relationships or alter the above relationships to fit what is most suitable to your particular occupation.

If work behaviors and strokes don't match, then these have to be altered so as to be appropriately connected. For example, if a sales manager wishes to get sales tips from his salespersons but ignores them or is critical of suggestions, then he will cease to receive them. The conditional negative stroke or lack of strokes will extinguish the behavior.

Unconditional strokes are much less preferred in a business situation than conditional ones for the prime reason already mentioned: Why "push" hard if you get the same strokes for not pushing hard. Unconditional *negative* strokes should be avoided like the plague in all situations. They are about as welcome in an organization as a new, large competitor with a far superior product. Unconditional negative strokes are indicative of a no-win situation. Regardless of what is done, it's wrong. Such environments lead to total frustration or outlets. Many go to other organizations to get the good strokes. Some take their frustrations out on the company in terms of sabotage or even industrial espionage in terms of leaking new product secrets. Others get into heavy political game playing for the purpose of overthrowing the powers that be. As mentioned already, managers win by getting top efforts from personnel, not by frustrating them.

There is no greater morale and productivity destroyer than placing subordinates in the no-win situation defined by unconditional negative strokes. Astute managers should be on the lookout for any office situations where this problem exists. To those reading this book, it may seem that only the dumbest of managers would let such a situation exist, but unfortunately unconditional negative strokes are alive and flourishing in many organizations—in some cases in organizations that should know better.

For example, some universities place professors in no-win grading situations. If they do not give enough good grades, it will be hard to attract new students, the administrators say. However, if they give too many good grades, professors are admonished for lowering universities' standards by rewarding poor quality work with quality grades.

We want to make it clear that *unconditional positive* strokes are useful in organizations only when used in conjunction with *conditional positive* strokes. *Only* giving good strokes to people, whether they are productive or not (unconditional positive strokes), will soon lead to the downfall of the business or organization. On the other hand, *only* giving positive strokes when an employee is productive (conditional positive strokes) or when you want to get something out of them can lead workers to feel that they are being exploited or manipulated. The impression will be accurate.

Employees who only receive strokes for producing and not for just being a part of the organization (Dorothy Jongeward and Philip

Seyer term these unconditional positive strokes) (12) often have reactions like:

> We're machines around here. As long as we are producing everything is fine. If we weren't their top producers, they'd probably discard us like worn parts.

> Mr. Jones, my sales manager, only talks to me when I sign up another prospect.

> I wouldn't work for those bastards if I could afford to work elsewhere.

> They are about as interested in us as they are in a new cup of that awful coffee.

Strokes, like boomerangs and rubber checks, have a way of coming back, even when you expect nothing in return (as in the case of unconditional positive strokes). I once had a stockbroker who would be on the lookout for and would report critical information in the *Wall Street Journal* or from whatever source if he felt it might affect my position in a given stock, even when I had not traded in many months. In the long run I made many more high commission trades with this broker than I did with a previous broker who never watched out for my stocks and who only called me to buy or sell. It became obvious to me that the second broker valued me more as a friend than as a commodity.

Overall, I would like to point out again that regardless of what type, positive strokes should be much preferred over negative ones. Positive strokes build spirit, self-confidence, and OK feelings. They also help develop rapport and team work between and among the parties involved. Negative strokes create hostility, put employees on the defensive, help destroy creativity and feelings of okayness, and tend to point out errors—not solutions. Extinguishing what a person should not be doing does not necessarily tell them what to do. In chapter ten, on leadership, I demonstrate how to give constructive criticism.

In closing, here is an effective stroking procedure or formula for getting new employees over the hump. Use it wisely and you will save yourself a great deal of time and money in start-up costs, reduced turnover, and improved morale and productivity.

1. *Stroke Desired Behavior Right After It Occurs and Make a Big Deal Over It.* Right after Mr. or Mrs. Doe completes the first project, makes the first sale, interviews the first employee, etc., make a "big deal" over it. For them it is a big deal. I am not suggesting here that you give what TA calls "candy" strokes or ingenuine strokes. In the long run, dishonest "candy" strokes—even positive ones—will be detected for the fraud they are and will be received with indifference or negative reactions. Remind employees that the first successes are the hardest ones. Managers should encourage new employees to practice techniques and methods in front of them and other co-workers where practical. Good points should be immediately applauded and complemented.

2. *Stroke Degrees of Success.* No one—in any profession or occupation—ever reaches perfection, and very few are ever overnight successes. Do not refrain from giving out positive strokes to newcomers who are not "tearing up the ball park the first time out the gate." Let them know that overnight success is very rare, and give them good strokes even when they approximate quotas. "Hey, Mr. Doe or Ms. Doe, XXX accomplishments the first few months is nothing to sneeze at. It's a darn good first effort in our organization."

3. *Up the Stroking Criteria.* Depending on what trend figures or experience tells you for a given field and the progress of the newcomer, up the stroking criteria over time. This time make a big deal over XXXXX amount of effort after three or four months. "Now Mr. Doe or Ms. Doe, your accomplishments are such and such. This is a great effort for the fourth month in the business. How about a few beers to celebrate?"

4. *Initially, Stroke Immediately; Then Intermittently.* Behavioral research indicates that reinforcement is most durable if given intermittently. Initially, new employees are on shaky ground and need confidence building. Immediate and consistent positive strokes at the outset help settle down the insecure child. However, after maturing somewhat in the field and reaching a certain desired level of performance, constant and immediate positive strokes might be viewed as

coddling, controlling, patronizing, or "candy." By this time the new employee knows enough about the field to give himself or herself good strokes for desired performance. On the other hand, we do not mean to drop good strokes altogether. Occasional unconditional positive strokes or being strokes are always good to remind the newcomer or anyone else that they are a valuable part of the team just because they are who they are. Also, periodic conditional positive strokes are good for any employee, regardless of how long they have been with the organization. If nothing else, it's a reminder that good efforts are still much appreciated. "Gee, Mr. Doe or Ms. Doe, that was an especially nice job you did yesterday." There are few persons who do not welcome with open arms special, intermittent positive strokes like this.

NOTES

1. Although the research is common knowledge in the field, one excellent article on the topic is: Donald P. Schwab and Larry L. Cummings, "Theories of Performance and Satisfaction: A Review," *Industrial Relations,* vol. 9, no. 4 (October 1970), pp. 408–430.
2. Richard M. Steers and Lyman W. Porter, *Motivation and Work Behavior* (New York: McGraw-Hill Book Company, 1975), pp. 277–279.
3. For an excellent discussion on how productivity leads to job satisfaction, also see: Schwab and Cummings, "Theories of Performance and Satisfaction: A Review."
4. G. Hugh Russell and Kenneth Black, Jr., *Human Behavior in Business* (New York: Prentice-Hall, 1972), p. 160.
5. Abraham H. Maslow, *Motivation and Personality* (New York: Harper & Brothers, 1954).
6. For an expanded discussion on applying TA to MBO, see: M. Michael LeBoeuf and Maurice F. Villeré, "Tambo—Applying TA to MBO," *Atlanta Economic Review,* vol. 25, no. 2 (March–April 1975), pp. 29–35.
7. Milton R. Blood, "Intergroup Comparisons of Intraperson Differences: Rewards from the Job," *Personnel Psychology,* vol. 26, no. 1 (1973), p. 4.
8. William F. Glueck, *Personnel: A Diagnostic Approach,* 1978 rev. ed. (Dallas, Tex.: Business Publications, Inc., 1978), pp. 239–240. Start-up cost figures taken from: Robert Sibson, "The High Cost of Hiring," *Nation's Business,* February 1975, pp. 85-86.

9. Earl R. Gomersall and M. Scott Myers, "Breakthrough in On-the-Job Training," *Harvard Business Review* (July-August 1966), pp. 62–71.

10. Parts of the formula to follow are similar to that generally recommended for workers by Jongeward and Seyer, *Choosing Success: Transactional Analysis on the Job*, pp. 86–87.

11. For an excellent discussion of instrumentality theory and research on motivational determinants of effective job performance in general, see: Victor H. Vroom, *Work and Motivation* (New York: John Wiley & Sons, Inc., 1964), pp. 211–288. Also see: W. Clay Hamner, "Worker Motivation Programs: The Importance of Climate, Structure, and Performance Consequences," in *Contemporary Problems in Personnel*, rev. ed. Edited by W. Clay Hamner and Frank L. Schmidt (Chicago, Ill.: St. Clair Press, 1977), pp. 256–284.

12. Dorothy Jongeward and Philip C. Seyer, *Choosing Success: Transactional Analysis on the Job* (New York: John Wiley & Sons, Inc., 1978), p. 96.

PERSONALITY AND THE ORGANIZATION

> Over time, those whose personalities and skills enable them to fit into the organization's human relations tend to stay on; those whose personalities conflict tend to leave—either voluntarily or involuntarily (1).

4

THE ORGANIZATIONAL WINNER

Some individuals are organizational winners. Their personalities, or individual styles of behaving and relating to others, are conducive to the achievement of their own personal goals and needs as well as those of the organizations. These organizational winners promote performance and morale through a spirit of cooperation, competence, and enthusiasm. They operate interdependently. They are competent enough to stand on their own two feet—performance wise and human relations wise— and yet are able to cooperate with others as work demands. As mentioned in chapter one, this individual acts primarily out of the maturity stage of personality growth.*

The organizational winner is motivated primarily by higher level needs in Maslow's model, including self-fulfillment, ego, and social. He or she is self-fulfilled by whatever they do. To them, work is also an end in itself and not just a means to other ends.

> I truly love what I am doing. I don't think I would get as much a kick out of anything else.

* See chapter one for the chart that discusses personality types by maturity stages.

You know, I wish everyone was as lucky as me. I love my work and the people I am working with. I know most people are bored or hassled by their jobs. But as for me, I am glad most of the time.

All I can tell you is that my work is a challenge, it's exciting, and fun to do much of the time. I really look forward to getting up in the morning and doing my job most days.

You want me to tell you why I think Mary is a winner on the job? I'll make it simple and to the point. She loves what she is doing. She does it well and she's a breeze to work with. From my standpoint, I look forward to working with Mary. I know I'll get an emotional lift whenever I team up with her.

One other primary characteristic of organizational winners is that they are learners. They are flexible and humble enough to learn new ways of doing the job as conditions dictate. Rather than being "locked-in" to set rules, techniques, procedures, and methodologies, they are receptive to new ideas, styles, and new approaches to the job. They actually embrace growth and change instead of devoutly resisting it. Change is an inevitable fact of life. Everything in the environment and within ourselves constantly changes over time—from biological cells to our top competitors. If we are not willing to adapt to these changes, we will most surely suffer some serious defeats down the road. Organizations and groups, as well as individuals, need adaptive mechanism—or they court disaster. There are many organizations and organizational members who have not survived because they would not change to meet competitive demands or changing times.

Many enterprises, especially those which have been in operation for many years, become too rigid to meet the first test of effective organization structure—adaptation to changing environment. . . . Some of the older companies provide ample evidence of these inflexibilities: an organization pattern no longer suited to the times. . . . Some of the railroads remained organized in territorial divisions originally determined by the daily mileage of a steam locomotive long after the diesel locomotive had made such divisions obsolete. Some of the defense plants of World War II still held fast to the complicated structures of their war-swollen industrial empires although their postwar operations were reduced by as much as 90 percent. The Ford Motor Company lost much of its efficiency and market before new management, under the founder's grandson, dispersed the centralized authority demanded by the late Henry Ford, Sr. (2).

Two noted management authorities, Harold Koontz and Cyril O'Donnell, comment:

> The most effective management is flexible management. Since the environment in which an enterprise operates is certain to change, and since the attitudes and motivations of people likewise vary, it can be no exaggeration to emphasize the importance of flexibility in managing (3).

Flexibility is one of the prime traits that has made Paul "Bear" Bryant of Alabama a coaching legend in his own time. The second winningest coach in the history of college football and the first coach ever to have over 100 victories in a decade (the 1970s), Bryant has always had the knack to shift styles of play and recruiting aims in order to meet competition and changing times. He has shifted formations, motivation techniques, and training methods—always with an eye on upgrading his squads to the latest and best in offensive and defensive strategies and tactics. When little, quick men got the job done, he used them. Now that big, quick athletes get the job done even better, he has quickly changed his recruiting strategy (4).

In TA terminology, the organizational winner might best be viewed in terms of an egogram (5). An egogram is a bar graph of an individual's (the concept can also apply to groups or organizations) personality by ego states. It describes how often the individual typically comes out of each of the five ego states.* Though an individual's egogram on the job may be somewhat different from the one he shows at home, I feel that people are basically consistent. As you get to know them well, certain ego states become apparent and prevail both on and off the job.

---

* Some in TA like to give specific mathematical percentages out of 100 percent. For example, some might describe an individual as coming out of the CP 12½ percent of the time, the NP, 25 percent, the A, 25 percent, the FC, 25 percent, and the AC, 12½ percent. If mathematical percentages are helpful to you in sizing up another's personality, then use them. I am cautious concerning applying mathematical precision to human behavior. I do not think human behavior can be reduced to precise numbers or mathematical equations. Sometimes individuals get hung up on numbers and lose the overall "feel" for the other person's personality in the process.

From my research on organizations, in terms of materials read and the contacts I have made in numerous workshops, I would say that the organizational winner (regardless of the type of organization or job*)—the high producer and happy and adjusted worker—would look as follows:

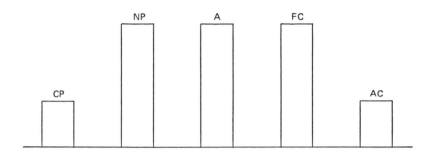

The larger nurturing parent, as I have already mentioned, is the key to the cooperative spirit in people. The nurturing parent, through its genuinely supportive and tolerant nature, builds a strong foundation of trust and spirit. Team work, cooperation, and warm social relations between and among organizational members are not possible without a large dose of the nurturing parent. The positive strokes the nurturing parent constantly puts forth help heal the hurts and reduce the friction and frustration that are a part of any organization.

The nurturing parent is also the key to developing the other winning parts of anyone's personality. With positive reinforcement through good strokes, self-support, and the view that mistakes are vehicles for learning rather than opportunities to punish, the nurturing parent generates the ideal climate within an individual for fostering a solid adult and a large free child. As already indicated in chapter two, the nurturing parent makes the large free child possible. It gives the personality the room to be creative and innovative. It nurtures the straightforward

* Like any general prescription on anything, this portrait may not be ideal for all jobs. For example, in a combat situation a larger, automatically complying adapted child may be necessary for survival reasons. Too much free child here could lead to disaster on the field of battle. Also, see chapter nine for the egogram of the effective leader that expands on the use of the same ego states but from a leadership perspective.

expression of feelings and thought. The nurturing parent is a cornerstone of the individual as well as a cornerstone of organizational integrity.

> You know, it is okay to be innovative around here. I mean they really are receptive and encouraging to new approaches. And it's okay to confront the boss about policies or procedures that aren't working. It's not like where I worked before. Suggestions were either ignored or viewed as a threat to the status quo. And confrontations and negative feedback! Oh, boy, if you disagreed with the boss, he'd figure a way to take it out on you sooner or later. Here, they help remove the obstacles to progress. At my other job they were forever thinking of ways to build bigger and more formidable obstacles.

The large free child is also indicative of an individual who is excited and enthusiastic about his or her work and his or her co-workers. Enthusiasm leads to high morale and productivity—the signposts of an organizational winner. As a manager mentioned to me once:

> I'll take a recruit with desire and enthusiasm over one with more ability anytime. You give me a B student who is committed to his profession or skill—whether it is accounting or welding—for he or she will make a much better go of it, for much longer, than the A+ student who is mildly interested. Enthusiasm, or the lack of it, is also contagious. You want a top notch department? You'd better keep the 'couldn't care less' types to a minimum.

With an abundance of creative ideas flowing in from the free child, and the self-confidence generated by the supportive nurturing parent, the adult computer is in the ideal psychological environment for functioning at its peak. When at peak functioning, the adult is in the best position to solve technical and interpersonal problems. Armed with good inputs and the freedom, as well as encouragement, to think through matters and projects clearly, work competence is assured. One excellent indication of a properly functioning adult is the ability to explain things and to simplify the complicated. Confusion and overcomplication are the results of a contaminated adult. Confusion is often used to foil the contamination of the adult. The true genius can explain the very difficult simply.

You know, when we give the computer section a problem to solve, I know we are going to get the best possible solution or solutions, given the data available and the time frame they are working under. Not only do they solve the problem, they explain the solution in a way that is easy to understand and does not leave you guessing as to how in hell you are going to implement their recommendations. They work with you every step of the way if necessary. You know, their expertise is even starting to rub off. For someone like me, who didn't know a computer do-loop concept from a donut, I can get most of the data I want out of the system without having to yell for help all the time.

When an individual functions with a lot of nurturing parent, adult, and free child, he or she is in the best position to learn and to adapt to change. Who else is better prepared to meet the challenges and demands of keen competition in a very fast-paced technological age than someone who is receptive (the large nurturing parent), alert and clear thinking (the large adult), and innovative (the large free child)? For a detailed discussion on how to develop these ego states in yourself, as well as in others, see chapter nine.

THE ORGANIZATIONAL LOSER

Somerset Maugham once said:

> We are none of us all of a piece: more than one person dwells within us, often in uneasy companionship with his fellows.

In TA terms, there are two fellows who cause most of our internal and external conflicts: the critical parent and the adapted child. The egogram of the organizational loser looks as follows:

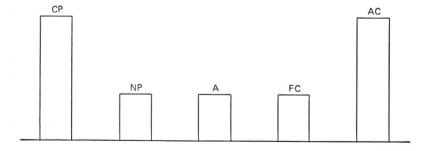

As already mentioned, the critical parent and the adapted child go together, as the other three do. The critical parent puts out the dictums and the adapted child buys into them, either through submission or rebellion. I have also noticed, in the organizational setting, that the individual who is very critical to his subordinates is also very submissive to his superiors. On our faculty at the University of New Orleans we have a professor who served as a briefing secretary to one of the top Army generals during World War II. He said that although this general played the "lording over," critical parent role to a tee with his subordinates, his was the very compliant child "yes-man" type when dealing with his superiors.

Although some critical parent and adapted child are needed in certain situations and with certain people, the excessive use of these leads to reduced productivity and poor morale. Being the chief dispenser of negative strokes, the critical parent creates hostility and ill feelings among organizational members. Individuals do not like to be put down and will often repay negative strokes with direct verbal retaliation or, indirectly, with work slowdowns, strikes, or even sabotage.* If the individual being attacked buys into the negativism of the critical parent figure, a lack of self-confidence and spirit results. Again, goodbye to productivity and morale, as the attacked individual sets into motion vicious negative dialogue between his own critical parent and adapted child.

> I guess I really am no good. My reports don't answer the right questions, the rationale is no good, and even my writing style is not understandable, as my boss says. I guess I will never amount to anything.

> With all the discounts I have received around here for so long, I don't need anyone to tell me how awful I am any more. I've gotten pretty damn good at using my own critical parent as my biggest critic.

The critical parent is also the biggest stumbling block to learning. Besides decreasing self-confidence, the critical parent is usually too opinionated to be receptive to ideas from outside sources. "I've been doing it this

---

* For a detailed discussion of how subordinates react to critical parent bosses, see chapter nine.

way for a hundred years and I am going to continue to do it this way." This is the motto of the critical parent, even in the light of improved technology and a rapidly changing environment. As demonstrated earlier, this inflexibility can spell the doom of an organization or an individual. Obsolescence is the necessary result of persisting in this type of thought pattern.

Often, too much power in the hands of one individual or a group can lead to this critical parent posture of inflexibility. Puffed-up with a false sense of power, the critical parent manages and behaves like a know-it-all for whom learning is obsolete. There are many who think, for example, that we may see a number of sports commissioners go by the wayside, due to their dictatorial censorship of constructive feedback and their inflexible view of new technology that could improve their respective sports.

Also, the critical parent avoids criticism directed toward itself or its policies like the plague. The result, as mentioned a number of times in this book, is that he or she is the last to get the necessary feedback to identify the problem or to solve it. The personnel director of a plant that was subsequently unionized responded to a survey on grievance procedures as follows:

> We don't have any gripes or grievances around here. Whoever gripes is terminated.

As indicated in chapter two (and these points are again discussed from a leadership perspective in chapter nine), the overly adapted child personality becomes the problem child of any organization either by becoming too submissive to make its own decisions or to solve its own problems or too rebellious to cooperate. Organizations can prosper much better without individuals who choose not to count (the overly submissive adapted child) or who choose to fight all the time (the overly rebellious adapted child.)

Also, as mentioned in chapter two, it is the critical parent and the adapted child who are involved in irrational, "get nowhere" game playing. These two ego states are always involved in one of the gamey Karpman roles (6).

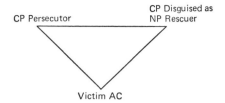

CP Persecutor   CP Disguised as NP Rescuer

Victim AC

Although ways of dealing with the critical parent or adapted child organizational member are also discussed in chapter nine, on leadership, I will now discuss points concerning the three game roles.

Avoid Being the Persecutor

He who persecutes today will be persecuted tomorrow. Remember—strokes, like rubber checks—have a way of coming back. Sow a lot of negative strokes, and this is what you will reap. There was a faculty member who felt that it was his job to point out weaknesses in the administrative and teaching practices of a university. Because he gave no specifics and no viable solutions, he was obviously the persecutor in a no-win game of "get the university." He later quit the university under a lot of pressure from the administration and the faculty. When he was officially censored by the university senate, it was clear that he had ultimately become the victim of his own persecutions.

Don't Play the False Rescuer

Whether you are boss, co-worker, or subordinate to someone else, do not feign help when you have no intention of giving it. Additionally, do not attempt to rescue individuals from work that they must learn to do. Sooner or later, the hypocrite who pretends to offer genuine aid, as a foil to exploitation, is uncovered at a very big price to himself or herself. Lie to your subordinates, your fellow workers, or your customers, and you lose their trust. When you lose their trust, you do not have much going for you. Wary, once-burned individuals make bad bedfellows when it comes to cooperation or commitment to what you want or need. As the cliché goes: "Screw me once, shame on you. Screw me twice, shame on me."

There is no way. I'll never buy from that s.o.b. again. (Facetiously): Oh, yea, he was my friend, getting me to buy before the stock ran out. In reality, he wanted to unload the merchandise at a greater profit to himself just before the prices were cut.

Do not rescue workers from jobs they will have to learn to do for themselves sooner or later. In the long run you will be hurting them, as well as yourself, by creating a symbiotic relationship.

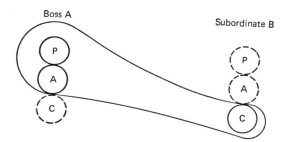

In the symbiotic relationship diagramed above, the parent and the adult of Boss A take on the duties and responsibilities for Subordinate B. This is demonstrated by the figure encircling A's parent and adult and B's child. In effect, symbiosis in TA means that one individual, in this case Boss A, takes charge of the responsibility (parent) functions and thinking (adult) functions of another individual, in this case Subordinate B.

The results are disastrous for both parties in the relationship. By playing mom or dad to B's child, A is depriving himself or herself of meeting some of his or her own child's needs.

You know, when I became chairman of the board I figured I would have more free time to travel and play golf. But every time a policy decision comes along I have to take our new president by the hand. Now I am doing two jobs instead of one. I am, in effect, chairman of the board *and* President.

The strain of meeting the individual's own needs is demonstrated in the diagram by the broken circle around Boss A's child.

By falsely rescuing, Boss A is helping to retard the growth of Subordinate B's parent and adult ego states, as demonstrated by the broken circles around these. The consequence is a deterioration in B's ability to take on responsibility (parent functioning) and to think independently (adult functioning).

The wise boss knows that he or she is doing no favors for subordinates by rescuing them from responsibilities that they must learn to take on sooner or later. If confronted by a subordinate or co-worker who wants to be coddled, let him or her know from the beginning that playing mom or dad to your own child is all the responsibility you want, and that it is not healthy for either of you to play foster parent to the other. Cut the umbilical cord by gradually getting subordinates to make their own decisions and to take responsibility for these. Believe me, you will be setting both of you free from a very unhealthy relationship. Successful programs dealing with alcoholic workers often require the participation in a rehabilitation program as a condition of employment (7). Falsely rescuing the alcoholic, by covering up poor performance or high absentee rates, only helps contribute to his or her drinking problem and a poorer work record for the department, as co-worker morale deteriorates (8).

Do Not Set Yourself Up
As the Victim.

Always be prepared. Sooner or later you will have to learn the job yourself. Cheating or trying to bluff your way through material will never pay off in the long run. Not only will you not derive the intrinsic satisfaction from knowing how to do a job and how to do it well, but you will be a slave to others who can hold their expertise over you as a powerful weapon. Use your adult wisely to explore the "ins and outs" of how to do the job, and you will be free from those who might use their knowledge to exploit you.

> I don't have to wait for Charlie to close out my books. I know how to do it myself.

Boy, for a long time I was miserable. I always had to check with Mary before I did anything. I was victimizing myself with all this dependence on her. Now I'm free to do my job at my own pace. Oh, I get feedback on new things when I need it, but I don't keep playing the helpless moron who has to keep being bailed out on what he should know already.

If you are in the kind of job that periodically requires presentations at meetings, or simply speaking out at meetings, do your homework and come prepared. The guy or gal who performs consistently well at such meetings is the one who comes armed with specifics and facts concerning problem identification as well as solutions. Meetings at which you have to present data on a new project often provide the only opportunity to make a meaningful impression on higher level organizational officials. Do not blow your chance at making good points with top bosses by coming in as a half-cocked submissive or rebellious child. The guy at the top, who might ultimately determine your career with the organization, might complement your victim role with long-term negative promotion strokes.*

A good TA exercise for graphically recognizing what ego states you are using and are tending to engage in is called five chairs.

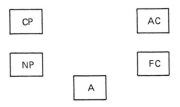

Arrange five chairs in such a way that each chair represents one of the five ego states. With a fellow worker, a friend, or a spouse, stage an ordinary happening or problem-solving episode from the job (like a business meeting). Do the episode the way you would naturally do it. Whenever you find yourself shifting ego states, shift chairs to

---

* An in-depth discussion on how to get the most out of committee and group discussions is treated in chapter eight.

the appropriate ego state. This exercise will quickly familiarize you with what ego states you predominantly use in your working relationships. Additionally, the exercise will give you a good feel for ego states in general. Part of the purpose of the exercise is to try to stay in the A, NP, and FC, regardless of what responses you get from the person with whom you are staging the episode.

In closing this chapter I will discuss some organizational characters you have probably met—and wished you had not. Ways of changing these organizational sappers of productivity and morale will also be discussed. Script analysis will be my vehicle for commenting on these typical organizational losers with whom all of us are familiar. Although any one of you reading this book, as well as I, may possess—to a certain extent—any one of a number of the characteristics portrayed by the scripts, it is the degree to which we possess these traits that might ultimately decide our organizational successes or failures. And, as you will see, any of these script traits can be changed for the better.

By familiarizing you with these typically "played" organizational scripts, I hope to accomplish two things: (1) If you can identify with one or a number of the scripts, I hope this chapter will make it easier for you to restage a more successful play for yourself; (2) By being aware of the scripts or roles played by others in your organization, I hope to put you in a better position to deal with their tactics and "moves."

Obviously, there are more individual scripts than the eight I will discuss in this chapter. I am simply trying to highlight the main ones. If there are others you can think of, feel free to construct such scripts based on the script elements that follow.

As indicated in chapter two, all of us are playwrights, directors, and producers of our own choosing. Very early in life we begin to design a life drama—a real-life play that has a plot, a theme, and an ending. Although the plot will to a large extent consist of the games we play, the essence of this life drama we have decided upon will center around injunctions and life positions. The injunctions limit options and provide the psychological limitations or "hang-ups" that we place on ourselves. An injunction like "don't be close" will keep an individual from developing rapport with co-workers or customers. As a result, the social rewards that come from close relationships will be difficult for this type of person to achieve.

The life position sets the stage for the theme, the ending, and the games of plot. For example, an individual who comes primarily out of the position I'm Not OK, You're OK will set himself or herself up to be a failure, or mediocre at best, as an employee. Such individuals will feel defeated before they even begin. They will play self-put-down games like "Kick Me." For instance, by coming unprepared for a business meeting, they may jeopardize promotional goals and thus confirm the theme of the play—failure.

By being aware of the various script elements that we decided for ourselves long ago, we may begin to take charge of the damaging aspects of our life dramas. With more realistic adult data at our disposal, we are in a position to more realistically redecide what we want to do with the rest of our lives. Rather than being compelled to act out early childhood decisions that might greatly limit our effectiveness and happiness, we can redecide for the better. One primary assumption of TA is that what was decided can be redecided. If changes were not possible, there would be little or no practical reason for having behavioral tools and therapies.

Of course, changing the momentum of a life script that was set into motion many years ago is not an easy thing to do. However, awareness—and a strong desire to change and practice—will set any of us on a more fulfilling course. As we become aware of our "hang-ups" and the games we persistently play, and if we practice—daily—altering at least one or two of these, we will become vastly improved organizational members and people.

Rome was not built in a day. Neither will you become the top organizational producer overnight. Work on only a few script elements at a time, and once you feel these are mastered, move forward to other changes. Many fail to change their scripts because they tire quickly from trying to do too much at once. Pace yourself and you will be much the better for wear.

To make people dramatically aware that positive change is possible for all of us, Muriel James and Dorothy Jongeward, two world-renowned consultants, discuss five case histories of well-known achievers who greatly altered earlier scripts in their text, *The People Book.* Their brief case studies included Eleanor Roosevelt, Golda Meir, Albert Einstein, Thomas Edison, and Martin Luther King, Jr.

Although each of these great persons seemed to be set on a dire losing course from childhood, all dramatically became winners. To quote the Greek philosopher, Heraclitus (540–475? B.C.): "There is nothing permanent except change."

Although Albert Einstein is revered by many as the most brilliant mind of our time, his early beginnings would not suggest this.

> Born to Jewish parents in an area where Jews were hated, Al was very slow in learning to talk. At school he was backward in his studies and in sports, and his father was ashamed of his lack of athletic ability. As a senior Al stayed out of school for six months with a nervous breakdown and one of his teachers claimed he'd never make a success of anything. Al, with no friends, lonely and shy, acquired odd mannerisms, made up his own religion, chanted hymns to himself, and was regarded even by his parents as very "different." He first failed the entrance exams to the university, and then repeated them successfully, but his record was not outstanding (9).

The analysis of scripts, as I present them, will consist of the following five elements: (1) *Life Course*—the narrative of the play; (2) *Life Position*—the feeling of okayness toward oneself and others; (3) *Injunctions and Attributions*—injunctions are "don't messages" or "hang-ups" and attributions are "do messages" that can hang us up by omitting other "do" possibilities. For instance, a person told to *think* his way through everything will lose out on *feelings* capabilities; (4) *Games*—the major games that help construct the life course.* (5) *Antithesis*—the resolution of the script or the way off the stage. (10).

---

* In this chapter I will only indicate the primary game roles of persecutor, rescuer, or victim played in the scripts. Typical organizational games are developed in detail in chapter five. It will be less confusing to the reader if specific games are left out of scripts until after chapter five.

EXHIBIT

Life Positions and Injunctions: The Cornerstones of Scripts

Life Positions—an individual's feelings concerning his or her own self-worth and the worth of others. Although individuals may shift periodically to any of the four OK positions, one will predominate. The chart, as follows, is an excellent brief graphical disposition of the typical feelings and roles played and behaviors that go with each of the four positions.

You're OK

Role = Sobber	*Role* = Solver
Behavior = Get away from	*Behavior* = Get on with it
Feeling = Scared	*Feeling* = Glad
	Only game-free position

I'm Not OK ——————— **1** | **2** ——————— I'm OK

3 | **4**

Role = Sulker	*Role* = Socker
Behavior = Get nowhere	*Behavior* = Get rid of
Feeling = Sad	*Feeling* = Mad
Because of their lack of trust in themselves, as well as others, those who are predominantly in this position rarely survive as viable workers.	

You're Not OK

Injunctions—"don't messages" we receive and accept at an early age that constitute our psychological "hang-ups" or discounts of our abilities and capacities. These discounts often come about through persistent verbal messages as well as how parents behave toward children. Although there are probably more, TA practitioners often speak of ten fundamental injunctions.

90

1. *Don't exist.* The growing child receives this message from parents*
who constantly get across the message: "If it weren't for you we would not
be caught in this awful marriage."

2. *Don't feel.* Through earlier reprimands and conditioning, children
learn that certain feelings are not acceptable. They are permitted, for example,
to feel sad but not mad or angry. Even if they appropriately express anger,
they are harshly reprimanded for expressing what their parents term as not
OK feelings.

3. *Don't be you.* This occurs when parents try to make their children
be something other than what they want to be. Messages, whether conveyed
verbally or behaviorally, such as the following, often lead to this injunction:
"Why don't you be a doctor like Uncle Joe?" "How come you are not more
like your brother?" "You'll be a great lawyer whether you like it or not."

4. *Don't make it.* No matter what the child does, it is never good
enough. A person with this injunction is rarely comfortable with success. He
or she always feels they could do better, or early on in their career they
may stop trying to succeed.

5. *Don't be close.* This injunction may come about if a child loses a
parent at an early age. The hurt becomes too great to let himself or herself
get close and hurt again.

6. *Don't be grown up.* This injunction is basically the same as don't
think. In the family environment, children are taught not to think and not to
make decisions for themselves. The discount here is addressed toward the
adult.

7. *Don't be a child.* This injunction is aimed at the free child. The
child is frequently discounted for having a good time. Those with a strong
don't be a child injunction feel uncomfortable with humor.

8. *Don't be well.* Frequently, this injunction develops in a family where
a lot of attention is paid to illness. Hypochondria may come about from a
strong adherence to this injunction.

9. *Don't be important.* This type of discount might develop in families
where children are treated as inferiors. "Children are made to be seen and
not heard" would be a primary message. "Now, don't be selfish. Let everybody
get what they want first." These are also frequent don't be important messages.

10. *Don't belong.* This injunction makes it hard to experience cooperation. A person with this injunction has a difficult time working with others.
The kid who is encouraged to feel like the "black sheep" or the family outcast
is a prime candidate for this injunction.

* Or any authority figures close to the child in the formative years, such as grandparents,
brothers, sisters, etc.

TYPICAL SCRIPTS OF
ORGANIZATIONAL CHARACTERS
YOU HAVE PROBABLY MET
AND WISHED YOU HAD NOT

The Hustler

Life Course. Hustlers are the types of individuals who will try to "seduce" you into doing their work for them. Often, they will glamorize the project to be done to the extremes in order to set the bait: "Oh, gee, if you get involved in this project with me, we will be stars at the company. The sky will be the limit around here." "I'm telling you, buddy, after this everyone will have to take notice." If you take the bait they will have a million excuses along the way as to why they cannot give you a hand with the project. Yet they will still push you to complete the work for them.

> Look, Mary, I would have made that second project meeting, but you know I had to help Joe on his deal. I'm really sorry—but, I'm in your corner. And we've get to keep plugging. I certainly won't miss the next meeting. (Of course, he does—with still another excuse.)

A number of the hustler's top excuses for not sharing the work load are:

> I've got so many projects going I just can't help now.

> Gee, you're the expert, not me. You better do it.

> Gosh, I completely forgot.

> I want to help on that end of things, but you know the cliché about too many cooks spoiling the soup.

The basic motivation of the hustler is to get a big name for himself or herself with organizational higher-ups by appearing to accomplish more than anyone *normally* could. In the short run he or she does *appear* to be the star of the organization. No single, hard-working man

92

or woman could accomplish—in the same time frame—what the hustler *appears* to have accomplished (by using a number of other people). However, in the long run, the word gets out and everyone who knows the hustler refuses to do work for him or her anymore. Ultimately, the hustler may be out of a job, because by using others he or she has avoided developing any marketable talents or skills of his or her own.

Life Position.   I'm OK, You're Not OK (I'll use you when I can to serve my purposes.)

Injunctions and Attributions:
Use others when you can.
Don't be concerned with how you shoot for the top.
Don't come off straight.
Manipulate others if you can.

Primary Game Role.   Rescuer (I'm only trying to help you by getting you to do my work.)

Antithesis.   The hustler learns that the only way to get lasting recognition and a true sense of accomplishment is to develop his or her own skills and to cooperate with others—*not* exploit them. As a result, he or she becomes secure enough in his or her own expertise to make exploitation of others unnecessary. The individual also begins to realize that "shooting for the top" at the expense of others makes the road along the way very miserable and lonely. Sensing now that the individual's offers to cooperate are genuine, support from other workers comes freely, abundantly, and in a lasting way. The social outcast and deadbeat has finally become a real member of the team.

The Critic

Life Course.   A synopsis of the script of the critic is described by Brendan Behan: "Critics are like eunuchs in a harem: they know how it's done, they've seen it done every day, but they're unable to do it themselves." I will go one step further than Behan. In many cases I do not think they have the know-how.

The critic generates a lot of nonconstructive criticism. Criticism that is constructive—that helps us learn and profit from our mistakes—does not appear on the agenda of the personality type about which I am talking.

Frustrated by his or her own lack of achievement, the critic tries to get temporary relief by putting others down. Such individuals employ a strategy that some psychologists term the "pulley effect." By putting others down, they feel they are raised up. Their motto is a twisted version of what is found in the Bible: Judge others first, lest you end up judging yourself."

Yet, with all their "ain't it awfuls" about everybody else and everything else, they accomplish little themselves. How do they find the time to be productive when they are all tied up with putting others' efforts down? Also, despite all their criticisms, they offer no practical solutions. When I asked one devout critic for his solutions to his discounts of another department, he said: "Oh, my job is to identify problems. I know nothing about solutions." At least he was honest.

In the end it becomes apparent to other organizational members that this frustrated nonachiever has nothing to offer them but a lot of negative strokes and bad feelings. They eventually shun him or her like a psychological plague. In the end the critic comes home to what he or she has avoided all along—a confrontation with the only person left, his or her own self.

Life Position. I'm OK, You're Not OK (That appears to be why criticizing you is my favorite pastime.) In actuality, the critic is covering up a feeling of inadequacy toward self.

Injunctions and Attributions:
Don't make it.
Don't belong. (Nobody else is good enough for my standards.)
Look for the negative in others.
Don't be grown up. (Putting others down does not promote personal growth.)

Primary Game Role. Persecutor (No one will escape my criticisms.)

Antithesis. The individual begins to realize that constantly criticizing others does not lead to close relationships or to a true sense of personal worth or accomplishment. Such individuals begin to work constructively on developing their own skills and talents. As a result they find they have less time and less motivation for putting others down. They are now having too much fun achieving. Now that they have achieved a certain level of expertise and a much more positive demeanor, others are attracted to them. They find that the constructive advice they are now able to give is well received and much more personally rewarding than the negative hot air they generated before.

The Moralist

Life Course. The moralist is allergic to tolerance. For moralists, the concept of "live and let live" belongs on a foreign exchange very distant from them. They are forever in the business of setting the standards for others to live by: "You should dress like this; you should arrange your office this way; remember, when calling on clients, do this." The ultimate message of the moralist is: "I am the standard against which all behavior is measured, and your job is to live up to my expectations."

Also, most of the standards set by moralists tend to be overly simplistic and polarized. They often preach to others in platitudes and through moralistic speeches. Everything is black or white, right or wrong, conservative or liberal, good or bad. Because of this superficial approach to organizational phenomena and problems, their solutions, if they come at all, are very short-lived at best. When asked for advice on how to solve difficult issues, none is usually forthcoming from moralists. Their commenting is often (thank goodness) restricted to trivia—like how to keep a neat desk or where to draw the margins on a report. Questions dealing with how to gather the data for the report and then how to analyze it make mutes out of them. They are too busy being superior to get down to the nitty gritty of doing the work.

Insulted by their superficial advice, intelligent people tend to avoid moralists when possible. The rest of the organizational members (bright lights or not) quickly tire of them setting themselves up as God. Moralists are often kicked in the corners somewhere, so that the only entities they can try to "lord over" are office machines, reports, or books—certainly not people.

Life Position. I'm OK, You're Not OK (I am all-wonderful and wise, who are you?)

Injunctions and Attributions:
Don't be you. (Be what *I* want you to be.)
Don't be important. (Only *my* standards are important.)
Do as I say.

Primary Game Role. Persecutor (Shame on you if you don't live up to *my* standards.)

Antithesis. The moralist, who by his or her need to lord his or her standards over others, demonstrates a strong desire for recognition and a sense of importance from others. Realizing that respect is a reciprocal thing—you only get it when you are willing to give it to others—he or she begins to tear down the superficial, pompous walls of the standard bearer and becomes a receptive and more accepting group member. Besides gaining in technical competence, such individuals learn that they do not have to play the all-knowing and pompous roles to be listened to and accepted. They just have to be human and accepting themselves.

The Pass-the-Buck Artist

Life Course. This personality type typically manages by abdication. He or she devoutly avoids responsibility. Afraid to fail and afraid to look bad in the eyes of others, this "gutless wonder" weasels out of anything slightly controversial or important. Like the puppet on the Mr. Bill Show, he or she always panics in the face of responsibility with an "Oh, no! Not for me. You do it."

The pass-the-buck artist usually deals with responsibility as if it were a hot potato. He or she passes it off quickly with never ending wooden leg excuses:

Gee, I don't have the time to handle this now.

I think this matter can more appropriately be handled in your ball park.

I'd like to render a judgment in this matter, but you are better qualified.

Gosh, thanks for reminding me. I'll get to it next week. (Of course, he or she never does.)

Look, I'd only be in the way. Why don't you settle these points among yourselves.

Oh wow! I don't know what to do. I'd better give this to my boss to settle.

You can't expect me to decide these kinds of things. They never give us the tools or the training.

Sooner or later the word gets out and the pass-the-buck artist is passed down the line to a job with a lot less authority and discretion. These individuals' lack of respect for themselves is finally translated into meaningless, get-nowhere positions. They will not have to pass the buck anymore. They will command so little respect that few will give them any "bucks" to pass.

Life Position. I'm Not OK, You're OK (Gosh, you'd better do it!)

Injunctions and Attributions:
Don't be grown up. (Taking on responsibility is too awesome a thing to do.)
Don't think.
Don't make it.
Let others make all the decisions.

Primary Game Role. Victim (I'd better be helpless or gutless or I'll fail.)

Antithesis. He or she takes a course in assertiveness training and learns how to stand up for his or her own needs and decisions. Such individuals learn that the surest way not to succeed is not to try at all. There has never been a putt sunk in the history of golf that was not stroked. They also find out that making mistakes can be turned into a vehicle for learning rather than for punishing, and that people who have not made any mistakes have not done anything. Not only do they grow in prominence and recognition on the organizational chart, but they also gain a very precious quality that makes living with themselves a lot more enjoyable—self-respect.

The Smoke Blower

Life Course. The smoke blower is the b.s. artist or great pretender par excellence. Such individuals pretend to do this and that, or to accomplish this or that, but after all the hot air or smoke clears, nothing happens. They work their "silvery voices" overtime so they won't have to do much work, period! They particularly appear to have bad cases of the "I'm gonna's":

> I'm gonna' write the first comprehensive book ever on organizational communication strategies.

> I'm gonna' be the first ever to exceed $1,000,000 in sales in the first six months.

> I'm gonna' balance the budget my first six months in office.

Of course, their achievements always fall very short of their "I'm gonna's." They always have a ton of excuses for their lack of accomplishment. "I would have been able to do this but, but, but, but, etc."

Craving recognition they must not have obtained in early years, and motivated by strong needs to impress higher-ups constantly, smoke blowers will blow their "personal horns" constantly—even over the smallest trivia. I recall a faculty member at a southern college who used to appear constantly in the university newsletter. Even if he talked to a few students over coffee in the school cafeteria, the event was practically cited as a noteworthy presentation.

However, after careful scrutiny, it became obvious to everyone—even those with power—that this individual's talk far exceeded his true achievements. Shortly after this observation, a decline in peer and boss recognition followed. In the end the smoke blower achieves no more than his or her hot air, and his or her organizational rewards match this mediocrity.

Life Position. I'm Not OK, You're OK (I've got to b.s. you to cover my lack of self-worth.)

Injunctions and Attributions:
Don't be you. (Pretend to be *anything* else.)
Don't make it. (Rather than do, *pretend.*)
Don't be grown up. (Exaggerate—like a little kid.)
Be important at any costs.

Primary Game Role. Victim (If I were not a deprived child, I would not have to slum for recognition.)

Antithesis. Smoke blowers are often too caught up in their own b.s. to realize that they are fooling no one but themselves. Someone who is mature and trustworthy gently takes them by the hand and points out their exaggerations and the futility of pursuing such a strategy. They learn to be quietly effective and to let accomplishments speak for themselves. They gain self-esteem; they gain lasting praise from colleagues and superiors. The craving for approval from others becomes a thing of the past.

The Hypocrite

Life Course. This is the type of individual who demands of others what he or she does not demand of himself or herself. Work standards rise for everyone but himself or herself. An anonymous individual wrote: "If some people lived up to their ideals, they would be stooping." A full professor, who had never published even an article, demanded increased research efforts from well-published associates with the comment: "My job is to police your efforts." Individuals who manage by hypocrisy either have a short tenure in office or cause serious morale problems. The above full professor was subsequently voted out as department chairman when his four-year term came up for renewal. Revolutions, strikes, union organization, litigation, and even industrial sabotage are sometimes the by-products of long-term, hypocritical leadership. Marie Antoinette's alleged infamous solution to the bread famine, "Let them eat cake," no doubt contributed to her decapitation.

The hypocrite causes a lot of turmoil and grief because he or she often plays the role of false rescuer. Pretending to be your friend, he or she—in reality—turns out to be your worst enemy. When the romance ends and the lack of integrity surfaces, the negative consequences are often explosive.

> We are going to nail that s.o.b. to the wall during the grievance hearing. We fulfill the specific criteria he said we needed to fulfill to be promoted. All during the year he pats us on the back and says we are doing fine. We've got it in the bag he says. But when promotion time comes, he recommends no one. His comment being: "Who can guarantee anything to anyone?" Well, we will guarantee him one thing. If there is any way to get his butt transferred or fired, we are going to work very hard to do it.

Life Position.   I'm OK, You're Not OK (That is why it is okay for me to knife you in the back.)

Injunctions and Attributions:
Don't be you. (Pretend to have much higher standards for yourself than you really do.)
Don't feel. (Just *pretend* to be concerned for others.)
Have anything *but* integrity.
Fools deserve to be taken advantage of.

Primary Game Role.   Rescuer (I'm your friend. Oh, excuse the differential standards and the knife in your back.)

Antithesis.   The individual learns (very likely through a very traumatic event like a strike or the loss of all potential friendships) that hypocrisy does not pay. In the long run it is much easier and much more productive to come off straight. Hypocrites spend a lot of wasted time and anxious moments trying to figure out, again and again, how to cover up another pretense. Finally, a watergate happens, and the price to pay is indeed a high one. The hypocrite also learns that followers ultimately respect and pay homage to those who know and do, not to those who simply hold the office and pretend.

The Workaholic

Life Course. This type of individual either knows little about time management or does not know how to assert himself or herself. Some workaholics have tunnel vision, locked in on activities but not on results or effectiveness. As salespersons they are busy drawing up prospect lists but not busy making sales. As researchers they are busy tabulating and analyzing, but file no reports. As managers they are busy having group meetings and one-to-one dialogue sessions, but make no decisions and set no policies. Some organizations reinforce mediocrity and ineffectiveness by rewarding those who make careers out of *looking* busy. I recall the case of one individual who was quickly promoted to the senior vice-presidency of a bank. He would often spend whole days shifting papers from one side of his desk to the other. This bank, despite its early accomplishments, is now bankrupt. Ineffective management precipitated its downfall.

Some workaholics are very effective and expert at what they do. However, because they cannot say no to others' requests, they unnecessarily burden themselves with too much work. In the long run the burdens continue to pile on and take their toll. Heart attacks, ulcers, strokes, nervous breakdowns, and poor family life are a number of potential consequences.

Life Position. I'm OK, You're Not OK (for the workaholic who squanders work time by pretending to look busy); I'm Not OK, You're OK (for workaholics who victimize themselves with others' work).

Injunctions and Attributions:
Don't make it. (Do a lot, but do not achieve anything.)
Always look busy.
Don't be a child. (Don't take time out to have a good time.)
Don't be important. (For those who let others shove their work off on them.)

Primary Game Role. Victim (Poor me! I'm either doing someone else's work or working my butt off but getting nowhere.)

Antithesis. He or she takes a course in assertiveness training and time management (11). Such individuals learn that all work and no play makes for little happiness and a short life span. They begin to use their adult a lot more when setting work priorities and objectives. With goals and results in mind, they find they achieve a great deal more on the job and have a lot more free time for family and friends.

The Politician

Life Course. This is the wheeler-dealer. As a leader, he or she gives out strokes—such as promotions, good sales territories, raises, and easy jobs—on the basis of political favors. The motto of the politician is: "I'll take care of my friends first, and my friends happen to be those who scratch my back when I scratch their's." Both productivity and morale suffer under political supervisors. Friction and alienation inevitably develop between the in-group (those on the "take") and the out-group (those not on the "take"). Usually, those on the "take" are the least productive members which, at best, disenchants the top-producing out-group members. They either leave for more equitable work pastures or slow down their productive efforts to match their meager rewards.

The politician subordinate is the apple polisher who will do anything but be quietly effective in order to impress superiors. If the boss says jump, he or she will ask how high. The politician sacrifices integrity, co-workers, family, and friends, but he or she never sacrifices recognition from on high. He or she very carefully culls out any work projects that are not politically self-serving. He or she recruits followers on whom to dump the everyday routine, drudgery jobs, promising them a piece of the limelight.

> George says I'll be sure to be promoted next year if I help out with the leg work on this big project of his.

When the politician cannot, or will not, deliver on promises he or she has made, the word spreads, and recruiting pawns becomes an impossible task. When the smoke finally clears, he or she is accurately seen as the self-aggrandizing weasel. Having developed some political savvy, but little work competence, the politician becomes the all-around loser, losing both friends and the sense of achievement.

Life Position. I'm OK, You're Not OK (I'll use anybody for my political ends.)

Injunctions and Attributions:
Don't feel. (Who cares if I use a few people along the way?)
Don't be close. (Just *pretend* to be close, using political favors.)
Be important and be recognized at all costs.

Primary Game Role. Rescuer (I'm only trying to help you get a little of the political glory too.)

Antithesis. The politician realizes, if he or she is a supervisor, that giving political favors does not lead to increased productivity. Giving strokes for being political and not for being productive increases political activity at the expense of effectiveness. The politically disposed subordinate also learns that using co-workers for self-glorification is a short-term proposition ending in less than favorable outcomes. Being ostracized from the work group is one of these outcomes. Also, he or she realizes that in the long run the development of work skills or expertise will pay the most solid dividends. Political favors, like the wind, blow this way and that way. They come and they go. Talent and skills cannot be taken away. Additionally, they make the individual highly marketable, in case the political climate becomes too intolerable.

NOTES

1. George Strauss and Leonard R. Sayles, *Personnel: The Human Problems of Management,* © 1972, p. 388. Reprinted by permission of Prentice-Hall, Inc., Englewood Cliffs, N.J.
2. Harold Koontz and Cyril O'Donnell, *Principles of Management: An Analysis of Managerial Functions,* 4th ed. (New York: McGraw-Hill Book Company, 1968), p. 416.
3. Koontz and O'Donnell, *Principles of Management,* p. 787.
4. For a provocative view of a very interesting organizational personality, see: Paul W. Bryant and John Underwood, *Bear: The Hard Life and Good Times of Alabama's Coach Bryant* (Boston, Mass.: Little, Brown & Company, 1974).

5. For a detailed discussion of egograms, see: John M. Dusay, *Egograms: How I See You and You See Me* (New York: Harper & Row, Publishers, Inc., 1977).

6. Karpman does not include ego states in his description of the drama triangle. See: Stephen B. Karpman, "Fairy Tales and Script Drama Analysis," *Transactional Analysis Bulletin*, vol. 7, no. 26 (April 1968).

7. William F. Glueck, *Personnel: A Diagnostic Approach*, rev. ed. (Dallas, Tex.: Business Publications, Inc., 1978), p. 708.

8. For an excellent commentary on dealing with alcoholic workers, see: Harrison M. Trice, "Alcoholism and the Work World," *Sloan Management Review*, no. 2 (Fall 1970), pp. 67–75.

9. Muriel James and Dorothy Jongeward, *The People Book: Transactional Analysis for Students*, © 1975, Addison-Wesley Publishing Co., Inc., chap. 1, p. 4. Reprinted with permission.

10. For a comprehensive view of script analysis and script elements in TA, see: Claude M. Steiner, *Scripts People Live: Transactional Analysis of Life Scripts* (New York: Grove Press, Inc., 1974).

11. For an excellent book on time management and how to overcome the workaholic script, see: Michael LeBoeuf, *Working Smart: How to Accomplish More in Half the Time* (New York: McGraw-Hill Book Company, 1979).

THE INTERPERSONAL LEVEL

Communication Strategies: Games Organizational Members Play

5

As mentioned in chapter two, the exchanges and transactions—the fundamental activities between and among personnel—have a great impact on the morale and productivity of any organization. If the exchanges and transactions are pleasant and productive, then the organization and the individuals prosper. If these exchanges and transactions leave personnel feeling offended and defensive, productivity and morale suffer. There is no more destructive interpersonal strategy than "games." This chapter deals with typical organizational member games and how to resolve them. Written exchanges between and among people (or TA and business correspondence) are covered in chapter six.

I want to make this very clear from the beginning: "Games," according to Transactional Analysis, are not redeeming strategies. In fact, according to TA, psychological games are irrational. They do not lead to the accomplishment of personal or organizational objectives. Games do not promote morale. They do not increase productivity. Their primary outcomes are negative. Games promote lower achievements, poor morale, hurt feelings, distrust, and poor communications. Nobody wins in TA games. Then why do people play them? According to to TA, there are a number of basic reasons for game playing.

1. *Where There Are No Positive Strokes, Negative Ones Are Soon to Follow.* When an organization or a company fails to recognize effective performance with positive strokes, people will often seek out negative strokes in terms of game strokes. Most people cannot tolerate a stroke vacuum. We all have a very strong and basic need for *some* type of recognition. If positive recognition is unavailable, we will often seek out negative recognition. The student who gets little praise from his or her teacher will often seek out negative recognition. Often, mischievous students are seeking the only recognition available—discipline and criticism. Employees who are conditioned to receive only poor treatment from managers will often set themselves up to be punished, even by typically nonpunitive supervisors.

2. *Games Come Out of Not-OK Positions.* People generally play games in order to reinforce Not-OK feelings about themselves or others. Some people in organizations will view other parties as Not-OK enemies to be dealt with. A given employee may rationalize, "I'm OK, but that co-worker, customer, or supervisor is a Not-OK enemy to be dealt with. If I don't get him first, he'll get me." The "screw" or "be screwed" attitude is typical of many game players. I am reminded of a car salesperson who got so wrapped up in "socking" it to prospects that he even put it to a member of his own family. He was heard to remark: "My sister came in to buy a car the other day. Boy, did I ever screw her on the deal she got!"

3. *Mine Is Better Than Yours.* An essential motive underlying most game playing is the need to impress. As children, most of us have clearly demonstrated to our friends how our bike was faster than their bikes, how our house was bigger than their houses, or how our parents were brighter than their parents. This desire to be one-up on someone else goes way back. Games often spring from this one-upmanship. Who has not heard an employee comment about another employee: "He thinks he can show me up! I'll teach that s.o.b. I'm always one step ahead of the bastard." Remember, however, that in TA games nobody wins. In the short run you may feel you are one-up on someone else. In the long run you will definitely be the worse for playing. Employees who have been "had" due to a game ploy won't be motivated to be more productive. They will use valuable company time to get back at other game-playing members.

4. *Games Are the Plots of Scripts.* Games are played in order to act out early script messages. The individual who feels beat—who views his or her life drama as one failure after another—will set himself or herself up for put-down games like "Kick Me," "Stupid," or "Ain't It Awful." As pointed out earlier, the essential plots of games revolve around at least two of the three roles in the Karpman Triangle (1):

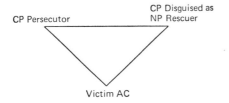

People who play games see themselves as persecutors, victims, or false rescuers. As pointed out before, a false rescuer is someone who is *not* genuinely trying to help someone else. He or she is *feigning* aid in order to take advantage of the other party. It is a "sneak up on them" ploy.

5. *Games Replace Boredom.* Everyone has a strong need to fill up his or her time in some kind of constructive way—for example, by doing challenging work. When work primarily becomes a means to other ends, but has little or no intrinsic value in itself, people are prone to game playing. Playing games is often the choice over meaningless, frustrating, or boring work. If employees are not periodically challenged with new ideas, new clients, or new approaches, organizational activity may become a vehicle for avoiding work through game playing. Proper training and management can help steer potentially bored employees into more exciting ways of pursuing their jobs.

One way of avoiding the economic and personal pitfalls of game playing is to be aware of various types of games. Games depend on their ulterior nature to survive. When the true, ulterior, negative purpose is disclosed, the game often goes up in flames—along with the game initiator. Games have three basic elements: (1) a series of complementary transactions on the surface, (2) an ulterior transaction, and (3) a negative pay-off that is delivered ulteriorly. Scoop out the "heart" of the game—its true, ulterior, negative purpose—and you have avoided a lot of wasted energy and grief to boot, whether you are a subordinate or a supervisor.

Although certainly not exhaustive, the following are some of the most typical games I could find concerning subordinates and supervisors. No doubt, there are many more than the ten that follow. However, a careful understanding of these games will at least familiarize you with some of the most commonly played organizational games. A good understanding of these will also help you in understanding other types of games people have tried to play on you. Once you are aware of the game process—basic strategies, roles, and ploys—you will be in an excellent position to rid yourself of one of the greatest productivity and morale burners around.

Although the games listed were found to be typical of the parties indicated (subordinate or supervisor), either of these two parties can play any of the games listed. For example, although I found "Uproar" to be typically initiated by supervisors, subordinates can also initiate the "Uproar" game.

TYPICAL SUPERVISOR OR MANAGER GAMES

"Now I've Got You, You S.O.B."

Supervisors generally play the NIGYSOB ("Now I've Got You, You S.O.B.") game a number of ways.

1. *Setting Objectives Too High.* Of course, the subordinate is caught deficient, and the manager can always come in and say: "Now I've got you. You didn't achieve the stated goals."

2. *Not Giving the Tools Necessary to Get the Job Done.* Some subordinates have deficient sales or incomplete projects or give poor presentations because they have not been properly trained and/or have not been given the support materials necessary to get the job done. Hence, the supervisor can say "Now I've Got You" again and again.

3. *Changing Performance Criteria During or at the End of the Review Period.* As a department head said to a professor who was

a candidate for promotion: "Gee, Mary, I'm sorry. You won't get the promotion to associate. Books don't count anymore as scholarly research."

4. *Requiring Objectives or Performance Over Which Subordinates Do Not Have Control.* "Now I've Got You. Why didn't you reach a decision with the other department heads over the purchase of the new computer?" The subordinate is left bewildered, knowing that he in no way has the authority to tell these other department heads what to do.

A prime solution for NIGYSOB is to remember that persecuting employees often ends more in negative than in positive results. People, like cats, don't like being "nailed to a corner." Push them too far and you may end up being the victim in terms of lower productivity and higher personnel turnover. Negative strokes, like positive ones, have a way of coming back to the source. The person you nail today may end up nailing you tomorrow.

"Uproar" (or "Who Can I Attack First?")

"Uproar" is an attack-defense game. "Uproar" players give their negative strokes by verbally putting others down. Although on the surface they may appear to be trying to resolve a problem, without an argument or some sort of verbal harassment "Uproar" players would not get their kicks. Common "Uproar" attack statements would include:

What's the matter? You're not up to par again.

Didn't you learn anything from the training program?

I suppose you want an extra hour off for lunch.

You guys are just plain lazy.

Hey, can't you keep your work area neat?

Supervisors are prone to play "Uproar" when objectives or quotas are not met. Anybody in the vicinity of their wrath will be attacked—

from secretaries to mail boys. The grumblings may be over insignificant things like unkempt desks or the use of too many paper clips.

Some bosses play "Uproar" because they believe in the "management by harassment" philosophy. I have already shown the folly and counterproductivity that result from such a management style (see chapter three). Others play "Uproar" in order to demonstrate to their subordinates or constituents that they have "fought the good fight." Union leaders will often "stir the waters" and get into heated verbal exchanges with employer representatives to indicate to the union membership that they are battling hard for the best possible contract.

Arguing or verbally attacking someone does not open the channels of communications and, thus, the path to solving problems or issues. It closes the channels. When attacked, people usually take on the defensive posture of the critical parent or the rebellious child. Rather than being receptive to listening, they concentrate on counterattacking. Emphasize solutions, *not* fault finding.

"Blemish" (or "Let's Sweat the Small Stuff")

This is the trivia game. In this game the boss is more concerned with minutiae—tiny details and inconsequential data—than with the important and primary objectives and purposes. I recall the case of the dean of a very large and prominent law school who spent over 80 percent of his time counseling students and going over individual grade sheets. In so doing he severely neglected his primary responsibilities of determining and overseeing school curriculum and research policies, faculty appointments, and promotional considerations (like fund raising and public relations work) in the local professional and legal community.

"Blemish" is not only a serious drain on the productive output of superiors. It can have a serious negative impact on subordinates as well. A past government official relayed how some State Department workers were stymied by the necessity of writing and rewriting cables many times, with the final draft being essentially the same as the first. Workers were putting in extra long hours, with no appreciable difference in the final product. The frustration and morale problems it caused among competent departmental employees were obvious and serious.

There is the case of a large computer company in which a top salesperson was seriously reprimanded for failing to wear a white dress shirt. Although dress codes—within limits—have their merits, inflexible and rigid dress codes can lead to the "Blemish" game.

Managers should always keep their primary objectives clearly in focus. If rules, regulations, and procedures become hindrances to the achievement of primary objectives, they should be removed or revamped. Additionally, employees are individuals. If caught up in a maze of trivia, their free child initiative and creativity might be destroyed in the process. Effective managers work diligently at developing employee potential and commitment, not at undermining these with "spin-the-wheel" activities.

"Cornered" (or "Heads You Lose and Tails You Lose")

There is probably no more frustrating and demoralizing situation in which to be caught than in this game of "Cornered," a game of unconditional negative strokes in which you are "damned if you do and damned if you don't." Bosses who want to constantly remind subordinates of their superiority will play "Cornered" by doling out tasks that cannot be accomplished. A "Cornered" game between a magazine editor and a staff writer proceeded as follows:

> Editor: Mary, now your article is too abstract.
> Staff Writer: When we talked before you said I had too many practical examples and that you desired more theory.
> Editor: You're getting close, but your article is still not up to par.
> After still another revision, Editor: I'm happy to see that you added more examples, but the article now needs a better balance between theory and practice. Why did you add so many examples?

Frustrating employees with intolerable "you can't win for losing situations" does not breed respect or support from employees. No "Cornered" scheme is foolproof. Employees, seemingly trapped, always have options that are much less than desirable to superiors including quitting, sabotage, unionization, litigation, and grievance channels. Impress your subordinates with your leadership qualities by supporting them and by helping them develop their talents in the most efficient and effective ways possible. Your superiors will be impressed also. Remember: pawns do not make for productive departments or organizational units.

"I'm Only Trying to Help You"
(or "I'm Your Friend")

This is the game of the hypocrite—the individual who feigns friendship but whose true purpose is to hurt you. "I'm Only Trying to Help You" is probably the most insidious game of all. Typical false rescuer remarks include:

> Gee, Joe, I'll help you by taking that old computer off your hands.
>
> (*True meaning:* I want that perfectly good computer for myself. I'm really only trying to help me.)

> Gosh, guys and gals, we held you back on promotions because we wanted you to feel worthy of reaching a higher rank.
>
> (*True meaning:* If those competent people ever get to our organizational level, we will lose a lot of power.)

> Joe, I'm your friend. Without me you wouldn't have those fine quarters to do research. I'm only trying to help, but we have no more research money.
>
> (*True meaning:* Screw you, Joe. I could not care less about your research aims. Why do you think I stuck you in the basement of the maintenance building!)

> Too bad, Martha, I really fought for that raise you asked for. The guys upstairs said money was too tight now.
>
> (*True meaning:* There is no way I'm going to recommend you or anyone else for a raise until I get a big fat one for myself.)

> See how I am looking out for your welfare. I got you a new XXX.
>
> (*True meaning:* I finally got rid of the last outdated and overstocked XXX.)

As pointed out in chapter four, those who manage by hypocrisy end up paying big prices for their false rescuer acts. False rescuers are on a collision course that leads to them becoming victims themselves and, thus, to a lonely existence. You may trick your employees once or so. However, after this they either won't believe you anymore and/or they will be out to "help" you like you "helped" them.

TYPICAL SUBORDINATE GAMES

"Kick Me: I'm Not Worth Much"

In extreme cases this is the game of the masochist. In this game the individual sets himself or herself up to be "kicked" or to receive put-downs or negative strokes. The obvious complementary game to "Kick Me" is "NIGYSOB" (the game of the sadist in the extreme). When these two team up, they can go on playing indefinitely.

Subordinates most often set themselves up for "Kick Me" by coming unprepared. Have you ever been to a briefing session with higher-ups where one individual has not done his or her homework? The result is the proverbial "kick" from one of the authority figures at the meeting:

> John, maybe you aren't ready for a project this size. Apparently, you are not even up to date on the A and B reports.

Some individuals, for one reason or another, consistently turn in projects or reports late in order to collect their put-downs.

> Joe, the next time your report is late, I'm reducing your project load until you can prove you can handle the work.

Other individuals will wait until the last minute and then haphazardly throw their prospectus, report, or work effort together. They are repeatedly reprimanded for careless, poor quality products.

"Kick Me" players, first of all, have to realize that negative self-labels are meaningless. No one is fated to be a victim. If we are victimized on a continuing basis, we *choose* to be victimized. We can also *choose* to be competent, reliable, and responsible. Believe me, good strokes feel a lot better than negative ones. No one demands perfection from you either.

However, adequate preparation, a reasonable amount of care and deliberation, and the meeting of reasonable time schedules are not too much to demand of anyone. Give yourself permission to succeed and you will never again flirt with the ultimate negative stroke or "kick"— termination.

"Wooden Leg" (or "My Excuses Are Better Than Yours")

"Wooden Leg" is the excuse game. Legitimate excuses are okay. The constant ones that keep individuals from producing are the ones I am concerned about here. "Wooden Legs" (or excuses for not producing) have included time, location, illness, tools, social events, staffing, relationships, etc.

Having been a college professor for ten years, I have heard quite a variety of excuses. Here are some "Wooden Legs" for not completing term papers on time:

I didn't have enough time.

Well, you didn't explain what you wanted well enough.

The library was closed during the vacation period. (The paper had been assigned three months in advance and there were numerous good libraries in the city.)

I couldn't do it. I didn't have the foundation courses.

How could you expect me to write a term paper? There are a number of seniors like me who have never written term papers in their lives.

You probably won't believe this. (I didn't.) I started to type the paper and my typewriter went haywire. I was on my way over to a friend's house to use her typewriter and I got a flat tire. When I went for help, someone stole the only handwritten copy I had from the car.

My girl friend has been sick. I had to spend most of my time with her.

They didn't have any of the books or articles I needed in the library.

Although the above excuses pertain specifically to college students, most of them are not much different from those commonly heard on the job. Contained in the above "Wooden Legs" are very common work environment themes: "I didn't have enough time;" "I didn't have the tools;" "I didn't have the training;" "I didn't have the experience;" "I lost it;" or "My home life or social relationships keep getting in the way."

Rationalizing away productivity helps no one, including the person doing it. Effective managers have an obligation to "nip" the excuse game in the "bud" when they encounter it. Sometimes circumstances can bring an abrupt and somber halt to "Wooden Leg" "bluffs."

> A branch manager of a bank, Mr. H., when quizzed about meeting his objectives concerning new accounts, would fall back on the branch's alleged poor location as his wooden leg. He was often heard to remark: "If I had the Lincoln Street Branch, meeting new accounts objectives would be no problem at all." At the unexpected departure of the Lincoln Street manager, Mr. H. was given the position. Unfortunately, he did not live up to his repeated prediction and the number of accounts actually decreased. His wooden leg dissolved and so did his job with the bank (2).

"Yes, But—Why Don't You?"

This is truly one of the most frustrating and time-wasting games any supervisor will ever encounter. In the "Yes, But" game, an individual asks for advice even though, in essence, he or she doesn't want any advice. The individual initiating the game gets his or her kicks by putting down the advice of the person from whom they are seeking it. The strategy of the game is based around the theme of the child who says to the parent: "See how much smarter I am than you." Of course, the ploy is a time waster. Why ask for advice not needed or wanted?

An example of the "Yes, But" game follows:

> A marketing assistant approaches the marketing director of a large bank on how to advertise the opening of a new branch.

Assistant: I feel overwhelmed. What suggestions can you give me for advertising the new Decatur Street Branch?"

Director: Why don't you look over past campaigns for new branches?

Assistant: I have tried that. And most of the stuff tried before is just old hat.

Director: Why don't you take out a whole page in the newspaper?

Assistant: Yes, that seems like the logical thing to do. But, honestly, few people read newspapers anymore. Even worse, the few who do will not read a dry ad about a bank opening!

Director: Why don't you send a mailout to all those living in the area.

Assistant: That sounds again like a good idea, but that may be your worst suggestion. Most mailouts end up in the round file—the trash can—before they are even read.

Director: How about having a jazz band on opening day? New Orleans people love to party.

Assistant: You almost sound like you are on the track, but, remember, the new branch is in the French Quarter. There are so many jazz places down there nobody will really pay much attention.

The solution to the "Yes, But" game is not to play it. If a subordinate attempts to hoodwink you into this big time waster, tell him or her you want to see his or her recommendations first, before you give any of your own. Most "Yes, But" players will "head for the hills" when you turn the tables on them. If you tend toward "Yes, But" games with your superior, remember that the strategy is purely short run. Over the long haul your boss will very likely put you in the "cheap seats" when it comes to raises or promotions for embarrassing him or her.

"If It Weren't for You"

This is a game in which one individual blames another for his or her lack of achievement. By placing his or her responsibilities on another, he or she can mask his or her true feelings of inadequacy. Common "If It Weren't for You" complaints include the following:

> If you had given me an adequate staff, we could have gotten the work done on time. (Yet, rarely was overtime pay ever used.)

If you had told me three months ago, things would have been different. (Giving her *five* months lead time in the past did not matter either.)

If you had only given me "Y" territory. (She was given "Y," and sales actually went down.)

If it weren't for those jerks, I would be receiving $5,000 more a year. (When it came time to file a grievance for inequity in pay, this individual could not even be solicited as a witness.)

If you had only given me a new computer. . . . (Guess what, he got one. However, productivity did *not* increase.)

There is no doubt that some complaints are legitimate. However, the "If It Weren't for You" player rarely, if ever, takes responsibility for his or her own deficiencies. Additionally, if there *are* legitimate and practical ways to resolve a complaint or a problem, he or she *never* takes a stand. If "It Weren't for You" players get their strokes from complaining, *not* from achieving. As one anonymous writer stated: "A chronic complainer gets all his exercise out of kicking." Your job is to ignore him or her so you won't get kicked.

"Between a Rock and a Hard Place"

In this game helplessness is feigned in order to prey on the sympathies of the other party. "Between a Rock and a Hard Place" is often used as a ploy to avoid work (3).

Gosh, boss, you know how much the men and I would like to get more directly involved in recruiting. Certainly, we can always use more top-notch, hand-picked engineers. However, we're caught in the middle. If we, for example, make direct contacts with recruiting agencies, personnel will claim we are taking away some of their responsibilities. They will make it hell for us when it comes to restrictive regulations on safety and equal employment. They are, after all, the ones who interpret the federal guidelines for the company. Additionally, if we make too ambitious a move to get new recruits, the Design Department will think we are trying to steal all the good engineers for ourselves. In the final analysis, we'd better leave well enough alone.

Or, consider this response to a public relations manager's request:

> P.R. Assistant: Well, Mary, I would love to write that speech for Mr. Jones, but if I do I won't be able to complete the handout for the convention. Also, Mrs. Pevy is giving a talk at the convention. If she finds out from Jones that we wrote his speech, we'll never hear the end of it. Before you know it, every Tom, Dick, and Jane in the organization will have us writing speeches.

Again, some gripes concerning work overloads or conflicts are legitimate. A careful study and appraisal of job duties and responsibilities, and how these interface with other jobs, will put any supervisor on firmer ground and will greatly reduce employee complaints. Even given a competently designed job scheme, some employees will *still* feign helplessness. Because this game can become cancerous in terms of undermining a manager's authority and his ability to lead, a few pointed suggestions that can help to abruptly and securely end this game are in order.

First of all, you can remind the employee that you are careful not to create unnecessary conflicts or overloads. Such problems lead to inefficiency and unhappy employees, which makes your job as a supervisor much harder and much less rewarding. Your superiors frown on poor morale and inefficiency as much as you do.

Secondly, state that there have not been other serious complaints. However, on the basis of this complaint, you will explore the matter further. Still, your work request must be completed until your investigation is finished. If the employee is simply playing a game, most will gladly do the work, fearing the outcome of an honest and thorough investigation.

Thirdly, it is always helpful to remind employees that by reasonably stretching their job responsibilities, you put a lot of confidence in their abilities. There are few better positive strokes to an employee's adult. Additionally, higher level jobs require a broader background. Developing reasonably broader talents is essentially in their best interest.

Employees who make a habit of "Between a Rock and a Hard Place" should be cautioned. In the short run they may finesse a few extra hours of work. In the long run they may get tagged as being allergic to work. Needless to say, the description will be accurate and their careers will be limited.

GENERAL STRATEGIES FOR GETTING OUT OF GAMES

Although I have given you some specific recommendations and strategies for dealing with the previously mentioned games, I would like to briefly discuss overall ways of steering clear of game playing. If you follow these suggestions, the prime productivity wasters (which is what games are) will not be significant problems for you or for your organization.

Be Aware

Games depend upon their ulterior nature for their existence. If you feel you are being put down, put off, or are "spinning your wheels," you are probably involved in a game. Often, the acknowledgment of this awareness to the other party will terminate the game.

> Look, Joe, I think we are spinning our wheels concerning advertising strategy. Go ahead and work up some suggestions of your own and let me react to them. At this time, it appears you are not receptive to my advice.

Such an acknowledgment of awareness might help terminate a "Yes, But" game, for example.

A few words of caution: Do not throw game labels or titles at the other party unless you know they are reasonably familiar with and receptive to TA terminology. Such labeling of another's behavior is a game in its own right and might lead to further discord.

Refuse to Play

It takes two to play games, and you do not have to play if you really do not want to play. If necessary, excuse yourself and leave the location of the game player.

Steer Clear of the
Three-Game Roles

Avoid playing the role of persecutor, rescuer, or victim. If you are out to get others, sooner or later you will be treated in kind. Feigning help and then taking advantage of the situation will win you a lot more enemies than friends. Coming unprepared or not trying, as victims often do, is an effective way to end up in the unemployment line.

Convert Negative Game Strokes
into Positive Ones

The ultimate pay-off of any game is a put-down, whether to yourself, to another, or to the organization. When you feel like "popping" someone else, stop and reflect before reacting. Practice constructive ways of correcting problems or problem people. "Can you explain it to me more fully?" gets much better results than "What you are saying sounds awfully dumb."

How you correct others can be a great asset *or* a great liability. If done properly, game playing can be significantly reduced and morale lifted to boot. If done improperly, the corrected party may take the criticism personally and may later strike back at the correcting party or organization through a reduced effort. Hurt adapted children do not make good employees. Also, improper correction can lead to a game of "Uproar," and *no* meaningful communication. Lemons can be made into lemonade. I have compiled a few tested rules for keeping employees from becoming defensive during criticism. These techniques will also work with supervisors, co-workers, and customers if you should have to correct them concerning data on a product, service, procedure, etc. These techniques are discussed in detail in chapter ten.

NOTES

1. For a review of the Karpman Triangle, see chapter two. It should be noted that Stephen Karpman does not assign ego states to the various drama roles in "Fairy Tales and Script Drama Analysis." *Transactional Analysis Bulletin* (April 1968), vol. 7, no. 26, pp. 39–43.

2. Michael LeBoeuf and Maurice F. Villeré, "Tambo—Applying TA to MBO," *Atlanta Economic Review* (March–April 1975), vol. 25, no. 2, pp. 30 and 33.

3. This game is frequently used as a ploy by labor negotiators. For a discussion on games and negotiating, see: Frank L. Acuff and Maurice F. Villeré, "Games Negotiators Play," *Business Horizons* (February 1976), vol. 19, no. 1, pp. 70–76.

TA AND WRITTEN COMMUNICATIONS

6

Despite the fact that very few organizational behavior books devote much time to business correspondence, I think and feel that a chapter on the subject is necessary. In workshops I have conducted, responses to data and exercises on TA and writing materials have been frequent and very positive. Many of the activities and behaviors of organizational members deal with the initiation of, or response to, some form of business writing. Writing forms include memorandums, letters, casual notes, reports, mail solicitations, etc. This chapter demonstrates how TA can be used effectively and efficiently in achieving the aims of any piece of business correspondence.

    Fundamentally, business writings have at least one of two primary goals: the conveyance of information and/or the solicitation of cooperation from one or more persons. Books dealing specifically with business writing spend a lot of time on the format and mechanics of various correspondence forms. For example, much time is devoted to how to head up a memo, the salutations and closes of business letters, or what should be included in the lead, body, and conclusion of a business report. Although all the above topics are important, there is a potentially more important ingredient—at least in terms of specifics and concrete examples—that is missing from most business correspondence books. This missing ingredient is the *psychological* aspect of the writing. You can have the neatest and most expertly organized business letter in the world, but if it makes the reader feel hostile or bored it will very likely have little positive impact on him or her. In order to motivate your reader to absorb and to respond favorably to what you write, the behavioral implications and features of business writings must be understood and employed appropriately. TA provides an excellent, concrete tool for quickly realizing these objectives.

Before getting into the specifics of applying TA to business writings, some comparisons of the psychological and organizational advantages and disadvantages of oral versus written communications might be helpful.

ADVANTAGES AND DISADVANTAGES: ORAL VERSUS WRITTEN COMMUNICATION

Feedback

In terms of feedback, oral communications have a distinct advantage over written communications. When communicating orally, as in face-to-face encounters or telephone conversations, feedback is immediate. If statements are unclear, for whatever reasons, the receiver of the transmission has the option to quickly clear up distortions through queries.

Gee, Mary, I am not sure what you mean by loose standards.

Did I understand you correctly when you said. . . ?

I see what you mean about such-and-such, but I need more clarity on issue X. Would you please elaborate?

The piece of written correspondence must stand on its own—at least for a longer period of time. In some cases the writer and the recipient may never meet, as in the case of a top executive officer sending policies down the chain of command to all supervisors, including those at the first level of authority. Two other obvious cases in which writer and receiver may never meet involve reports dispensed by governmental agencies for public consumption and mass mailings for advertising purposes.

Because immediate feedback is often not available, much more thought and precision must go into written materials. The adult must play a primary role in all business correspondence.

Some people prefer writing to face-to-face communications in order to avoid feedback. Positive or negative strokes are immediately available when transmitting data orally to another. Some organizational members would like to delay or to avoid the praise (or mainly criticism) that might be forthcoming. However, using written communications as a cop-out to avoid face-to-face confrontations will very often lead to more explosive negative strokes in the long run. Rather than defusing the critical parent or rebellious child emotions immediately, delay through writing can give these ego states more time to fuel up on their own anger.

> The s.o.b. could have at least told me in person. Wait 'till I see that guy next week. I'll nail him good. Plus, this memo gives me more time and ammunition to nail him with.

Permanence

Compared to oral communications, writing is permanent. What you say will quickly fade from the scene after you say it. However, what is written is there in black and white (or red, blue, green, etc.) for all concerned parties to view and review.

There was the case of an applicant for an engineering job who wrote a somewhat sarcastic note along with his application data to the personnel director of a large construction company concerning his opinion of the company's recruiting process. What he did not know was that he had an excellent chance of landing a fairly coveted position with the company. His apparent snap decision to sarcastically comment cost him that job and possibly other jobs. (Recruiters in the same region and field often keep in close touch.)

"You know," commented the personnel director, "when I read his dossier, at first I was very impressed with his record. But, in the second reading, I noticed some very sarcastic remarks concerning our style of recruiting. I am proud of what we have done to improve the recruiting process around here. I'll be damned if any s.o.b. of a new recruit is going to discount all our efforts. Who needs a guy like this working for you?"

The individual involved may simply have wanted to give some constructive feedback to the personnel director for improving recruiting techniques. Such feedback could have been given much more appropriately and effectively in person. With the aid of immediate feedback, negative impressions—like the intent to be sarcastic—could have been quickly dispelled.

Do not get me wrong. I am not trying to scare you, the reader, into being overly fearful or timid in conveying yourself on paper. I am simply saying that a little more attention paid to the psychological implications of writing is an easy and effective way to change potential lemons into lemonade. The dividends, in terms of cooperation, morale, and profits, can sometimes be enormous.

Positive strokes on paper are also permanent. People who go out of their way to complement others, through writing, are not easily forgotten.

As one school teacher stated:

Teaching can be a thankless job. If you get any feedback at all, it is usually negative—gripes about grades and so on. But every once in a while, I get a student who really appreciates my efforts to educate. When he or she goes to the trouble to write a sincere thank you letter, it not only lifts me the day I receive it. It's a great lift for a long time to come. I keep such letters displayed on my bulletin board as a source of encouragement to other teachers. If I can ever be of aid to such a student—with letters of recommendation, for example—you can bet I will.

Documentation

My father, an attorney, has desk stationery headed by humorous quotes. One such quote reads:

Confucius say, "Poor handwriting is better than good memory."

Whether the above saying was actually from the lips or writing instrument of the wise Chinese philosopher or not, I do not know. However, there is an abundant amount of truth in the statement, as any experienced lawyer will tell you. It is very difficult to enforce oral contracts. Witnesses sometimes have a knack for forgeting important details if there is no written document to remind them.

During the performance appraisal process, for example, it is always wise to document important happenings as they occur during the year (whether these involve exceptionally good or exceptionally poor performance on the part of the employee). Stashed away in the employee's file, such documentation not only refreshes the supervisor's memory but also makes dealing with employee disagreements a far easier task (1).

Cues

Oral communications provide audio and visual cues, such as tone of voice, voice inflection, hand motions, and facial expressions, that greatly help in properly interpreting the information transmitted. Without the aid of such cues, it is sometimes difficult to determine whether ideas conveyed are to be taken seriously or not, which ego state is conveying the message,* and the general emotional tone of the communications.

Of course, written materials, as I shall discuss, do have cues for distinguishing emotions and ego states, such as phraseology, punctuation marks (like an exclamation point), and other literary devices such as underlining. Even given these considerable devices, written materials can never match the spectrum of contextual cues available through oral communication.

Chain of Command

When it comes to passing information down the chain of command, particularly if there are many authority levels involved, the written medium cannot be surpassed. However, short memories, individual frames of reference, and semantical interpretations often severely distort

---

* For example, the phrase "open the door" could be an adult request, a parent command, or a child's pleading, depending on how it is expressed.

original transmissions. Distortion becomes very evident as a colonel's order is passed down a military chain of command in a communication story known as "Halley's Comet."*

Halley's Comet

A Colonel issued the following directive to the Executive Officer:
Tomorrow evening at approximately 2000 hours Halley's Comet will be visible in this area, an event that occurs only once every 75 years. Have the men fall out in the battalion area in fatigues, and I will explain this rare phenomenon to them. In case of rain, we will not be able to see anything, so assemble the men in the theater and I will show films of it.

Executive Officer to the Company Commander:
By order of the Colonel, tomorrow at 2000 hours Halley's Comet will appear above the battalion area. If it rains, fall the men out in fatigues; then march to the theater where the rare phenomenon will take place, something that occurs once every 75 years.

Company Commander to Lieutenant:
By order of the Colonel in fatigues at 2000 hours tomorrow evening, the phenomenal Halley's Comet will appear in the theater. In case of rain in the battalion area, the Colonel will give another order, something that occurs once every 75 years.

Lieutenant to Sergeant:
Tomorrow at 2000 hours the Colonel will appear in the theater with Halley's Comet, something that happens every 75 years. If it rains, the Colonel will order the comet into the battalion area.

Sergeant to Squad:
When it rains tomorrow at 2000 hours the phenomenal 75-year-old General Halley, accompanied by the Colonel, will drive his Comet through the battalion area in his fatigues.

Numbers reached

Important, but maybe too obvious to mention, is the fact that written material can obviously reach many more people, more quickly, than

---

* I received this story from a student in a management course some eight years ago. The original source is unknown.

oral, face-to-face transmissions. Also, you can only call so many prospects or employees in a given day. However, many thousands can be reached in a few hours or days by way of written transmissions, depending on the distance and the mode of transmission (that is, telex or the post office). Of course, audio-visual aids such as cassette tapes or video tapes can also be used to convey a great deal of information very quickly to many parties. However, such transmissions require a lot more equipment on the part of the receiver (projectors, video cassette systems, tape recorders, etc.) and the mode of transmission can be overly time consuming and expensive. A training film for explaining how to conduct appraisal interviews to supervisors may be very practical and feasible. However, making a video tape to relay price changes to parts people scattered around the country would be totally inappropriate cost wise and time wise.

HOW TO WRITE EFFECTIVELY IN ANY FORM OF ORGANIZATIONAL CORRESPONDENCE

Know and Motivate Your Audience

For your writings to be effective in soliciting the desired response, they must zero in on the needs of the audience. Too often, management's efforts to gain cooperation from workers fall short because they communicate their own needs rather than the needs of the workers. For instance, examine the following memo:

Date: August 1, 1981

From: Plant Manager
To: Production Workers

Ladies and Gentlemen, you should be as excited about the new production facility as we are.

With our added capacity and new machinery, you should be able to increase productivity by 30 percent.

Be devoted employees and help make the move to the new plant a smooth and a quick one.

The memo conveys very clearly and concisely the needs of the writer, the plant manager, but it states very little about the needs of the readers of the memo, the production workers. Naturally, the plant manager would like productivity to increase 30 percent with little down time due to moving to the new facility. Such an accomplishment would mean many good strokes to the plant manager, with possibly a raise or even a promotion in the bargain. However, what motivates the plant manager may be quite different from what motivates the plant workers. If the plant manager wishes to gain the cooperation of the workers, the memo should stress how the move will affect the workers' needs.

An excellent and efficient way to get a "feel" for readers' needs is to construct a stroke chart. The chart may be constructed easily from your own background and from knowledge of the reader. In the case of a large audience you may wish to do some formal or informal field research, depending on the importance of the piece of written correspondence. In the case of the plant manager he or she may wish to check with first-line supervisors to get a reading of the motivational climate of the workers before constructing the stroke chart. A direct mailing to 100,000 readers may require some formal market research before constructing the stroke chart. For simple, everyday one-to-one or one-to-a-few memos, the stroke chart might be done mentally, thus requiring little more than a brief reflection on the needs of the reader or readers.

A stroke chart for the production workers mentioned in the previous memo might look as follows after the plant manager checks with a number of first-line supervisors to see what might best motivate the workers to respond favorably to his or her memo. Also, management research data on how workers respond to change situations would also be helpful here.*

Because of the plant manager's better understanding of the production workers' needs via the stroke chart, he or she is now ready to construct a memo targeted to those needs. There is no better way to gain a favorable response from your readers than by catering to *their* needs and concerns, not to your *own.* The following memo will be much more effective in gaining cooperation from the production workers.

---

* This type of data may be easily gathered from basic management and organizational behavior textbooks found in almost any college or public library.

STROKE CHART
Production Workers

Needs	History and Background	Types of Strokes to Give
Physiological[a]	Extra pay can always be used during these inflationary times—that is, grocery bills do not get cheaper.	If possible, give extra money strokes that can be used to meet a number of needs.
Safety & security	Most workers are insecure about changes. Some fear they may lose their jobs to machines. Others fear they will have a hard time learning the new job or that production rates will be pushed unreasonably high.	To the scared adapted child, give security strokes about job security and the ability to adapt to the new job.
Social	Some feel they may be relocated away from friends.	Not really a big issue for most. Arrangements can be handled here, individually, by supervisors so that nobody's child feels separated from friends (that is, during lunch, etc.) who are not moving to the new factory.
Self-fulfillment	Some will respond favorably to the change if they are given an opportunity to give inputs concerning using the new equipment.	Input should be solicited from any who can help facilitate the change. This will provide good strokes to the employee's adult sense of competence and further understanding of the change.

[a] For a review of Maslow's needs, see chapter three.

Date: August 1, 1981

From: Plant Manager
To: Production Workers

Ladies and Gentlemen, the new production facility will be of great benefit to you as well as to XYZ Corporation. In this memo I would like to outline these benefits and to address myself to concerns that a number of workers have over the new facility.

1. *No jobs will be lost.* The rumors about workers' jobs being replaced by some of the new equipment is totally false. You are our most valuable asset. If anything, the increased profits to be realized by the move to the new facility will mean more jobs. Down the road I may be asking you to see if you have any friends who are interested in working at XYZ.

2. *Ease of production.* Every production worker who has tested out the new equipment says it's a dream compared to the old equipment. You will have little trouble adjusting to the new equipment. In fact, workers tell us it is much easier and more convenient to operate than the old equipment. Although you will be able to produce more with less effort, new production standards will be easier to meet than current standards. Again, you will be involved in setting these standards at a pace comfortable for you. Also, any suggestions or feedback from you concerning how to make adjustments to the new equipment even easier are greatly welcomed and appreciated.

3. *Extra pay.* Part of the extra productivity that will be realized by the new equipment will mean higher pay checks for all. Within the first year this could mean an extra 20 percent in pay to everyone on the production line, with no extra effort on your part. This should take some of the sting out of inflation for you.

Your supervisor will be meeting with you next week to discuss the details of the move to the new facility. If you have any concerns or questions regarding the move, feel free to express them. If you are not happy and secure about the move, XYZ Corporation isn't either.

Thanks again for your continuing help and support. Without fine workers like you, XYZ would not be the top manufacturer it is today.

Notice how the second memo focuses immediately and thoroughly on the needs of the readers—the production workers. Fears and concerns over job security, adjustments to new equipment, and production rates are frankly discussed and thus reduced. Also, extra benefits to the worker—in this case more pay—are also introduced. Genuine praise for past efforts is given also. If the praise is not *genuine,* forget it. Candy or ingenuine strokes can easily be detected, and their hypocritical nature does more harm than good to relationships. Channels of communication and feedback are kept open to help deal with employee difficulties through the statement: "If you have any concerns or questions regarding the move, feel free to express them." Such a statement is not only a good nurturing stroke to the reader, but it also helps establish the climate of mutual support and cooperation between you and the reader—the primary aim of almost any form of organizational writing.

Meet the Reader on His or Her
Own Personality Level

Address your correspondence to the personality of the audience. If you are dealing with an adapted child reader who is concerned or scared about a given issue, let your pen take him or her by the hand via the nurturing parent. If the audience is predominantly adult, make your statements concrete, logical, and factual. Support data in the form of statistics and research, with solid rationale behind points, would best appeal to an adult audience of scientists. If writing to a predominantly parent reader, you might want to stress the "shoulds," "musts," "rules," and punctuality of the matter.

If the matter you wish to relate is significantly important, you can get a more precise "feel" for your reader or readers by constructing a strokegram by ego states. (To refresh your memory on strokegrams, see chapter three.) If the reader is someone you deal with on a continuing basis, such as an employee or a client, you have a file you can refer to and update for future correspondence. The strokegram will do two things for your writing. First of all, it will clue you in on the egogram or personality structure of the reader by ego states. Secondly, it will tell you the strokes to give to get the most favorable response from such a person. As mentioned earlier, you get what you stroke. Stress clear thinking and recognize your reader for being a clear thinker and you will appeal favorably to the reader's adult. Stroke an employee who cares a lot about customers and you will not only make a good impression, but you will help the employee maintain this nurturing parent posture. Stroke a co-worker for being a "kick" to be around and you are on your way to an even closer relationship and more free child humor to cheer you up when you need it.

A strokegram for a fictitious employee, Kathy Davis, reads as follows:

STROKEGRAM

Ego States	History and Background	Types of Strokes to Give and Appeal to Make
Critical parent	Not much C.P. If excessive, it is on herself. Tends to push herself a little too hard. Sometimes tries to put 14 hours in a 10-hour day. Feels she has to be extra good because she is a woman.	Stroke her for her hard work, but let her know you do not want her to "burn out" by pushing too hard. Make sure she takes full advantage of her vacations. Let her know you don't demand any more of her because she is a woman.
Nurturing parent	Shows a great deal of concern and caring for clients and other employees. Because she has no children, she says her maternal instincts have to come out somewhere.	Caring like she does is great for her, the organization, and other employees. Keep on stroking and appealing to her nurturing parent in this regard.
Adult	Alert, bright—likes to take charge. Had to take full responsibility for herself at an early age after her mother's divorce. Particularly aware of how to adapt to client sensitivities. Although mothering, knows when to back off.	Manage and appeal to her adult by self-management. Except for general guidelines or specific requests by clients, let her take full charge in handling accounts. Make suggestions to her in memos with good, concrete adult data, but never use commands or "talk down to" statements.
Free child	Boy, does she ever love to party, which is great, because she knows how to set up a great	Stroke her periodically for making the separation between work and play, but let her know

STROKEGRAM *(continued)*

Ego States	History and Background	Types of Strokes to Give and Appeal to Make
	party. Her parent keeps her child in charge during work hours. Has a good sense of humor—loves a good joke. Although she can set up the most formal affair perfectly, off the job and among co-workers she prefers to be casual and be on a first name or nickname basis.	you like her free child play qualities—brightens up the office and is appealing to customers. Go casual in writing appeals.
Adapted child	Because of the financial straits she and her mother were in after her mother's divorce, she is very security conscious. As good as she is at her work, she needs to know she is needed and her job is secure.	Reduce her adapted child fears by periodically reminding her she is a great asset—a much-needed asset—to the organization.

Memo to Kathy Davis (with strokegram in mind):

Date: May 15, 1981

From: Bill Jones, Public Relations Director

To: Kathy Davis, Public Relations Account Executive

Hey, I just wanted to get it into print that you did a great job in handling Mr. Brown's account. He was particularly pleased with how you immediately took charge and made all the flight, hotel, and food catering arrangements without a hitch, leaving him a lot more worry-free sightseeing time. The program agenda you wrote up kept all conventioneers in the right place at the right time like never before. Believe me, Mr. Brown has been a "hard cookie" to please in the past.

Off the record—how about lunch to celebrate *you* tomorrow. If I don't give special strokes to my top-notch helpers, some other agency is going to steal them away. Also, I've got some great new jokes to share with someone who appreciates them. See you tomorrow at noon.

Bill Jones, the public relations director, zeroed in on the key personality dimensions and needs of Kathy Davis with the skill and adroitness of a human relations expert. With the aid of the strokegram, in the first sentence he zeroed in on Kathy's casual way of relating to others. In the last paragraph he led off with a casual expression, "off the record," again hooking Kathy's free child. He later built upon this free child appeal by addressing Kathy's sense of humor as demonstrated by her love for jokes. He helped reduce her adapted child fears over job security and helped solidify her loyalty in the remaining sentences in the last paragraph. What better positive recognition to give a valuable employee than to celebrate *her* as something very special, and top-notch to you as well as to the organization.

Ego States to Address and Those to Avoid in Any Form of Organizational Correspondence

Of course, what I have to say in this section is a general rule. There may be times, circumstances, or individuals that require different treatment in order for you to gain the desired results. However, I would say that at least 90 percent of effective business writings, regardless of their nature (memos, business letters, reports, etc.), adhere to general guidelines.

Come out of and address the following ego states: the free child, the adult, and the nurturing parent.

The Free Child. The free child stimulates enthusiasm and excitement over the problem, issue, or product written about. As discussed in detail in chapter nine, on leadership, effective leaders are like good salespersons—they are enthusiastic. Prospects buy from salespersons who are truly excited and interested in the product or service they are selling. Subordinates put out extra efforts for enthusiastic bosses, not for bored ones. Enthusiasm is contagious, and readers can catch it from writers. Interesting, exciting, and stimulating writing obtains many more favorable responses from readers than dull, dry statements. It is a wise rule to lead with the free child. Cultivating interest and desire early never hurts.

The Adult. The body of the correspondence should be written in the adult. The adult conveys facts, data, benefits, problem areas, etc. specifically and concretely. Employees, co-workers, and customers are better educated today than ever before. "B.S." will often land your writing where it belongs—in the trash can. Give dates, places, descriptions, and the who's, what's, when's, where's, why's, and how's of the issue when needed. Back your statements with solid rationale when available. People are more willing and more able to cooperate when their adults are fed meaningful material with which to work. One reader comments on a supervisor's written request:

> Okay, now I know what she is talking about and why it is so important that we fill this order immediately. I really don't mind rush orders that much when things are explained to me. When I'm kept in the dark— as with some half-baked requests I've had—I often end up getting things delayed through foul-ups.

The Nurturing Parent. Although useful throughout, always remember to close with the nurturing parent. The nurturing parent demonstrates a sincere concern and interest in the reader. People reciprocate in kind to those who are concerned about them. Closing with nurturing parent statements like "If I can be of further assistance, please do not hesitate to call," "We can help you by calling . . . ," "To benefit from our . . . , please call . . . ," "Thanks again for your assistance," "If you have any further questions, feel free to get back in touch" also help pave the way for future contact with the reader, whether he or she is a co-worker, employee, or prospect. If affordable, sending a self-addressed and stamped envelope is a great nurturing parent stroke in itself when soliciting responses (research data or prospect replies) from extra organizational readers.

The Adapted Child. Avoid the adapted child in almost all situations. Readers are turned off by writers who stammer like they do not know what they are writing about or who pour out their failings unnecessarily, hoping possibly for a miraculous rescue by the reader.

Do not use written material as a vehicle for game playing. Do not set yourself up as the helpless adapted child victim or you will receive negative strokes—especially rejection—from the reader, *not* cooperation. I recall the case of a job applicant who wanted very much to work in New Orleans. Her experience and academic credentials were excellent. In her résumé she included a statement saying that she had asthma and that she wondered whether working in a high humidity climate like New Orleans would be bad for her health. She was not given the job. Although the employers were not medical doctors, and although they had no specifics on her type of asthma, they did not want to incur a lot of training time and expense only to have Ms. X leave suddenly, claiming she needed to move to a drier climate. Obviously, if Ms. X was truly concerned about her health, she should have checked with a doctor, *not* her potential employer. However, the adapted child rarely uses discretion.

The Critical Parent. Unless you are addressing very small children, the critical parent has *no* viable place in your writing. In fact, there is probably no better way to turn off your audience than with patronizing, scolding, or critical remarks like "You need permission from this office in all cases," "Let me tell you what your problem is," "If you cannot handle the job . . . ," "As you are well aware," "If you had taken the time to check your manual, you would already know . . . ," or "Don't give me that. . . ." The average response to critical parent remarks like the preceding ones is from the rebellious child. This means counterproductivity, *not* cooperation.

> (Sarcastically): Oh, I have to get permission every time from Big Daddy. He's always got to impress you with his power.

> If he keeps telling me I have problems, I'll give him some real problems to worry about.

> If I am so damn well aware, why in the hell is she writing to tell me so?

> (Facetiously): Right, I just pull price changes out of the air. Who needs a manual? Heck, we only have 2,000 products. I'll show the s.o.b.

Let your writings leave permanent expressions of problem resolution and mutual support with the reader, *not* accusations and fault finding. Writings often precede face-to-face communication. Putting down a foundation of hostility in advance does *not* pave the way for smooth interpersonal exchanges or problem solving later.

Get to the Point Quickly

Most organizational members are already burdened with too much mail and other reading materials. Yet, many writers feel that if they don't "cover the whole world" much of the information they wish to convey will be lost. Actually, more is lost through "information overkill" than through condensation. Comprehension tests indicate that little is lost in information value when writings are condensed—even when condensed by more than 80 percent. College students reading an abbreviated version of a semitechnical article (one-sixth as long as the original) only scored two percentage points lower than the group reading the full-length version (2).

By failing to write succinctly, writers often turn off the two most important ego states in the reader: the adult and the free child. By badgering the reader with reams of data and explanation, the adult in the reader becomes overburdened with trivia and thus has a difficult time separating important information from the "chaff." Thus, he or she becomes confused in terms of what and how to respond effectively to what you have written. If the reader's adult is more than sufficiently taxed by everyday problems and previous correspondence, his or her angry free child may take over and choose to discard these longer writings in favor of shorter ones.

> I've had enough. I will not read anything that looks like beating around the bush. If push comes to shove, I'll take a three-paragraph memo over three pages any day. Frankly, I'm getting bored.

Believe me, it *is* hard to gain the reader's free child interest in what you have to say if you bore him or her to death with unnecessary wordiness. One principal way of cultivating the reader's cooperation is by showing genuine nurturing parent concern for the reading burden under which he or she must labor. Keep your ideas and data crisp and to the point and you'll receive more dividends in terms of favorable responses than you ever imagined.

Sometimes writers get sidetracked into adapted child mumblings and indecisions and other ego state concerns that can best be handled in face-to-face communications, where immediate feedback and audio-visual cues such as parent nurturing (as demonstrated by a smile and a warm handshake) are available. Unless you want to document material (by yourself and/or the reader) for further reference, many things can be most appropriately and effectively expressed orally. Notice how the vice-president of operations gets detoured in the following memo.

Date: November 15, 1981
From: Mr. O, Vice-President of Operations
To: Mr. T, Director of Training
This is to confirm our 3:00 P.M. meeting Wednesday in Conference Room 15A to discuss your proposed program on Transactional Analysis. I have some mixed feelings about TA. I am uncertain as to whether terms like "Parent, Adult, and Child" might be viewed as childish by many of our line managers. Oh, I know you are an excellent trainer and that many firms have had a great deal of success with TA, but I can't help but wonder about TA terminology and its implications. I would estimate that you have some experience in the TA area? This brings me to another point. Will the program be handled in-house or through outside trainers? Our training budget is meager now since it is the end of our accounting year. Well, I know you would not try to put our department in a fiscal bind. See you Wednesday.

Except for a confirmation of time and place for documentation purposes, the rest of the material is superfluous and could be most appropriately handled at the meeting—with less antagonism to boot. The question "I would estimate that you have some experience in the TA area?" is not going to endear Mr. T to Mr. O. The memo could have simply read:

Date: November 15, 1981
From: Mr. O, Vice-President of Operations
To: Mr. T, Director of Training
This is to confirm our meeting Wednesday in Conference Room 15A. I am looking forward to discussing your ideas on TA as a training tool for line managers.

Ego State Editing

After drafting your piece of writing, circle key words and edit out inappropriate ego states. Adapted child or critical parent expressions add little productive value to what you have to say and may do a great deal of harm, as mentioned earlier. Particularly patronizing, sarcastic, or bungling expressions may stick in the minds of the readers and overshadow an otherwise effective piece of writing. It will only take you a few extra minutes to weed out these rhetorical cancers. These few minutes may mean the difference between success and failure, between a sale or no sale, and between cooperation and hostility.

The David Brown Memo

Read the following memo carefully and then answer the questions and directives following it. This exercise should be an excellent aid for you in integrating the material discussed in this chapter. With a little practice, you will find your psychological style of writing to be greatly improved.

1. Out of what ego state is the writer coming? You can get a concrete handle on this by analyzing each sentence and then giving an overall impression of the paragraph. However, simply adding up the number of times the writer comes out of a given ego state does not necessarily mean a given paragraph or the whole writing will be dominated by this ego state. Emotional ego states like the parent and child often have a greater impression on the reader than the emotionally neutral state of the adult. A few choice critical parent expressions at the close of a letter or memo, for example, may overcome the impact of a basically unemotionally stated adult description. One who has received obviously sarcastic or belligerent comments in a letter or memo need not simply add these up to feel their impact.

2. Toward what ego state is the writing addressed? Along with question one, this can be analyzed sentence by sentence and then paragraph by paragraph, keeping the above consideration in mind. Sentences and paragraphs can be quickly coded with ego state initials like CP-AC, A-A, NP-FC, etc.

3. Ego edit out any particularly undesirable ego state expressions by circling these.

4. Draw a line through any unnecessary words, phrases, or statements— condense.

```
Date:   October 10, 1981
From:   David Brown, Dean of Arts and Sciences
To:     College Faculty
Re: Midterm Examinations, Fall 1981
Regarding the midterm examinations schedule, the following direc-
tives pertain thereto.
Exams are to be given on the dates enclosed. Any deviation from
this schedule cannot be made without permission of this office.
Rarely, if ever, is permission given.
Exams, as usual, are to start exactly on the hour. To avoid any
confusion with normal class times that start ten minutes after the
hour, announce this deviation from the normal schedule in ad-
vance to your classes.
Examination forms are to be filled out with number 3 pencils as
indicated on the grade sheets. If you do not use #3 pencils as
indicated on the computer grade sheets, the grades will not be
picked up by our computer scanner. Do not—and I emphasize
again, fill in the grid areas in ink.
Students who are scheduled to take more than two examinations
on the same day may appeal to have these extra examinations
taken on different days. Clearance for such changes must come
directly from this office and cannot be made by instructors individ-
ually.
As always, midterm examinations must be given to all students,
graduate and undergraduate. No exceptions to this rule will be
tolerated.
```

5. Overall, how effective do you feel the memo will be in gaining cooperation from the reader?

6. Rewrite the memo in order to make it most effective and succinct.

Although the solutions I present below may not totally agree
with yours, the "meat" of the solutions should be close. Interpretations
of a writer's intent will vary with the reader's familiarity with the subject
and with his or her relationship with the writer. However, certain ego
state overtones and expressions will be consistently obvious to most
readers. I have taken the liberty to number the paragraphs, because
this makes it much easier to analyze them separately.

EDITED VERSION OF MEMO

From: David Brown
Dean of Arts and Sciences
To: College Faculty   Date: October 10, 1981

Re: Mid-term Examinations, Fall, 1981

A-A   (1) ~~Regarding the mid-term examination schedule, the following directives pertain thereto.~~

CP-AC   (2) Exams are to be given on the dates enclosed. Any deviation from this schedule can not be made without ⟨permission⟩ of this office. ~~⟨Rarely, if ever, is permission given.⟩~~

A-A   (3) Exams, as usual, are to start exactly on the hour. To avoid any confusion with normal class times which start ten minutes after the hour, announce this deviation from the normal schedule in advance ~~to your classes.~~

CP-AC   (4) ~~Examination forms are to be filled out with⟨number 3 pencils⟩as indicated on the grade sheets. If you do not use number⟨#3 pencils⟩as indicated on the computer grade sheets, the grades will not be picked up by our computer scanner. ⟨Do not - and I emphasize again,⟩ fill in the grid areas in⟨ink.⟩~~

A-A   (5) Students who are scheduled to take more than two examinations on the same day may appeal to have these extra examinations taken on different days. Clearance for such changes must come directly from this office ~~and cannot be made by instructors individually.~~

CP-AC   (6) ~~As always, mid-term examinations⟨must⟩be given to all students, graduate and undergraduate. ⟨No exceptions to this rule will be tolerated.⟩~~

Questions 1 & 2. Questions 1 and 2 can be answered most appropriately together. Taking it paragraph by paragraph, my rationale follows:

Paragraph one. I analyzed this paragraph as adult to adult. Basically, David is simply stating what is to come in the memo. However, I am giving David the benefit of the doubt, as I find the wording "pertain thereto" somewhat affected and patronizing.

Paragraph two. In the first two sentences he is simply pointing out the "rules of the road"—or giving out adult to adult information. However, the last sentence overcomes this with its heavy critical parent

142

overtones, indicated not only by the wording but by the underlining, which again emphasizes his authority position. Hence, I read this paragraph as predominantly critical parent to adapted child.

Paragraph three. Except for the recommendation that professors announce time changes to students in advance (which some may take as a parent scolding a child over something he or she already knows), I find this paragraph a basically adult to adult conveyance of information.

Paragraph four. This paragraph is blatantly critical parent to adapted child. The triple underlining, the repeated emphasis, and constant "nots" reminds one of a critical parent verbally spanking a small child.

Paragraph five. Again, "rules of the road" are laid out in a fairly straightforward adult to adult fashion.

Paragraph six. The memo closes in a very critical parent to adapted child fashion, as evidenced by the triple underlining and the harsh autocratic sentence at the end.

Overall, the memo is clearly one of critical parent to adapted child. Although the adult to adult paragraphs equal the critical parent to adapted child paragraphs, the scolding and autocratic demeanor of the parent to child statements greatly overshadow the unemotional adult statements.

Directive 3. On the edited version of the memo, particularly obnoxious statements, phraseology, and grammatical expressions have been circled. All these involved critical parent forms of expression. I found the triple underlining and the repeated statements concerning David's reluctance to tolerate deviations from his dictums particularly unnecessary and tyrannical.

Directive 4. As you have probably noticed, I have primarily eliminated all obnoxious ego state phrases and paragraphs one, four, and six. Paragraph one had already been mentioned in the line above it. The fourth paragraph, besides being demeaning, is unnecessary, because this data is included on the grade sheets. The last paragraph is also unnecessary. "As always" tells me that everyone already knows they must give midterms to all students. New teachers are briefed on examination requirements as a part of their orientation sessions.

Question 5. Although the great majority of the members of the college faculty are professional enough to properly discharge their duties concerning grading, some might resist David's childish treatment of them by turning in grades late or by rebelling against his commands in the letter (such as the use of pencil versus ink). Certainly, his excessively demanding approach to the faculty will not endear them to him. It will add a hostile atmosphere at other times when cooperation is needed, as in college committee work.

Additionally, David's memo is clearly not on target. Many go into college teaching for reasons of academic freedom, which guarantees them the right to pursue matters of higher intellectual pursuit at their own discretion, without interference from others—including authority figures. Thus, faculty members are conditioned to resist a parental or an autocratic approach to exercising organizational policies. They are accustomed to running their own shows in the classroom and in research and, thus, are more disposed to be treated as adults. The memo should have been targeted adult to adult and not parent to child. Also, there is no data in the memo that appeals to the needs of the faculty—for example, information on how the dean can help facilitate grade processing for the faculty.

Directive 6. Rewritten memo:

Date: October 10, 1981
From: David Brown, Dean of Arts and Sciences
To: College Faculty
Re: Midterm Exams, Fall 1981

Midterm exams are upon us once again. Here are some suggestions and information that will aid you in the grading process.

Scheduling of exams. Enclosed is a schedule of exam dates. For coordination reasons, would you please check with us if you plan to change from this schedule. For example, students who are scheduled to take more than two exams on the same day may schedule the extra exams on different days.

Starting times. Unlike normal class times, exams start on the hour and not ten minutes after the hour. You may wish to advise students in advance of these time changes.

If you have any questions concerning any aspect of the exam procedures or need any type of assistance, please feel free to contact the college office at your earliest convenience.

Note how the rewritten memo completely alters the demeanor of the first memo from one of hostile autocratic dictums to one of mutual aid and support. By making suggestions instead of commands, the message is clearly adult and not critical parent. Also, sprinkled throughout—and most effectively at the end—are nurturing parent statements designed to pave the way for cooperation by offering aid and assistance to the readers. Italics are used sparingly and only as a vehicle for clarifying and organizing adult data—in the paragraph headings. Obnoxious reminders of the dean's authority over the faculty through triple underlining or the underlining of authority statements have been deleted.

NOTES

1. Maurice F. Villeré, G. Kent Stearns, and Kenneth J. Lacho, "The Human Side of Performance Appraisal," *Business* (Nov.–Dec. 1979), vol. 29, no. 6, p. 46.
2. Joseph R. Razek and Maurice F. Villeré, "Five Do's and Don'ts of Business Communication," *Louisiana Business Survey* (July 1978), vol. 9, no. 3, p. 11.

THE GROUP LEVEL
Group Dynamics

7

Groups, such as committees, have been the butt of many jokes and much ridicule. Milton Berle once commented: "Committee—a group of men who keep minutes and waste hours." As one anonymous writer put it: "To get something done, a committee should consist of no more than three men, two of whom are absent."

Yet, in spite of the numerous criticisms lodged against groups and how they function, much of what happens in an organization is done through groups, particularly committees. A survey, with 1,200 organizations responding, revealed the following: 94 percent of the firms with over 10,000 employees use formal committees; 64 percent of those with less than 250 employees also use formal committees (1). Those results do not include all the things done through informal groups and other types of work teams.

Whether we like to believe it or not, groups are an integral part of organizational life and are here to stay. This chapter, with the aid of TA, explores some of the aspects of group dynamics. Questions to be addressed here include: What is a group? Why do groups form and what keeps them together? How do groups function (including their dynamics and ways of communicating)? Chapter eight deals with decision making and problem solving in groups.

A group consists of at least two individuals who (1) interact with each other, (2) are aware of each other, and (3) view themselves to be a group in the sense that the members have similar purposes or overall objectives (2).*

In his text, *Organizational Psychology,* Edgar Schein elaborates on the definition of what constitutes a group and what does not:

> The size of the group is thus limited by the possibilities of mutual interaction and mutual awareness. Mere aggregates of people do not fit this definition because they do not interact and do not perceive themselves to be a group even if they are aware of each other as, for instance, a crowd on a street corner watching some event. A total department, a union, or a whole organization would not be a group in spite of thinking of themselves as "we," because they generally do not all interact and are not all aware of each other. Work teams, committees, subparts of departments, cliques, and various other informal associations among organizational members would fit this definition of a group (3).

As can be seen by Schein's comments, groups are psychologically distinct from individual behavior or organizational behavior in concert. When individuals function and interact in a group setting, they behave differently than they would behave alone. When we are being observed by others, when we have to defend our own viewpoints, when others apply social pressures to the positions we take on an issue, and when we have an audience with which to share our ideas and feelings, we will naturally perform differently. The dynamics of the various ways of relating in a group setting under group pressures will be discussed shortly. Now, I would like to discuss some of the reasons that cause individuals to form into groups in the first place. A better understanding of group motivating factors will shed some light on why groups are so prevalent in organizations and why they are very likely to remain in the limelight.

---

* This idea does not mean that individual group members have to agree on subobjectives or the means of accomplishing objectives. For example, a fact-finding committee might be formed to suggest ways of upgrading the educational level in a given community. Though the overall group objectives would be the same, suggestions for accomplishing this may range from improving primary education to a better public library system.

WHY GROUPS FORM OR COME ABOUT

Social Needs

Men and women are social animals. They need and crave love, support, friendship, and general companionship. As mentioned earlier, organizational members are paid high premiums (in terms of salaries, bonuses, etc.) if they are placed in jobs that isolate them from family, friends, or even their community. The free child in all of us needs the warm feelings that come from affiliation strokes. Few of us are hermit types. Almost all of us need the nurturing we get from being with others. Support groups, groups to which individuals can go to share their "hurts" and "wounds" over everyday work life turmoil, are being used by a number of organizations as a way to reduce turnover and improve morale. As one group member put it:

> This is a high-pressure outfit. If I didn't have some buddies I could rely on to help 'lick some of the wounds,' I would have gotten out a long time ago. Around here, one can be human and still be effective.

Whether or not organizations provide formal vehicles—in terms of support groups—for sharing feelings and frustrations on the job, such groups *will* develop, informally. The affiliation needs in the child are strong and will not be denied.

Ego Needs

Through group membership individuals can gain status and recognition from others (including peers, bosses, or subordinates). The child in us needs to feel important in the eyes of others. By holding positions of importance in groups, and by the impressions we make on others during group presentations or discussions, we have very tangible and immediate ways to receive prestige strokes.

> Mary, that was a fantastic presentation you gave on time management. I am going to apply some of your ideas starting now.

148

I know there is no more money involved in being elected committee chairperson—and probably a lot more work. But, frankly, I feel quite honored to be elected to the head of the operations committee. I never realized before how much others valued my opinions and my administrative abilities.

Security Needs

Through unions, for example, employees are in a better position to maintain job security. In fact, the most important thing in any collective bargaining agreement is the issue of job security. Without contracted rights concerning terminations, layoffs, and job territories—the secureness of the job itself—pay and fringe benefits are meaningless. Without a job, members have nothing over which to bargain. This need for security explains why unions will spend thousands of dollars on arbitration and legal fees over a $20 claim that involves a job territory issue. By uniting into groups or unions, employees have the power and resources to offset the power and resources of a large organization. *One* individual would have little, if any, success in combating injustices on the job at General Motors. However, the United Automobile Workers has the muscle and resources to provide increased security and benefits to workers. As the cliché goes, "United we stand, divided we fall."

One individual who files a grievance where no union exists may be viewed as a troublemaker and a complainer, and his position with the organization may be a short-lived one.

> Don't take Joe seriously. He's just biased against his boss and he complains about things whether they are going well or not.

On the other hand, if a *whole section* files a grievance over the way they are being treated, they will no doubt receive a lot more attention.

> Gee, they can't all be wrong. They must have a legitimate gripe. And there is no way we can afford to fire all of them anyway.

The insecure adapted child is a very strong motivator toward group formation.

An Adult Ego State Decontaminator

Through groups, individuals can check out their adult perceptions of the work environment. Thus, groups help perform the important function of validating adult data in order to overcome possible parent prejudices or child exaggerations.

> I guess you guys are right. Mack isn't out to get me. You say he gives all new people a hard time. I'm relieved now that I have checked with you guys.

> Yes, I guess I have been a little too strict in my performance standards. Now, how do you go about giving more equitable ratings?

> I figure now I have been taking work too seriously. Thanks for the chat and the opportunity to compare notes.

A Sounding Board

Sometimes our child is frustrated over something that has happened on the job. We just want to get out some angry or sad feelings, or even share some happy things. We don't want any adult answers— just a good audience. The informal group can be a great listener.

> Okay, we hear what you are saying. We'd be damn angry too if that happened to us. Doesn't it feel good to let it out?

A Testing Ground

Many times the group, acting as a kind of proving ground, helps us test out adult ideas or free child intuition. Rather than embarrass ourselves in front of the boss, or jeopardize our chances with a prospect or a client, we can test new approaches or strategies with co-workers.

> Well, look, I think we all agree on a few points. We think you ought to canvass all medium to large businesses in the area first and you should go through the purchasing directors. However, your research on the new territory will go more quickly and effectively if you first introduce

yourself and your purpose through a direct mailout before telephoning for preliminary data-gathering interviews.

To Meet Parent or Adult Authority Requirements

Sometimes, in order to accomplish the task at hand, other individuals are required to be a part of the decision. For example, you may wish to purchase a large computer for your department. Organizational rules may require that this decision to purchase be discussed by a budget committee if the amount involved is in excess of, say, $25,000. Banking decisions involving commercial loans to businesses or individuals require the sanctions of lending officers and sometimes the board of directors, depending on the size and the nature of the loan under consideration. Therefore, whether we like it or not, authority constraints sometimes exist that obviate individual decision making or problem solving.

The Only Feasible (or Most Effective) Way of Getting the Job Done

From a practical adult standpoint, sometimes the job can only be feasibly accomplished through a group effort. I recall seeing a game show on television that required, as one of the challenges, that all four tires on an automobile be changed in two minutes—without the use of a jack—in order to break an existing world record. It would be virtually impossible for a *single* individual to accomplish this task at all, in more or less than two minutes. A *group* of five, consisting of three football players and two auto mechanics, broke the existing record by about ten seconds. The three football players lifted up an end of the car while the auto mechanics changed the tires. Although most organizational tasks would obviously not require a challenge so bizarre, many require a group effort for an effective solution. Without an effective team effort, few basketball, football, baseball, or hockey teams would be successful against keen competition. Without a group effort, few advertising agencies could make meaningful proposals on a complex ad campaign. Commercial artists and copy writers, as well as account executives, must be involved in such proposals. Books are published efficiently and effectively through a group effort. Authors, editors, and marketing personnel must all be involved if there are to be significant unit sales.

HOW GROUPS FUNCTION

Through reading and experience, I have found two theories that I feel and think best explain the dynamics or happenings in a group: exchange theory and script theory.

Exchange Theory

Exchange theory basically says that the interactions between and among group members can be explained in terms of the exchanges of things of value that take place. In fact, group members will only continue to interact as long as the rewards exceed the cost or, in other words, as long as the exchange is profitable. In TA terminology, individuals attempt to maximize the positive difference between positive and negative strokes. For instance, individuals will continue to belong to a certain group because it is more profitable in terms of positive strokes to do so than to belong to a different group or to be a loner. Single people may prefer singles groups rather than sitting at home alone on certain nights. Blue collar workers may find it more profitable in terms of their financial security, as well as their job security, to bargain in concert rather than individually. University faculty members often form research teams in order to handle consulting jobs or in order to publish research articles. They often find that their activities will be most profitable, in terms of number and quality of publications and lucrative consulting jobs, when working as a team rather than working alone. Research or consulting projects requiring expertise from a number of disciplines (that is, management, marketing, finance, and business law) may require a group effort if there is to be any success at all.

How group members communicate, to whom they communicate, and how frequently they communicate may also be explained by exchange theory. Individuals communicate most frequently with those who have the most to offer them in terms of positive strokes. Members gravitate, then, toward the most profitable exchanges. Members in a research group will tend to direct statements most frequently to members who have the most expertise or research knowledge strokes. Members of a garden club will direct a lot of their communication toward those with an abundance of gardening technique and arrangement strokes. Members on an endowment committee for a charitable institution will direct their communication toward the wealthiest group members.

Besides seeking out knowledge or money strokes in terms of the primary objectives of the group, members will also communicate, at least informally, with other members on the basis of their position or status on the organizational chart and in terms of their strokegrams. (For a review of strokegrams, see chapter three.)

In discussing group dynamics, Joe Kelly, a noted authority on organizational behavior, states:

> The relation between status and communication has been investigated in a large number of different researches. The findings of these investigations may be summarized in three propositions:
> 1. Communication is likely to be directed towards high-status members. For example, on balance nurses prefer to talk to doctors.
> 2. Communication is likely to be directed towards individuals of equal status. If doctors are not available or "open" for communication, nurses prefer to talk to nurses.
> 3. Where equality of status is uncertain, communication will tend to be avoided. If two nurses are competing for promotion and there is a marginal difference in qualifications, seniority, and so on, then contact will be avoided (4).

It is because of this phenomenon of organizational status that I will not permit supervisors and subordinates of the same organization to participate in the same group exercise during one of my TA and organization workshops. I find that subordinates become too involved in monitoring and responding to supervisor communication to get relaxed and meaningfully involved in the task at hand.

The strokegram is probably the best clue as to how individual members will communicate in a group setting. Construct strokegrams of individual members of your work group or committee and you will readily see what I mean. By tying together an individual's egogram and his needs, the strokegram will indicate clearly which exchanges are most profitable to the member's personality and needs. An individual with a strong need to nurture and a large nurturing parent will seek other more helpless members (for instance, in terms of knowledge on the topic at hand or in ability to articulate points) to bolster.

> Look, guys, Mary may not have the same formal education you guys do, but she damn well cares as much about the kids as any of us. Come on, Mary, tell us more.

The predominantly adult member will communicate with those who can best meet his or her needs for solid evidence and rationale.

> Suzy, you seem to make a lot of sense. Tell me more about the how's and why's of such an approach.

The individual with the large adapted child and strong security needs will be tailoring his or her exchanges toward those who can relieve their anxieties.

> I don't know about buying this apartment complex as one of our primary investments. The real estate market is heavily inflated now and may go way down. And a tenant who gets injured on the premises may sue us right into bankruptcy. Let's listen to what Joe has to say before we even think about such an investment. Frankly, I'm scared. Joe, being an accountant in the insurance business, will keep us from going off the deep end.

Script Theory

You may also view groups in terms of the roles or scripts played. Some individual, usually the formally assigned leader, will play the role of taskmaster with the purpose of pushing group members toward goals as quickly and as effectually as possible. Another member, usually informally emerging, will try to take care of morale needs. At times he or she will attempt to temper the taskmaster's push toward productivity.

Look, if we take a 15-minute break for coffee, we'll get a lot more done. I think we all need a little rest right now. We've hammered on the topic long enough. Our minds will be clearer after the break.

Another group member may play the role of joke maker in order to add comic relief to some of the more serious matters undertaken by the group. Another may play a negative script "dummy" role and ask the same questions over and over again, even if decisions on these questions have already been made and resolved.

In addition to individual member scripts that clue observers as to what parts of the group process will be played out by whom, are overall group script messages and themes that also affect the behavior of members. These themes or messages are often termed the norms or standards of conduct of the group. In effect, these norms are similar to script injunctions and affirmations except that they are applied at the group level. For example, on the assembly line we know that there are norms or script injunctions that say: Don't rate bust or produce more than the quota set up by the production people and don't rate chisel or "drag your feet" either. Some of these standard ways of behaving or script messages are formally stated in bylaws and policy statements. Others are informal, but no less adhered to than the two above.

Actions speak louder than words in groups also. Norms, only *formally* stated or written, take back seats to norms based on *actual* behavior when it comes to influencing group members (5). A teacher may *formally* tell his or her students at the beginning of a semester that he or she encourages questions. However, when students ask questions they are ignored or ridiculed. From then on few students will waste their time or risk further embarrassment by asking questions.

Additionally, group norms may be constructive, unlike script injunctions or affirmations that always have negative implications. The norm suggesting that all members not speak at once would make coherent decision making impossible if not followed.

Group members communicate more freely and more effectively and are more close knit when overall norms are collaborative rather than competitive (6). In a collaborative group, problem-solving activities concentrate on adult questions such as "What can we learn from this?" or "How can we improve this situation?" In the competitive group, emphasis is placed on childish competition, such as "If I am right, then you must be wrong." or "My answer is better than yours." Under cooperative norms, members attack issues and problems as a team. Under competitive norms, important issues and problems often go by the wayside as members concentrate on competing against and attacking each other. In the long run shyer members, who may have the most to contribute in terms of expertise and resources, drop out of the discussion in deference to the more aggressive group bullies. The ins and outs of developing effective problem-solving groups follows in chapter eight.

Groups are a very necessary part of organizational life. They are here to stay. A familiarity with the stroking patterns of members and the scripts they play out provide keen insights into how they function.

NOTES

1. Rollie Tillman, Jr., "Problems in Review: Committees on Trial," *Harvard Business Review,* 38 (May–June 1960), pp. 6–12 and 162–72.
2. Edgar H. Schein, *Organizational Psychology* (Englewood Cliffs, N.J.: Prentice-Hall, Inc., 1965), p. 67; Carl L. Kell and Paul R. Corts, *Fundamentals of Effective Group Communication* (New York: Macmillan, Inc., 1980), p. 3. Kell and Corts stipulate in *their* definition that the communication between and among members must be cooperative. I left this out of *my* definition, because much of what happens in some groups is anything *but* cooperative.
3. Edgar H. Schein, *Organizational Psychology,* © 1965, p. 67. Reprinted by permission of Prentice-Hall, Inc., Englewood Cliffs, N.J.
4. Joe Kelly, *Organizational Behaviour: An Existential-Systems Approach,* rev. ed. (Homewood, Ill.: Richard D. Irwin, Inc., 1974), p. 664. © 1974 by Richard D. Irwin, Inc.
5. Lawrence C. Porter, "Group Norms: Some Things Can't Be Legislated," in *Readings Book for Laboratories in Human Relations Training,* 1972 ed. Edited by Cyril R. Mill and Lawrence C. Porter (Washington, D.C.: NTL Institute for Applied Behavioral Science, Associated with the National Education Association, 1972), pp. 34–35.
6. Lawrence C. Porter, "Group Norms: Some Things Can't Be Legislated," pp. 35–36.

GROUP PROBLEM SOLVING

A camel is a horse designed by a committee.
Anonymous

8

There is a lot of truth to the above cliché about group problem solving. Too often committees are formed for no specific purpose; too often they are designed to avoid reaching a decision about a certain matter. For example, a certain governmental agency may form a citizens' committee to discuss building a new bridge or some other public works project. Not having the funding for the project, the governmental agency carefully selects members who would have a hard time agreeing on *anything,* and then they set the meetings for once every six months. Ten years roll by without even a single proposal from the committee concerning the project. The governmental agency *appears* to be getting valuable public input on a key community project but, in essence, it is playing a stalling game.

On occasion a committee may make solid recommendations for solving an organizational matter in record time, only to find that the recommendations are ignored by top management.

We bust our behinds to develop a new fringe benefit program for the entire corporation. I'll bet we must have put in 500 man hours and studied fifty different surveys and reports of companies similar to ours. Cost wise and benefits wise I'll bet we have the best and most thorough benefits package in the industry. And what happens? Rather than read our report, the president shelves it and goes duck hunting. I understand now he never really planned to change benefits anyway.

If committees are formed to play stalling or pretense games, then they will be basically worthless as a problem-solving tool and will hurt morale to boot. As mentioned earlier, games—especially hypocritical or pretense games—leave no one the winner in the long run. Organizational members will become conditioned to treat committees as "make work," just as management does. Absences will be high and meetings will be infrequent. When a project comes along that management *truly* deems important, it will often be treated with the same indifference found in other committee projects.

Before bringing a committee together, make sure it has some usefulness. Save game playing for sport, *not* for valuable work time. Disband any currently standing committee that has outlived its purpose: to perform.

Treat committee recommendations or proposals as pieces of gold. Thousands of dollars of man hours—at a minimum—may be involved. Michael LeBoeuf, author of *Working Smart,* points out:

> When it comes to meetings most of us behave as though we had never heard that time is money. Meetings are terribly expensive and most of us believe that this is the number one time waster. How much does a meeting cost? Calculate the per-hour salaries of those on a committee and add them up. It's very common to have meetings that cost thousands of dollars per hour. However, most of us don't tend to think of meetings in dollars and cents. Consequently, one reason for so many useless meetings is that we fail to recognize the cost (1).

COMMITTEES HAVE THE POTENTIAL TO SOLVE PROBLEMS BETTER THAN INDIVIDUALS

As indicated in chapter seven, committees often perform valuable services, and sometimes their use cannot be avoided. Committees, like other organizational resources, can be extremely valuable assets if properly used. Although almost invariably slower working, groups have the potential to make better decisions than individuals working alone. First of all, there is more adult and child involvement when one has to defend decisions in front of others. When an individual has to defend his or her ideas in front of others, they naturally tend to be more careful about what they say. A little bit of anxiety tends to sharpen the functioning of the adult.* Having an audience to review what we say will help us to fine tune the organization and presentation of our ideas.

> When I work through problems alone, I sometimes tend to get very sloppy in my thinking. The group challenges me to stay on track and to keep my ideas clear and to the point.

Also, in front of a group, there is more emotional free child or adapted child involvement to perform better.

> The group just plain won't let me slack off. Plus, frankly, I've been through too much with these guys to let them down.

> You want to know why I come prepared for my group presentations? It's very simple. I don't like making an ass of myself in front of my peers.

Secondly, adult feedback from members helps keep individual errors to a minimum. If assumptions are faulty, logic is somewhat suspect, or facts are unclear, another member can help clarify and rectify these. Members can even perform editorial functions by catching mistakes in grammar or arithmetic, which is especially helpful if a report must be filled by the committee.

Thirdly, more resources (or two or more heads) are better than one. As mentioned in chapter seven, some projects even require a number of individuals with different expertise in order to be successfully completed. In the planning of a new model car, experts in engineering,

---

* See chapter three for a review of the relationship between anxiety and ego state productivity.

marketing, and finance—must at least—be involved. Even if group members have the same or similar expertise, through the group process each is able to feed off the ideas of the others. The famous brainstorming technique developed by Alex Osborn for business organizations is based around the notion of group members feeding their ideas off the ideas of others (2).

> You know, if Joe had not suggested a fund raiser, I would have never thought of the idea of a Las Vegas party that ended up going over real well.

Finally, competing viewpoints can help offset critical parent biases. Each of us, regardless of whether we wish to admit it or not, has certain biased ways of looking at things. We were all carefully taught by our parents to prejudice our thoughts on certain topics or on certain ways of approaching specific problems. These critical parent dictums, although possibly helpful at times, may contaminate our adult functioning through tunnel vision. Thus, our normally objective view of an issue or an approach to a solution may be impeded. Critical parent "blinders" (3) may take on many irrational forms.

> I don't care what anyone else says. Black is the only color for our radio cases.

> She could be the greatest administrator in the world. I would still never elect a woman president.

> I am a conservative. There is no way I would elect a democrat to congress.

> Look, fellows, there is only one way to build a mouse trap. Watch me again and I'll show you.

> I don't care if we can get 15 percent on our money in treasury bills, I always leave 40 percent of our cash reserves in demand deposits in the bank.

> Hire whomever you wish for the secretarial job, provided she is a woman.

Bunker and Dalton's research on the effectiveness of groups versus individuals in problem solving revealed:

A more objective view of the problem resulted from competition between the private prejudices of group members. . . . When arguments were stated so they appealed to persons of one persuasion, those in opposition were anxious to detect their error. In this way, liberals counteracted conservatives, Republicans offset Democrats, and "independents" guarded against critical lapses on the part of fraternity members. Groups were forced to become more objective, and this, of course, increased their chances of drawing valid conclusions. The significance of this one factor alone would be hard to overestimate (4).

FEATURES OF EFFECTIVE PROBLEM-SOLVING GROUPS

In spite of all the advantages that groups have over individuals in reaching quality decisions, we know very clearly that some groups function much better than other groups and that some individuals do a much better job than some groups do. From research and my own experience in many group meetings, I have found that effective problem-solving groups have the following characteristics.

First of all, they are conscious of and deal effectively with both adult task needs and the emotional needs of members. Effective groups know what their goals are. Objectives are carefully formulated early on so that all members understand the things the group is trying to accomplish and how it plans to accomplish them. Input is gathered from all members in the shaping and setting of objectives. This furthers understanding and acceptance by the members.

The adult of all members is also concretely involved in the group process itself. Suggestions are periodically taken by members, or the leader, as to procedures and methods for achieving objectives. For example, if the group decides to use brainstorming as one vehicle for finding solutions to problems, Osborn's basic rules of freewheeling (or suspending judgment or criticism until after ideas are generated) and the striving for a quantity of ideas are strictly adhered to. Members are consciously aware that adhering to this process is the best way to stimulate adult free thinking as well as the creative juices of the free child. Later, criteria are set up for measuring the validity, practicality, feasibility, and originality of the ideas generated (5). Throughout, effective problem-solving groups are keenly aware of their task needs both in terms of objectives and the group processes needed to achieve them. Members of an effective fact-finding committee in a large organization are frequently heard to discuss issues as follows:

> All right! I hear what you are saying, but are we about the business of doing primary research on this ourselves or reporting the findings of other departments? Let's get clear on this matter before we proceed further. Once this objective is clearly understood, then we can go about the business of figuring out the best approach for gathering research data and compiling it for whoever is to read it.

In keeping with task needs, members are also keenly aware of time constraints. A balance is struck between giving adequate consideration to matters and reaching workable solutions in a reasonable time frame. Although group members are not pressed to come to decisions prematurely, without adequate adult reflection and understanding, a reasonable and somewhat flexible time frame is fairly closely adhered to. Premature decision making is often indicative of one of the most destructive of group phenomena.

> A curious psychological phenomenon seems to dominate a great many of the thinking processes that go on in business meetings. This is the phenomenon of *premature closure*, in which the members of a group switch too soon into a convergent thinking mode and jump at a particular conclusion, usually under the influence of a few strong personalities. Psychologist Irving Janis gave this phenomenon the name of *groupthink*. It results, Janis believes, from insufficient awareness on the part of the group members that they are engaged in the process of making a decision and a lack of inclination to entertain diverse alternatives.
>
> Janis studied the interpersonal dynamics among the members of President John F. Kennedy's cabinet and advisory staff members during the Bay of Pigs disaster, involving American encouragement and support of an invasion of Cuba by a group of exiles. . . . According to Janis, several of the members began to have serious doubts about the wisdom of the undertaking, but they never expressed their ideas forcefully because of the strength of the developing consensus and because of the subtle signals they received from the in-group members telling them that they had better join the consensus or risk their status as Kennedy's confidants (6).

On the other hand, without deadlines and timetables the group process can easily degenerate into "getting nowhere bull sessions" or wasteful stalling games discussed at the beginning of this chapter. Such groups help verify Milton Berle's comment (given at the beginning of chapter seven): "Committee—a group of men who keep minutes and waste hours."

In order to avoid unnecessary time wasting and "bull shooting," my brother installed a two- to three-minute time clock on any member discussing points in a public service organization over which he presided. Because of this he claimed that his organization was able to discuss and implement many more good ideas and programs during his tenure as president of the organization. Other members testified to the unusual number of rewarding accomplishments for the year also. Although input was encouraged from all members, the time clock forced committee members to organize their thoughts carefully before presenting them.

In addition to dealing effectively with task needs, effective problem-solving groups are skillful at dealing with the emotional or child needs and feelings of its members. As mentioned earlier, if the child ego state is ignored it can work to contaminate adult thinking. In effective groups members, along with the support of their leader, work to cultivate an interest in the topic or problem at hand. In addition, the group is careful to deal with the frustrations and the feelings of its members. These are not brushed aside, because pent-up child feelings, if not dealt with, can interfere with adult reasoning. If members are bored or feel they have been pushing too hard on a project, it is wise to deal with these feelings. Otherwise, members may push for a solution just to terminate the project, even if the solution is only a half-baked one. Taking a break—or a little humor on the part of the leader—may be just the thing needed to release child tensions and to get things back on an adult track. I can tell you clearly, from teaching for more than ten years, that it is far more satisfying and productive to vent students' feelings throughout the semester than to run too tight a ship. From my own experience, attendance and the number of meaningful exchanges in the classroom are both greatly reduced in overly strictly run classes. Also, the probability of having very disruptive behavior on the part of one or more members increases if feelings cannot be openly aired along the way. We all live at the feelings level. The child in all of us will not be denied. Work with the child ego state and you gain enthusiasm and creativity, great assets to adult thinking. Ignore the child ego state or try to "sweep it under the rug" and you invite not only dissatisfaction on the part of group members but a strong likelihood that they will vent their frustrations later on when they start solving problems and getting on with the issues at hand (7).

A barber shop chorus meeting was disrupted for over fifty minutes when the time was badly needed for rehearsing. This critical delay resulted because a late-arriving member's request to vote again on the date for a concert was ignored. Even though, rationally, it made no sense to have a second vote (the vote count was 48–2 the first time), until this member's hurt feelings were taken care of, through another quick show of hands, arguments between him and the other members persisted. Rationally arguing with a hurt child who felt left out did not work, even though this excellent singer was forty-five years old. Sometimes, unless you deal with the child ego state first, regardless of the chronological age of the individual involved, you will not be able to engage the adult. How permissive a group leader should be is discussed further later in this chapter.

Secondly, disagreements, regardless of what ego state they come from, are not "shoved under the rug." In an effective problem-solving group, it is okay to have different viewpoints on issues. The group process is viewed as a forum where viewpoints, ideas, and approaches are freely shared and examined. In other words, the process is opposite to groupthink, where there is overt or covert pressure toward single-mindedness. Because it is okay to disagree, the group is able to use the resources of all its members. In effect, the group functions as a group, not as a committee of one or two trying to shove its ideas down the throats of others.

Ideally, the best decisions are reached when there is a lot of adult and free child involvement. As mentioned earlier, with the adult and free child involved you combine clear thinking and pragmatics with creativity and the true needs and feelings of the members. Thus, the task needs and the emotional needs of the group are best met in this fashion. Although the feelings of critical parents and adapted children should also be aired, so they won't later squabble among themselves and interfere with problem solving, a skillful leader will tone down their interruptions and will always be working toward as much adult and free child involvement as possible.

A very direct and effective way of gaining meaningful disagreement, through predominantly adult and free child involvement, is to clearly set the stage like the following chairperson of a social services group:

> Look, we are here to bring the best services possible to our clients. Each of us has a lot to contribute to the other. So don't be afraid to disagree or take issue with what others have to say. However, I only have one rule regarding disagreements. You can take issue with another's ideas or approaches, but not with him or her personally. We are here to openly exchange ideas, not to have personality conflicts. We are all on the same team.

By prohibiting name calling or any other personality confrontation that has nothing to do with solving issues, members are free to test out new ideas without fear of reprimand or ridicule.

Thirdly, a nurturing parent supportive climate that respects all members' views is established early and maintained. This is the key essential to any effective problem-solving group. Without this characteristic, the rest is impossible. Members cannot feel free to openly exchange ideas and feelings if they are in a psychologically antagonistic environment.

> The boss calls us in to brainstorm on a new advertising campaign for a client. So I start the ideas flowing. So what happens? He chews my head off with: 'That's the most stupid thing I ever heard.' Needless to say, no one suggested any more novel approaches. Then he proceeds to give us a sermon on the lack of cooperation on our part and on how he has to make all the decisions himself. The s.o.b. is about as sensitive as a stone wall. You don't get teamwork by openly insulting the members of the team.

Supportive groups exhibit the following characteristics.
(a) Ridicule is at a minimum. Critical parent put-downs in the form of ridicule or sarcasm toward the ideas of any group member, even if the ideas seem extreme, are almost nonexistent in effective problem-solving groups. Under the threat or the presence of ridicule, some of the brighter (but shyer), more adapted child members will likely capitu-

late. As a result, the group, in effect, has caused some of its top resources to become dropouts. One member in a group dominated by two critical parent personalities put it this way:

> You know, we could come up with a lot better designs for passenger cars and trucks if those two s.o.b.'s didn't snub out each new idea with their pompous arrogance. To tell you the truth, Larry and John are our best designers, but they are too new and too shy to stick their necks out in front of the more senior pompous asses. It's like our design group has had two right arms cut off in the form of Larry and John. To put it in medical terms, we are a group that has amputated itself.

(b) The life position of all members toward one another is I'm OK, You're OK. In effective problem-solving groups, every member is viewed as a valuable resource with something to contribute. Positive strokes abound to reinforce this life position. People listen with care to one another, a very valuable positive stroke in itself. Good listening, as mentioned before, is contagious and promotes further listening.

> You know, I thought committees were a big waste of time until I got on that personnel policy committee. We do a hell of a job. You would think we were competing against other corporate groups for some large cash prize. It's hard to put into words, except to say that all of our members count. Oh, we may tease one another periodically, and we joke around a fair amount. But when it comes to developing a new policy or changing an old one, everybody's input counts. We really work as a team. What I say counts as much as anybody else. I guess, to put it in simple words, we respect one another. Our accomplishments bear this out.

(c) Criticism, when given, is always constructive and deals with issues, *not* personalities.* In supportive groups, negative feedback is not programed out. Even the most liberal nurturing parent knows that it is not supportive to withhold negative feedback that might help someone. If a boss permits a subordinate to slide in his or her duties, without confronting him or her, the boss is not being supportive. The subordi-

---

* For an in-depth discussion on how to give constructive criticism, see chapter ten.

nate, in the long run, will be terminated and will have acquired some bad habits to boot. Supportive groups have tactful ways of giving negative feedback to members. Group criticism emphasizes solutions to concrete problems faced by the group, *not* a psychological analysis of members of the group. Additionally, if the group is struggling through some thorny issue it remains close-knit and concerned with alternative solutions. Supportive groups do not degenerate into blaming tactics such as faultfinding or making scapegoats of members.

> I know things are not working out as we had planned. We are two weeks behind schedule. But we've accomplished a lot. Let's see if there is still a better way to deal with the logistics issue. Now, more than ever, we must hang tough. With all the responsibilities we have in this project, I just have one thing to say. I am damn proud of all of us. Believe me, we're going to handle this logistics thing and handle it well.

(d) Group norms are cooperative, not competitive. The supportive group spirit is one of togetherness and "how can we solve these issues?" rather than one of members warring against one another for the limelight under the philosophy of "I win my points if you lose yours."**
(e) The leadership is supportive, permissive, and enthusiastic. The effective group leader does not quench new ideas through too much strictness. Additionally, the effective group leader does not try to act as a committee of one. He or she realizes that his or her main role is to facilitate input from others, not to act as a star or a lecturer (8).

> We have these departmental meetings to discuss curriculum matters. And what happens! The chairman uses the committee as a captured audience to lecture to. If he wants the benefit of our ideas and feelings on the matter, that is one thing. If he wants to use us as a doormat for one of his boring speeches, that's something else. He wonders why committee attendance is way down. Our time can be used much more valuably somewhere else—like preparing for classes and research.

If there are difficulties with some members (permissiveness to extremes can disrupt the functioning of *any* group), the leader handles these

** Refer back to the end of chapter seven for a review of group norms and their impact on group effectiveness.

matters leniently but effectively—away from the meeting room. First of all, the leader checks to see if the disruptive behavior is a one-time or seldom occurrence and if it is truly harmful to the group or simply a normal release of child tension. As discussed earlier in this chapter, a periodic release of child ego state tensions is an aid to effective group problem solving, not a hindrance. If the occurrence of disruptive behavior is repetitive and significantly harmful to the functioning of the group, the leader takes the disruptive member aside for corrective purposes. Chastising delinquent members in front of the group often makes the rebellious type even more rebellious and is likely to cause other shy, but bright, members to remain on the sidelines in future discussions. Additionally, individual matters, like the disruptive behavior of a single group member, can best be handled one-on-one. In this way valuable group time is not wasted and no member is embarrassed unnecessarily.*

> We had a group member who seemed to act like a spoiled child. After presenting his viewpoint on a given issue, he would sit on one of the sofas away from the meeting table and read the newspaper. When this happened again at our second meeting, I took him aside and asked him if he was aware of how his behavior was affecting the group. If we all sat back and read newspapers we might as well not meet, I told him. He said that this practice of speaking and reading was the norm of another committee he was on. I informed him that it was not the practice of *our* committee and that some members were concerned about his apparent lack of interest in what they had to say. I suggested that if he could not get more involved in the meeting, it might be wise that he not attend the meetings. He agreed and shaped up pretty well at the third meeting. I don't want to give the wrong impression. We're a fairly hang loose, easy going group, but we also have a job to do. Disciplining members is something I rarely have to do and something I hate to do. But on a few occasions with new members, person-to-person chats have prevented prolonged emotional hassles for the group.

Finally, decisions involve all group members and are not based on "steam-rolling" or majority rule. Effective groups attempt to gain agreement from all members. Sometimes a unanimous decision is very difficult to achieve. Getting *all* members to agree on *all* issues *all* the time is impossible. However, if the group is a supportive one at least all members

---

* For specifics on how to deal with problem employees, see chapter nine.

will have some input into the decision, and they will not feel that other members are trying to take advantage of them through a quick vote or through pressure tactics. When pressure tactics or political maneuvers are employed to outvote a given faction of the committee, the minority always has the option of proving the majority wrong when implementation time comes. Even if the tactics are not deliberately sinister, the impact on the group's problem-solving efforts can be disastrous. Certainly, group members will not feel enthusiastic about a decision to which they did not feel a party (9).

Take the time to get all the concerned ego states of members involved, particularly the adult and the free child. In this way not only will good decisions be made but they will be implemented properly also. Members will better understand the rationale behind such decisions and the needs they meet. They will be much less prone to use their rebellious child to sabotage decisions or projects.

TA AND GROUP EXERCISES

In closing this chapter I would like to recommend three group exercises that I have found very useful in relating TA concepts to group communications and decision making.

Five Chairs*

There are basically two ways that five chairs can be used as a group exercise. First, select a topic (or topics) of interest with the help of the workshop participants. Stress before voting on a topic that you want a controversial topic that most people would be interested in discussing. Ask for five volunteers (or more if you break the free child into the natural child and little professor and the adapted child into the rebellious and submissive child) who will sit in chairs facing the audience. Have each member of the five chair committee keep a card in front of him or her with the initials on it of the ego state he or she will be portraying during the exercise. Print the initials on the

* To refresh your memory on the basic five chairs exercise, see chapter four.

cards large enough so that the audience can clearly see them. For example, the individual who holds up a large "NP" will be playing the role of the nurturing parent on the committee. The individual who has the card labeled "CP" will be playing the critical parent, and so on. Suggest that the individual who sits in the middle of the committee play the role of the adult and the chairperson. Set a time limit, say twenty or thirty minutes, for the committee to resolve the issue before them. Make the time limit fairly flexible so that the committee will not feel rushed. For example, if nothing is resolved in twenty minutes give the committee another ten minutes. When I first saw this exercise done in a workshop conducted by Muriel James, the renowned TA author and past president of the International Transactional Analysis Association, Inc., some six years ago,* she invited members of the audience to replace any committee member whose role they had an urge to play. The exercise went very well, with audience participation extremely high.

I have conducted a number of these committee exercises in which I kept the original committee intact until the problem at hand was resolved. Then I've asked for committee, as well as audience, feedback on how they felt the discussion and problem solving went. Using either approach, I have found audience participation to be very high.

Through this exercise a large number of workshop participants can actively get a feel for what ego states dominate a given group discussion and what pressures regarding navigation and resolution are placed on a chairperson, particularly if squabbles between the critical parent and the rebellious child are permitted to dominate the discussion. This exercise also illustrates very graphically how critical parent biases or adapted child fears can contaminate creativity and rational problem solving.

The other approach to the five chairs group exercise is more similar to the original five chairs exercise discussed in chapter four.

The basic difference between this exercise and the one discussed in chapter four is that different people play each ego state. Again, the adult is the chairperson of the committee, and a time frame is set to resolve some topic of interest selected by the audience. Enough commit-

---

* Although the basics of the exercise are the same, I may have made some changes from the one I originally saw Muriel James conduct.

tees are formed to accommodate all workshop participants. If there are twenty-five participants, five committees participate in the exercise simultaneously. Committees should be separated sufficiently to prevent too much noise pollution.

I have also found this multiple committee format to be excellent in giving participants a feel for how ego states affect group problem solving and a feel for the demands placed on a committee chairperson.

The one committee approach to the five chairs exercise mentioned first has the advantage of audience feedback to the committee. The latter multiple committee exercises make it possible for all participants to take part in the exercise, which is particularly good for shy members of the workshop who may feel intimidated if placed on "stage." In many workshops I have beneficially employed both approaches, usually leading in with the single committee approach.

The Critical Parent
Biases Exercise*

In this exercise paper head bands with parent biases written on them are placed on the heads of participants. Although seen clearly by other group members, the critical parent statement on the head of a given participant is unknown to him or her. The group is instructed at the beginning of the exercise to deal with a given participant in terms of his or her respective head band label, but not to tell that participant what the label says. Typical critical parent labels or messages might be: "ridicule me," "disagree with me," "agree with me," "laugh at me," "ignore me," etc. One group, acting as a control, will not have head bands. Typically, the control group arrives at solutions much more quickly, more cooperatively, and more adequately than the groups with head bands. Regardless of whether the exercise invovles a mental puzzle (as you see in mental game books), a simple crossword puzzle, or a problem related to the work the participants normally do (for example, solving some personnel or marketing problem), the groups with the headbands have a lot more difficulty reaching correct or appropriate solutions. Before the exercise terminates most group members

---

* This exercise was suggested by a number of graduate MBA students during a group presentation. The original source is unknown.

have figured out their head band labels based on their interactions with other members during the exercise. None like the derogatory labels placed on them.

From participation in the exercise and the discussion that follows, all workshop participants get a very good feel for how parent prejudices can disrupt the group problem-solving process. By mentally placing biased, Not-OK "ignore" or "ridicule" labels on other group participants we, in effect, have created some unnecessary conflicts and may contribute to minimizing the impact of those members on the group process.

The Personnel Exercise (10)

In this exercise participants are asked to hire or fire a group of fictitious people based on some background information about them. In addition to ordinary work experience and educational data, typical information about the subjects to be selected or rejected might include age, sex, religion, race, national origin, and so on. Heated debates often ensue over the critical parent prejudices of individual members. After a certain period of time members begin to become more aware of their prejudices and to see how these prejudices can interfere with their rational or adult ability to solve the real issues at hand: to select the most qualified person for the job and to terminate those who would have the greatest negative impact on productivity and morale. Because of the heated debates that might ensue, this is an exercise that especially requires a workshop leader skilled in dealing with interpersonal dynamics.

NOTES

1. Michael LeBoeuf, *Working Smart: How to Accomplish More in Half the Time* (New York: McGraw-Hill Book Company, 1979), p. 128.
2. Alex F. Osborn, *Applied Imagination,* rev. ed. (New York: Charles Scribner's Sons, 1957), p. 84.
3. William V. Haney devotes a whole chapter in his book, *Communication and Organizational Behavior,* to this process of limiting our view of problems. See: William V. Haney, *Communication and Organizational Behavior: Text*

and Cases, 3d ed. (Homewood, Ill.: Richard D. Irwin, Inc., 1973), pp. 460–474.

4. Douglas R. Bunker and Gene W. Dalton, "The Comparative Effectiveness of Groups and Individuals in Solving Problems," in *Managing Group and Intergroup Relations,* edited by Jay W. Lorsch and Paul R. Lawrence (Homewood, Ill.: Richard D. Irwin, Inc., 1972), pp. 206–207. © 1972 by Richard D. Irwin, Inc. A number of the ideas in this chapter were at least partially suggested by the above source, and I heartily recommend it to anyone further interested in pursuing the topic of group problem solving.

5. For an excellent, concise discussion on setting up a brainstorming session, see: Leland Brown, *Communicating Facts and Ideas in Business* (Englewood Cliffs, N.J.: Prentice-Hall, Inc., 1961), pp. 129–130.

6. Karl Albrecht, *Brain Power: Learn to Improve Your Thinking Skills,* © 1980, pp. 239–240. Reprinted by permission of Prentice-Hall, Inc., Englewood Cliffs, N.J. For an in-depth treatment of the groupthink phenomenon, see: Irving L. Janis, *Victims of Groupthink: A Psychological Study of Foreign-Policy Decisions and Fiascoes* (Boston: Houghton Mifflin Company, 1972).

7. For an excellent discussion on dealing with emotional problems in groups, see: Harold J. Leavitt, *Managerial Psychology: An Introduction to Individuals, Pairs, and Groups in Organizations,* 2d ed. (Chicago: University of Chicago Press, 1964), pp. 257–261.

8. For an expanded discussion on permissive group leadership, see: Harold J. Leavitt, *Managerial Psychology,* 2d ed., pp. 266–267.

9. Harold J. Leavitt, *Managerial Psychology,* 2d ed., pp. 263–264.

10. This type of exericse is typically found in personnel books. One of my favorite case books on personnel is: William F. Glueck, *Cases and Exercises in Personnel,* rev. ed. (Dallas, Tex.: Business Publications, Inc., 1978).

A PROFILE OF EFFECTIVE LEADERSHIP

> Almost every influential thinker from Confucius to Bertrand Russell has attempted some analysis of the differential exercise of power of individuals over one another, which characterizes all social life (1).

9

Interest in what makes effective leaders, proficient directors, and guides of the activities of others has grown. The courses of societies, governments, corporations, and public institutions have been significantly altered by changes in leadership. Success, both monetary and personal, is accorded to those in the top leadership positions. Next to exceptionally highly compensated entertainers like Johnny Carson or athletes like Pete Rose, the top salaries go to the *leaders,* whether the organizations are governments, business enterprises, or labor unions.

Leadership ability is equally important to the individual. Except for some staff jobs and a few specialist and professional jobs, the great majority of individuals working in organizations will find their achievement horizons severely limited if they have not begun to master the skills required to direct and guide others. A persistent diet of "follow the leader" is a sure way to very limited responsibilities and a dead-end job. When students and seminar participants ask how to avoid mediocrity in an organization, the best advice I can give is: develop leadership skills.

Leadership skills, however, have eluded many people who do not understand how to develop them. Haven't you been puzzled at times, like some of my workshop participants and university students, over such questions as: "How do I go about acquiring leadership skills?" "Aren't great leaders just born, not made?" "What qualities must an effective leader possess?" "Are there certain styles or leadership approaches that work better than others?" "What situational factors affect the leader-follower relationship? For example, aren't some groups of workers or types of jobs easier to direct than others?" "What are some proven ways of dealing with difficult employees?" "How can you correct a good employee without hurting his or her feelings?" "What is a constructive approach to criticism?"

Three areas of concentration have evolved in the study of what makes an effective leader: (1) the trait or personality approach to leadership; (2) leadership style, or the leader's characteristic way of dealing with his or her subordinates, particularly with respect to sharing responsibility; and (3) the situational approach, or how factors such as the nature of the job and the time element affect leadership success.

Using TA as my primary tool of analysis, I discuss the trait and leadership approaches in this chapter. Chapter ten completes the leadership style analysis and will include the situational approach and correction problems.

Despite considerable research, there is no concrete evidence that leaders possess certain *specific* personality traits such as sociability, interpersonal sensitivity, dominance, qualities of the introvert or extrovert, conservatism, or liberalism (2). Yet Stogdill, one of the most respected authorities on the topic of leadership, contends that leaders do, in fact, have certain *overall* observable qualities or personality characteristics that distinguish them from followers. He is joined in his findings by many other top researchers and practitioners. These characteristics cannot be broken into individual atomistic parts, as Stogdill terms the specific trait approach, but are qualities in response to certain situational demands (3). For example, to link the impact of the leader's introvert qualities to the group performance of a research team of scientists is difficult, if not impossible. However, it *is* possible to see how a leader's overall intelligence as a researcher—his or her adult ability to solve research problems and to respond to subordinate's questions—will affect the output of his or her research group.

In TA terminology, the overall qualities of an effective leader—one who brings top productivity and morale to the work group—emphasizes the adult (intelligence), the nurturing parent (support), and the free child (enthusiasm). In terms of an egogram, the effective leader's portrait is as follows.

PORTRAIT OF AN EFFECTIVE LEADER

THE PORTRAIT OF AN EFFECTIVE LEADER

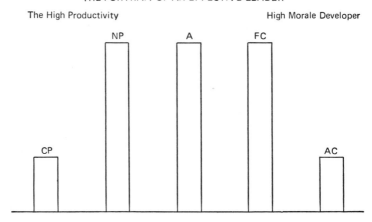

QUALITIES OF AN EFFECTIVE LEADER

The Adult Leader

The effective leader is reasonably intelligent. He is at least as intelligent as his followers, which permits him to stay on top of the technology or know-how required by the job and to answer the questions of his subordinates. He is a better than average problem solver, both people wise and task wise. *The effective leader keeps the adult as executive of his personality.* With the adult in charge, a leader can appropriately and accurately respond to situational demands or problems, whether these involve people, things, timing, or "red tape." He quickly gets to the who's, what's, when's, where's, why's, and how's of situations in order to separate causes from symptoms. The adult leader also documents critical happenings with subordinates, good or bad, for further reference—if needed—for such things as appraisal reviews. He realizes that "poor handwriting is better than good memory," especially when employees need correcting. The adult leader is prudent enough to foster the development of the adult in his subordinates, both by example and by involving them in the solution of their own problems. He challenges rather than spoon-feed his employees and, thus, he doesn't "err on the side of underestimating people's ability to solve their own problems." (4)

Having the adult as executive of the personality does not mean the effective leader comes out of the adult ego state constantly. A *constant* adult leader would be cold, insensitive, and boring. With the adult as executive, he or she has easy access to rational thinking. There is little child or parent contamination to get in the way. In other words, exaggeration and prejudice do not interfere too often in getting on with solving the problem at hand. By having the adult in charge, the effective leader is in the best position to activate the other ego states when necessary and appropriate. When it is time to laugh or joke with employees, he or she can easily shift into the free child. If a depressed employee needs confidence building, the effective leader can clearly diagnose the problem through the eyes of the adult and then appropriately engage the nurturing parent. When it's time to be firm, even the critical parent can be used as an asset.

The Nuturing Parent Leader

The effective leader is supportive and has a genuine interest in his or her subordinates:

> He is supportive, friendly, and helpful rather than hostile. He is kind but firm, never threatening, genuinely interested in the well-being of subordinates and endeavors to treat people in a sensitive, considerate way.
>
> He shows confidence in the integrity, ability, and motivations of subordinates rather than suspicion and distrust (5).

Likert's comments represent one of the most accurate descriptions of the nurturing parent that I have ever read. The effective leader has a large nurturing parent, an unconditional, positive regard for his subordinates. He or she has a genuine interest in developing subordinates, *not* in using them. The support and trust generated by the nurturing parent leads to high productivity and morale on the part of the followers.

A climate of high support and trust sets into motion a mutually constructive cycle. With very rare exceptions, relationships are reciprocal. A person is treated as he or she treats others. If a leader wants respect, he must give it. A leader, at least in the long run, cannot expect trust and support from followers in whom he or she is disinterested. Subordinates will work extra hours, even without extra compensation, for the leader who really cares about them and *shows* it.

On the other hand, the leader who is openly hostile or disinterested, who undermines his or her subordinates, who uses them rather than develops them—the predominantly critical parent leader—will also be treated in kind. Workers will cheat on the quality and quantity of productivity, they will deliberately be tardy, or they will even in some cases resort to sabotage in order to get even with a hostile, critical parent boss.

Even a causal observer in an organization can appreciate employee remarks such as the following:

> I'd do anything for Jim. He's demanding, but he cares. If you're caught in a down-and-out situation, he's there to help even if he has to pitch in himself.

> Mary went out of her way to help me with that new project I was working on—even after hours. She's the best boss I ever had. I'll make sure this work unit looks good.

> All I can say is I really enjoy working here. This hotel is a together group. Management asks for suggestions on how to make our work easier and more productive, and they actually use them. If the suggestions aren't feasible, they tell us why. At other hotels, suggestions were about as welcome as mass cancellations.

> Why should I care? You tell my s.o.b. boss your problem. If he doesn't ignore you, he uses the information to make the problem even more difficult.

> There is no way. I wouldn't work an extra two minutes for these jerks. All they give a damn about is saving face in front of their own bosses.

High expectations lead to high productivity. This is another reason why the supportive nurturing parent leader gets high productivity from his or her employees. He or she has high expectations.

It has been demonstrated in the classroom setting that the expectations of teachers will affect the performances of students. In one study, elementary children's I.Q.'s rose remarkably when teachers were falsely informed that their test scores indicated the children had high potential for academic work. The rationale of the researchers for this finding was that

> . . . The teachers involved, having high expectations of the selected children, tend to treat them with more respect in the sense that they show them that more is expected of them, and the children identify with this role of one of whom greater things are expected and begin to work harder to live up to it. (6).

Performance benefits accure to the high-support leader in any organization.

> By and large high trust tends to stimulate high performance—so say the overwhelming majority of over 4,200 supervisors I have questioned in 29 organizations of varying kinds and sizes. These supervisors feel that a subordinate generally responds well to his supervisor's confidence in him. He tries to justify his boss's good estimate of him. And, axiomatically, high performance will reinforce high trust for it is easy to trust and respect the man who meets or exceeds your expectations (7).

For the supervisor who has low trust in his subordinates, the result is the opposite. As Haney puts it, "more often than not the subordinate responds with minimal compliance and resentment. 'If that's all he thinks of me I might as well give it to him—I won't get credit for doing any more.' " (8)

The nurturing parent leader has more than an overall feeling of concern and high expectations for his or her workers. He or she is actively involved with ascertaining what employee needs are and what can be done to meet them. He or she periodically takes "readings" of employee grievances and needs, either formally in appraisal review sessions or informally. Such a "readings" process makes excellent adult sense also. Periodically airing out gripes and needs, such as a problem like bleeding steam from boiler system, prevents a morale explosion in the form of a strike or sabotage.

The nurturing parent leader does his or her best to meet employee needs, just as a good salesperson tries to cater to the demands of a good customer. *To the true nurturing parent leader, employees—in a very real sense—are top-notch customers.* What better way to treat the most valuable and often most expensive factor of production, labor?

Conversely, to the critical parent boss—the hostile or indifferent boss—management is its own best customer. For this reason such bosses obviously get low returns from their subordintes. In essence, it is easier and more productive to work with people (the supportive approach) than to work against them (the hostile approach).

Because the nurturing parent is in the business of developing his or her workers and *not* in the business of exploiting them, criticism is constructive and is aimed at finding solutions, not faults.

> Joe, you have done an excellent job in area A. Can we work to improve you in area B?

The nurturing parent is no "patsy" or "easy touch" either. If the need arises, the nurturing parent can be a firm disciplinarian also. The nurturing parent's genuine interest in his or her people necessitates firmness at times, just as the parent who must protect his or her child from being burned with matches. However, the correction approach is not simply a critical parent slap on the fingers. The nurturing parent uses more concern and adult in the correction process (9).

Sometimes tough discipline is essential for being a supportive, nurturing parent leader—because the job *requires* it. I recall a coach who had almost thirty injuries in a game against a Big Ten school. His philosophy was: "College football is like fraternity football. Just go out and have fun, men. Don't worry about too much practice or conditioning." Needless to say, he was not a supportive leader. His lack of genuine interest, even in his players' basic physical needs, led to an 0–10 season and a lot of badly beaten up people. Under his leadership there were no achievements—only injuries.

Nurturing parent support facilitates rapport and communications with subordinates. Nurturing parent bosses are concerned and receptive. Being excellent listeners and approachable people, they receive a more accurate view of what is troubling employees and the immediate feedback necessary to prevent problems from blowing out of proportion through delay.

The leader who is the last person to be informed is the critical parent boss. His or her critical and demeaning posture causes employees to go on the defensive.

> Boy, there is no way I can confide in that guy. He would chop my head off.

> Let the s.o.b. find out for himself. I plain don't feel like getting yelled at.

> Now, let's see. How can I put the situation so the boss won't blow her stack? I know. I won't tell her.

Bob, a very bright professional type who works for a large governmental agency, will sometimes spend a day or two shuffling his report papers around to delay having to report negative news to his predominantly critical parent boss. As Bob told me: "If there is any way around that horse's ass, I'll find it. Hell, his exploding at me doesn't solve the problem anyway."

Do not let yourself become the captain of a ship who is the last to see that it is sinking. Keep your nurturing parent firmly in control. By so doing, you will get feedback quickly enough to prevent molehills from turning into mountains.

If you are concerned that every Tom, Dick, Jane, and Mary will come in to tell you their every little problem if you are too nice a guy, don't worry. Most people only approach their boss over serious concerns. If you do have a few problem children in this area, tell them that you are very receptive to what they have to say, but that you want to hear their solutions along with the facts of the problem. Such a tactic is actually supportive, because it will help keep this overly adaptive type from becoming too dependent upon you. As this type of employee begins to use his or her adult more in solving problems, he or she will bring only meaningful matters to you.

Here is how a supervisor can develop more of the nurturing parent.

First of all, give more positive strokes to yourself as well as to others. In becoming a supportive leader, charity truly begins at home. It is much easier to be kind to others when we are kind to ourselves. When the critical parent starts putting out internal negative strokes, don't buy into them. Each of us can choose to be his or her own

PERSONALITY PROFILE CHART.
Ms. Jones (Personnel Assistant)

Ego State Profile	Steps for Change
Parent: Has a hard time taking on responsibility, particularly in people matters. It is very hard for her to make a preliminary evaluation of job candidates unless I lead her by the hand. She is too critical of herself.	*Developing the parent:* Let me get her own input on all of this first. Ultimately, the change has to come from her. But I'll make it known that her evaluations are very good, and if I disagree with her, I'll tell her that too.
Adult: She has a good head. She is great at developing job descriptions. She needs work on her interview techniques.	*Developing the adult:* I'll send her to that interviewing institute. She'll learn more there than I can teach her. It will also help keep her from becoming too dependent on me. Additionally, they use more of a self-teach adult approach, and they are great at demonstrating interview techniques.
Child: A little too shy and insecure. Too much adapted child. I've seen her joke during coffee breaks. I know she would feel more relaxed with people—in her interviews, for example, if we could bring out more of her free child humor. Such a posture would help her relax and would bring out more responses in interviewees. 5/16/80	*Developing the child:* Maybe joking with her more will help. Plus, I've got to stroke her for confidence whenever I get a chance. Additionally, I won't make any review comments until she has completely committed herself on an evaluation. I know she is hung up on this notion that she is playing God by evaluating candidates. But someone has to do it, and we need conscientious people like her.

worst enemy or his or her own best friend. Certainly, life is much more enjoyable and, as research indicates, much more productive when we tune into the positive "tapes" of the nurturing parent and tune out the negative "tapes" of the critical parent.

Secondly, cultivate a genuine interest in your subordinates. Find out their likes and their dislikes and their strengths and their weaknesses, just as you would uncover those of any good customer. Develop a personality profile on each employee by ego states to help your plans for strengthening good parts—the nurturing parent, the adult, and the free child—and also to help reduce or compensate for the weaker elements—like an overly submissive or overly rebellious adapted child. Update this chart periodically to reflect changes, and date these (as any good record keeper does). Remember, you have no more precious resource to keep track of than your personnel.

Thirdly, demonstrate confidence and trust in your subordinates by getting them involved in solving their own problems. An effective leader knows when to cut the umbilical cord and let his or her people grow. When the leader comes up with too many of the answers himself or herself, this prevents employee growth. Such a lack of employee involvement often leads to negative symbiosis (10). Over time, both parties to the relationship become frustrated. The supervisor frustrates his own free child by ending up doing his subordinate's job as well as his own. Thus, he limits his free time to do what his free child really wants to do. The subordinate is not given the opportunity to develop his parent sense of responsibility or his adult capacity to solve problems on his own. *Steer clear of playing "mom" or "dad" to your subordinate's "kid."* You are not being supportive by rescuing subordinates from responsibilities you know they must shoulder sooner or later (11).

The Free Child Leader

The final, overall quality of an effective leader is enthusiasm. *The enthusiastic leader is excited about the job and about the people doing the job.* Such a leader is eager to take the initiative in problem solving when it is required. However, more importantly, his enthusiasm stimulates the workers to be more productive and more creative. Enthusiastic bosses elicit stimulating reactions from employees:

I didn't know my work could be so interesting until I worked for Mary.

I can't say that Jim is any brighter than any of my previous bosses. Oh, he knows the technology of what we are doing quite well. I guess it's his demeanor. He's always got a smile on his face, and he is really excited about the work we are doing. It's hard to be sluggish around a boss like that.

I never realized how important our product is until Pete gave me the low-down on it. Man, when you come out of his office, if you never sold much before, you will then.

The enthusiastic leader is like a good salesperson. He or she is as excited about his or her work as a top-notch salesperson is about his or her product. Enthusiasm is contagious. Prospects rarely buy from salespeople who are not sold on the product themselves. Leaders who couldn't care less foster a similar attitude in their followers. The rationale is: "If my boss is not excited about what I am doing, why should I be?"

Harold J. Leavett, a noted authority on managerial psychology, states that history clearly tells us that one of the most important ingredients of effective leadership is enthusiasm. Cold, impassionate leaders do not inspire extra effort on the part of followers (12). You can help stimulate this free child enthusiasm in yourself as well as your employees by a number of means.

First of all, be receptive to creative ways of making the work and the work place more exciting, more interesting, and more effective. If feasible, solicit suggestions from the employees on novel ways to improve their own jobs or on ways of doing them better in less time. Such creative involvement will help ease the boredom of more routine jobs.

Secondly, supply any information that would help cultivate the employee's interest, not only at the outset of the job, but periodically. Information that adds to the employee's sense of purpose and excitement is particularly helpful. Background material on developments in the technology of the job and the importance of this technology is useful. Particularly, information on the relationship of the employee's job to the overall operations of the organization is good food for free child interest. Meaninglessness, a lack of purpose in one's job, is one of the biggest causes of poor morale, especially in large organizations.

As organizations get larger, individuals have a difficult time seeing how what they do relates to the overall purpose of the organization (13). For example, how does putting nuts and bolts together on an automobile door ultimately contribute to company profits at Ford or General Motors? In some cases, the worker's task appears so irrelevant and distant from overall organizational objectives that he or she feels like a very small anonymous cog in a large wheel. Free child enthusiasm cannot survive long when the felt sense of contribution is so meager.

Cultivating enthusiasm in the subordinate not only reduces Not-OK morale feelings in the free child. It helps to stimulate adult thinking and hence productivity as well. An excellent way of getting adult "gears" into full swing is through the excitement of the free child. Excellent teachers are often that way because they entice the student's child involvement in the subject with stimulating introductory material before getting into the drier adult content.

Thirdly, whenever possible refrain from "Poor Me, Ain't It Awful" and other bad mouth pastimes and games in front of employees. No one can be a ball of enthusiasm all the time. However, an excellent way to steer clear of fueling a morale pit is to keep a tight upper lip around subordinates when you feel low emotionally. Then, when your emotional black cloud clears, you won't have a longer lasting employee morale cloud with which to contend.

GOODBYE CRITICAL PARENT AND ADAPTED CHILD LEADERS

The critical parent and the adapted child have no place in the portrait of an effective leader. No doubt, there are some employees whose attention can only be gained by a solid, swift kick, but overall the critical parent plays *no* constructive role in your leadership tactics and strategies.

The reactions to critical parent bosses are painfully obvious:

You can't make any suggestions to him. He already has all the answers.

You're right, I don't tell her if something is not working out—she'll chew my head off.

> I don't feel any obligation to that s.o.b. He couldn't care less about me.

> Why try? If you do something right, you don't get complimented. But do one little thing wrong and he'll let you know fast.

Two major drawbacks to the use of the critical parent in a leadership role, as mirrored in some of the above remarks, are that it brings out the worst in the subordinates—either the overly rebellious or overly submissive child—and it closes off valuable feedback from subordinates.

Unlike the nurturing parent that creates a constructive climate of mutuality, the critical parent creates an adversary climate. Critical parent bosses treat their employees as if they were enemies to be dealt with. They go in to "nail" people, not to solve problems. The result is that negative feelings are mutual, often expressed through the rebellious child in the subordinate. Although subordinates may not directly express their rebellious feelings in face-to-face confrontations with the boss (perhaps fearing quick dismissal), there are sometimes other and even more brutal ways to vent frustrations.

I recall the case of a southern-based organization that was having some serious morale problems, evidenced by a very high turnover rate and even industrial sabotage. Skilled machine maintenance personnel, who cost the company many thousands of dollars to train, were leaving in droves to join competitors and other industries. The company found that the turnover rates were much higher for some supervisors than for others, and that the morale factor was directly related to how supervisors confronted work complaints or problems. Those with the most serious morale problems led off their confrontation sessions with comments such as:

> Okay, you s.o.b., ten minutes late again. I don't even want to hear a word from you. Next time, you're fired.

Notice the typical critical parent style. The motivation is to "nail" the employee, the enemy. Valuable feedback from the employee that might help resolve the difficulty is programmed out.

"Nailed" verbally to a corner, like a hemmed-in animal, some employees choose to verbally shout it out with the boss in a reciprocal "Uproar" game that some communications experts term the "pendulum effect." The "pendulum effect" is described as an escalating verbal conflict in which neither party is really listening but is arming himself or herself with "comebacks" to the next oral barrage. Over time the pendulum, representing the argument, registers larger and larger swings from center, indicating further communications distance between the parties (14). When a critical parent boss and a rebellious subordinate come together, the result is attacking and counterattacking, not learning or the sharing of information. The higher the critical parent boss "ups the ante," the higher the rebellious kid in the subordinate responds. In the process neither gets closer to the other or to the solution of the problem. As shown in the following diagrams, each ego state grows in response to the attack from the other.

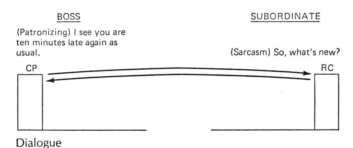

Dialogue
1. *Boss (patronizingly): I see you are ten minutes late again, as usual.*
2. *Subordinate (sarcastically): So, what's new?*

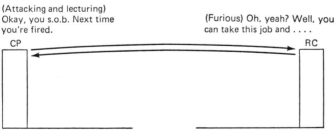

Dialogue
1. *Boss (attacking and lecturing): Okay, you s.o.b. Next time you're fired.*
2. *Subordinate (furiously): Oh, yeah? Well, you can take this job and . . .*

Most of the maintenance workers in this organization chose to express their rebellion through even more hurtful means, like industrial sabotage. Some placed extra nuts and bolts in the engines of trucks. Others put sugar in the gas tanks. Others deliberately ordered materials late, which slowed down other parts of this serial production process in which the completion of one man's job depended upon the completion of another's job.

The most effective maintenance supervisors—those with the lowest turnover rates and the highest productivity—employed well the tact of the supportive nurturing parent combined with the adult. From the outset of the confrontation they acknowledged that the subordinates were valuable employees, which helped disarm any rebellious child defenses. Then they employed the adult to explore the causes of the problem and to see how the problem could be resolved. Rather than coming in armed with preordained critical parent opinions and labels, these bosses solicited the aid of the subordinates in solving their own problem.

Boss	Maintenance Worker
"Charlie, you have put in ten years with our firm and you are one of our most experienced and valuable employees. I hope you know that."	"Gee, thanks, Boss."
"However, I have a difficult matter I want to discuss with you. Maybe you can help me with it."	"Okay, Boss."
"In the last couple of weeks your attendance record has left something to be desired. What is the difficulty and how can I help you solve it?	"Well, Boss, to tell you the truth, my wife's car broke down and I have had to bring the kids to school. The part on her foreign car has finally come in and things should be back to normal by tomorrow."
"Okay, good. I knew there was a good reason for your tardiness. You are one of our most reliable workers. Look, if you should ever have difficulty in getting to work	"Sure, Boss, any way I can help you out. You surely have been good to me. I forgot about the serial production thing. I don't plan to be late again. If something unex-

on time in the future, let me know in advance. You know we work in serial here, so if you're late everybody else down the line gets slowed up. This way I can schedule one of the other guys in early and you can work the last minutes for him."

pected comes up, I will let you know."

In this confrontation, not only did the *present* problem get solved, but the foundation was laid for alleviating any *future* problems. Additionally, rapport was improved—*not* further strained. The handling of criticism is so crucial to the leader-follower relationship that in the next chapter a whole section is devoted to how to give constructive criticism to subordinates.

Even worse than engaging the rebellious child in a subordinate is hooking into their overly submissive child. Supervisors who employ an excessive amount of critical parent tend to create a climate most conducive to overly adaptive "yes-men" and "whimperers"—employees who are afraid to take on job responsibilities and risks, even when necessary, and who are often given to creating conflicts for others in order to cover themselves. Whenever

. . . the climate is hostile and threatening communication tends to suffer—not only is there a tendency toward miscommunication with malice aforethought, but in such an atmosphere true feelings are suppressed lest one be punished for revealing them. When an organization member slips no one 'carries him'—on the contrary he may serve as a useful scapegoat for others who seek temporary relief from criticism of themselves. By and large one's communication (as well as his behavior in general) is dominated by the need to protect himself rather than the desire to serve the interests of the organization (15).

Following are some recommendations for steering away from the counterproductive critical parent.

First of all, replace negative strokes with positive ones. As demonstrated in chapter three, this boosts morale and fixates employee efforts on productive behavior rather than on rebellious behavior.

Secondly, if you are very upset or angry with a subordinate, with-hold your confrontation session until your critical parent emotional "smoke" has had a chance to clear. The critical parent's "hot air" interferes with adult rational problem solving and often ends up with a lot more "hot air" in return from rebellious employees. Count to a hundred, punch on a pillow, or schedule the session for another day—but leave the critical parent at home. It has no constructive role in your effectiveness as a leader.

Thirdly, when dealing with a difficult disciplinary case, use the adult in place of the critical parent. Some leaders are afraid to abandon the critical parent for fear they may be taken advantage of by subordi-nates. As I have already shown, the critical parent often adds fuel to the fire by further stimulating the rebellious child in the subordinate. Additionally, the adult—because of its cold, impersonal nature—is a firmer disciplinarian. Yet, the adult does not aggravate the employee's rebellious child because it does not "nail" the subordinate to the wall with negative labels. The adult acts as a disciplinarian by clearly convey-ing the requirements of the job and the consequences of failing to meet these requirements. In this way the adult supervisor does not treat the subordinate as a bad child who needs to be punished but as an adult who has the option to choose his or her own mode of behaving with the responsibility of the resulting consequences. By not "nailing" the subordinate with labels, the adult takes the wind out of the rebellious child's sails and at the same time sobers up the subordinate's adult by making the consequences evident.

For example, if a maintenance worker insists on taking advantage of a supervisor's nurturing parent nature with further absences, the supervisor's adult may firmly quench further rebellious behavior with:

Look, Bob, you have still been repeatedly absent on these dates. Although you are an excellent maintenance worker, we can only tolerate up to XXX amount of unexcused absences per year. After XXX amount you will be officially reprimanded. After two such official reprimands in a year you will be laid off without pay for a month. After the third repri-mand you will be terminated. (Shifting into the nurturing parent) As I said before, I am on your team and I will do everything in my power to help you succeed. (Back to the adult) However, ultimately the choice—the responsibility—is yours. (Back to the nurturing parent) I hope you don't let me down. But mainly you have an obligation to yourself. I hope you choose wisely.

Blending the nurturing parent with the adult even further reduces the tendency to cultivate a rebellious response or attitude in the employee. With the adult in charge, no firmness is lost. In fact, the nurturing parent, by demonstrating a sincere concern for the economic well-being of the employee, should help further stimulate the subordinate to take constructive action—in this case to cut out absences.

This approach of using the adult and the nurturing parent instead of the critical parent even works very successfully with less mature subordinates—for example, in the school setting. I have had a lot of success in gaining cooperation and better efforts from the few problem children undergraduates I have encountered while teaching by using the adult and the nurturing parent approach. The critical parent approach led either to the students dropping my course or to further aggravation of some kind.

Further, as I tell my workshop participants, if you keep away from the critical parent as much as possible you will probably significantly reduce your chances of getting heart disease. It is the ranting, raving, yelling, and emotionally explosive critical parent boss who keels over at an early age from a heart attack.

Effective leaders avoid the adapted child as much as possible. The adapted child is indicative of the "wishy washy" manager who lacks self-confidence and who is overly submissive. Subordinates are very reluctant to follow leaders who don't know where they are going or how they plan to get there. And who can blame them? Who wants to stumble off the bridge with his boss?

The typical adapted child boss responds to employee questions with comments such as:

Men, I will do my best to explain the new order system. Now, ah, ah, ah. What I think will be happening . . . well now, let's see, what were we doing before . . .

Frankly, I would like to give you permission to order that new computer, but I just don't know if we can afford it. But, then again, it could be very useful and stammer, stammer, stammer.

A faculty friend of mine told me about a meeting she attended at which the dean addressed the college faculty to explain new graduate admission requirements.

> I attended the meeting with the graduate council that I think determines the guidelines. And I am still confused. I know I should know what the requirements are. But I mean, it should be simple. But with all these accrediting agency requirements and all . . .

The dean went on and on, making constant excuses for himself and confusing the faculty more than informing them.

Additionally, the adapted child leader often brings disappointment to employees by not standing up for them in meetings with higher authorities in the organization. Being overly submissive, he or she yields to the demands of more assertive peers who are after a piece of the same allocations of money, equipment, and vacation time. For instance, some departments consistently fail to get a fair shake on office expenses and salaries because their submissive bosses are afraid to go to bat for them with superiors.

A boss who uses too much adapted child needs shoring up in at least one of three areas: his or her technical knowledge of the job; a misguided need to know it all; or his or her lack of assertive posture.

Often, bosses are not in a position to answer subordinates' questions properly because they are not adequately prepared. No one says the leader must know everything about a job. No one has perfect knowledge of anything. However, the fundamentals should be learned adequately. If you are planning a meeting with subordinates, at least learn that particular subject matter well before addressing them. There is nothing to be gained by further confusing them and embarrassing yourself. If you don't know all the answers, openly admit it, but tell them you will find out the answers and give them at the next meeting. Subordinates appreciate an honest admission of ignorance. It is natural to distrust anyone who pretends the impossible: to know it all. If you have a problem child subordinate who repeatedly tries to get his or her kicks from embarrassing you despite your private attempts to reconcile difficulties, have him or her report back to the group with the solutions to his or her own questions.

Some leaders, like many professionals, put too much pressure on themselves by thinking they must have all the answers. A good leader should be an expert guide. He or she should be reasonably abreast of the technology and the know-how of the job. But a leader is a guide, *not* an answer machine. The leader who tries to answer all the questions will be depriving his or her subordinates of developing their own adult problem-solving skills.

Leaders are effective when they remember that their job is only one of the jobs in the group. A primary function of leaders is to help others to carry out their roles, *not* to carry out their roles for them (16).

Some bosses take on an overly submissive adapted child posture because they confuse being assertive with being aggressive. Such bosses are afraid they will hurt others' feelings or infringe on the rights of subordinates if they take a more forceful stand. Again, these leaders confuse aggression with assertiveness.

The aggressive person (as shown in the following chart) stands up for his own rights but also tramples over others' rights in the process. The aggressive person comes out of the critical parent ego state and plays the Karpman game role of the persecutor. Cooperation, morale, and productivity suffer as a result of his or her punitive tactics, as subordinates go on the defensive in an attempt to protect themselves or to counterattack.

A LEADERSHIP VIEW OF ASSERTIVENESS

	Submissive	Assertive	Aggressive
Interpersonal Strategies			
Ego States	Adapted child	Adult, free child, nurturing parent	Critical parent
Game Roles	Victim	None	Persecutor (or false rescuer)
Leadership Styles	"I can't make a stand."	"I will make a stand without hurting theirs."	"I'll bust their stand."

The submissive leader comes out of the adapted child and plays the role of the victim. He or she is not very effective because he or she fails to stand up for his or her own rights as well as the rights of subordinates. As a result, he or she gets walked over in meetings with superiors and subordinates, sowing seeds of distrust and lack of confidence.

The effective leader is assertive, standing up for his or her own rights, but not at the expense of others. The assertive leader comes solidly out of the adult, the nurturing parent, and the free child, and he or she plays no games. Hence, everyone concerned benefits from such leadership.

CONCLUSION

The effective leader emphasizes the wisdom of the adult, the genuine support and concern of the nurturing parent, and the contagious enthusiasm of the free child. He or she inspires productivity, confidence, mutual respect, cooperation, and a keen interest in the job. He or she says goodbye to the stammerings and insecurities of the adapted child and the punitive tendencies of the critical parent. Everyone truly comes out an OK winner under his or her stewardship.

In closing this chapter, I would like to share with you three recommendations that will make changing yourself (if you deem it necessary) a smooth and rewarding experience:

1. Program the idea of nonchange out of your adult.
2. Take the changes gradually.
3. Have some reward for the free child as you change.

The assumption of nonchange is an example of adult ego state contamination. Everything in this world, including the cells in your body, is in a constant state of change. Unless you are devout in clinging to the past or devout in your commitment to nonchange, you can change as much for the better as you wish and as you are willing to apply yourself. Considering their backgrounds, who would have thought that the courageous civil rights leader, Dr. Martin Luther King, Jr., or the brilliant scientist, Albert Einstein, would achieve greatness? King had attempted suicide twice before the age of thirteen. Einstein was a slow learner and was backward in his early studies. One of his earlier teachers remarked that he would not amount to anything. He originally failed his college entrance exams (17).

Often, the only thing that stands between you and positive change is that put-down artist in your head, the critical parent. View his assumption of nonchange and negative messages as just so much idle chatter and you will be happier and more prosperous for it.

Take the change gradually. Rome was not built in a day—and neither were you. Persistently work at changing one or two little things at a time and you will be amazed at the results. It is not necessary

> . . . to make wholesale, abrupt changes in your behavior. You will only find it frustrating and probably unbearable. The best and most lasting way to implement change is gradually, smoothly, and systematically (18).

At a gradual rate, the change will be more smoothly accepted by your subordinates. The Dr. Jekyll and Mr. Hyde leader, who is Mr. S.O.B. one day and Mr. Nice Guy the next, will make employees feel unsettled and wary.

You might solicit the aid of a fellow supervisor, a trusted and mature subordinate (with a large nurturing parent, adult, and free child), your spouse, or a good friend in making changes. Let him or her help you in the construction of your current egogram with specific feedback on ego state behavior you might be unaware of such as certain unconscious mannerisms. Over time he or she can help you gauge your progress.

Sometimes even small, unintentional gestures can make a difference. I remember one middle-level manager who, although very supportive at heart, had an obnoxious critical parent mannerism when trying to explain something to his work section. He would critically shake his finger at his employees. A change in this simple, unintentioned mannerism turned his explanation sessions with his people from lectures into more meaningful and relaxed knowledge-sharing experiences.

Give yourself a reward. When making a change in yourself or when achieving anything, have something in it for your free child. Even if the reward is inexpensive and seems trivial, OK child strokes provide a large incentive to keep going. Remember, you live at the feelings level. Feeling good while changing makes it quite a bit easier and often insures your completion of the task. After I finish a chapter on a book, my wife and I celebrate by going to a favorite restaurant. If you feel you might cheat, let your wife, or friend, or whoever is helping you clue you when adequate progress has been made, and then celebrate with him or her. The celebration of positive change with a friend is a super free child stroke in itself.

One last comment: Do not let your critical parent hassle you if change is going slowly or if you are not achieving perfection. Do not

> . . . expect to be perfect. There will be days that you will not or cannot do the things you feel you should or could have done. Some days you simply may not give a damn. . . . No matter what happens, simply resolve to keep trying. Improving your effectiveness is much like playing golf. Theoretically, the perfect golf score is eighteen, but to reach that would mean a hole in one on eighteen consecutive holes. Obviously, no one will ever come anywhere near that. However, this fact doesn't stop millions . . . from trying to improve their score each week. As you strive to work smarter, take a similar approach. Resolve to improve, but realize that this is an area where you will always be able to improve (19).

NOTES

1. Lindzey/Aronson, *The Handbook of Social Psychology,* vol. 4. © 1969 by Addison-Wesley Publishing Co., Inc. Chap. 1, "Leadership," p. 205. Reprinted with permission.
2. Gibb, *The Handbook of Social Psychology* vol. 4, pp. 216–228; David R. Hampton, Charles E. Summer, and Ross A. Webber, *Organizational Behavior and the Practice of Management* (Glenview, Ill.: Scott, Foresman & Company, 1978), pp. 596–598.
3. R. M. Stogdill, *Handbook of Leadership* (New York: Macmillan, Inc./Free Press, 1974), pp. 81–82.
4. Thomas Gordon, *Leader Effectiveness Training L.E.T.: The No-Lose Way to Release the Productive Potential of People* (Wyden Books), © 1977 by Dr. Thomas Gordon.
5. Renis Likert, *New Patterns in Management* (New York: McGraw-Hill Book Company, 1961), p. 101.

6. B. R. Bugelski, *The Psychology of Learning Applied to Teaching,* 2d ed. (Indianapolis, Ind.: The Bobbs Merrill Co., Inc., 1971), p. 173.

7. William V. Haney, *Communication and Organizational Behavior: Text and Cases,* 3d ed. (Homewood, Ill.: Richard D. Irwin, Inc., 1973), pp. 14–15. © 1973 by Richard D. Irwin, Inc.

8. Haney, *Communication and Organizational Behavior,* pp. 14–15.

9. I discuss in detail how to use the nurturing parent and the adult instead of the critical parent for firmness in dealing with a problem employee later on in this chapter and in the next chapter in the section dealing with the correct way of correcting.

10. For a detailed review of the symbiotic relationship and the means of terminating it, see chapter four.

11. Chapter ten adds specific pointers on how to appropriately let out the reins of responsibility.

12. Harold J. Leavitt, *Managerial Psychology,* rev. ed. (Chicago, Ill.: University of Chicago Press, 1964), pp. 266–267.

13. Robert Blauner, *Alienation and Freedom* (Chicago, Ill.: University of Chicago Press, 1964), p. 22.

14. For an extended discussion of the pendulum effect, see: William V. Haney, *Communication and Organizational Behavior,* pp. 362–365.

15. William V. Haney, *Communication and Organizational Behavior: Text and Cases,* 3d ed. (Homewood, Ill.: Richard D. Irwin, 1973), pp. 14–15. © 1973 by Richard D. Irwin, Inc.

16. Leavitt, *Managerial Psychology,* p. 266.

17. Muriel James and Dorothy Jongeward, *The People Book: Transactional Analysis for Students* (Reading, Mass.: Addison-Wesley Publishing Co., Inc., 1975), pp. 4–5.

18. Michael LeBoeuf, *Working Smart: How to Accomplish More in Half the Time* (New York: McGraw-Hill Book Company, 1979) p. 3.

LEADERSHIP STYLES AND FACTORS AFFECTING THESE

10

Leadership styles and the factors affecting the usefulness of one style over another have been the subjects of hundreds of books and thousands of articles in the field of organizational behavior. Utilizing a TA perspective, I will weave into *this* discussion some of the most fundamental and practical theories and data available on the subject. This chapter is designed to give you some specific and easy to understand ways to deal with almost any leadership situation in a practical and effective way.

TA AND LEADERSHIP STYLES

Almost all books on the subject of leadership or organizational behavior agree that there are two fundamental styles or methods of leading: democratic and autocratic. These styles have been discussed under many different labels. Labels describing the democratic approach to leading have included theory Y (1), participative, human relations, and the modern approach. Labels describing the autocratic style have included Theory X, traditional, bureaucratic, and production oriented.

Yet, in spite of the diverse labeling, there are still only *two* fundamental ways of getting others to follow our lead. Both leadership styles or approaches revolve around the central issue of authority. They deal with the leader's method of sharing his or her power and authority with his or her followers. As you will see, how power is shared with followers will have a significant impact on a leader's success or failure.

LEADERSHIP STYLES

	Autocratic	Democratic
Method of Sharing Responsibility	Non participative	Participative
Style of Relating to Subordinates	Parent to child	Adult to adult
Life Position toward Self and Followers	I'm OK, You're Not OK	I'm OK, You're OK
Method of Communicating	Top down	Two-way or open
Overall Predominant View of Followers	Multi-injunctional. Followers are often viewed as irresponsible, lazy, stupid, and incompetent. Primary injunctions placed on followers are: don't think, don't feel, and don't be you.	The viewpoint is mainly supportive and positive. Followers are assumed to be responsible, self-motivated, intelligent, and competent.
Behavior Demanded of Follower	Obedience	Self-reliance and initiative
Motivation of Followers	Money	Money plus higher-level needs like ego and self-actualization

Those who lead successfully are frequently destined to plot the courses of organizations—and possibly even societies—in the future.

The two styles of leadership may be viewed as opposite ends of the same continuum, with many managers demonstrating a clear preference for one style over the other.

The Autocratic Approach

The autocratic leader typically takes a parent to child approach in dealing with employees. He or she, in one word, demands *obedience* from followers. As the cliché goes, "Subordinates are to do or die but not to question why." A good worker is viewed as a robot who does exactly as he or she is told and who is only motivated by money. In TA terminology, the autocratic leader strongly prefers obedient, submissive, adapted children.

> When I tell them to jump, I expect them to do it now and with no questions. We don't live in a democracy around this place. It's my job to make the decisions around her and the workers' job to follow them to the letter. I don't make suggestions to workers. I give orders.

As a result of his or her dictatorial critical parent approach, the autocratic leader often creates a hostile relationship with his or her followers and often brings out the worst in them: rebellion or oversubmissiveness. (See chapter nine for a review of the reaction of subordinates to critical parent bosses.) However, as I discuss later in this chapter, some workers have predominantly adapted child egograms. They shun responsibility. They prefer that the boss makes all the decisions.

Because the autocratic leader views the typical worker as Not-OK—as irresponsible, unmotivated, incompetent, and stupid-he or she has little option but to make all the decisions. "If I share significant authority with followers, they most surely will screw up" is the thinking of this type of leader.

One boss, very close to being a pure type of autocratic leader, put it this way:

> If I delegate any authority to my workers, I lose. First of all, most are too stupid to do the job competently. And even if they were competent,

most are simply too lazy. I mean if I don't spell everything out in black and white and don't push like hell to get things done, everything will go to hell in a basket.

Frederick W. Taylor, a prime exponent of the autocratic approach and considered to be the founding father of scientific management, spoke of the typical worker's desire to produce as characteristically lacking:

> There is no question that the tendency of the average man (in all walks of life) is toward working at a slow, easy gait, and that it is only after a good deal of thought and observation on his part or as a result of example, conscience, or external pressure that he takes a more rapid pace.
> There are, of course, men of unusual energy, vitality, and ambition who naturally choose the fastest gait. . . . But these few uncommon men only serve by affording a contrast to emphasize the tendency of the average (2).

Although the autocratic approach to leadership flourished during the turn of the century when the average worker was much less educated and much less affluent than he or she is today, there are still many managers and supervisors who still take this very narrow and negative view of their human resources. Research even indicates that under some circumstances, with certain types of people, the autocratic approach yields the best results in terms of both productivity and morale (3). The details of these moderating circumstances and factors will be discussed shortly. One thing is for sure: To function effectively the autocratic leader must have a broad base of work experience and a thorough knowledge of his subordinates' jobs. Through his or her top-down, closed communication approach, valuable feedback and knowledge from those often in the best position to know—those actually performing the jobs under him or her—are programed out.

The Democratic Approach

At the opposite end of the continuum from the autocratic approach is the democratic style of leading. The assumptions of what followers are like and the style of relating to them are dramatically different in the democratic approach.

The democratic leader views the typical worker as competent, self-motivated, and responsible. As a result, he or she treats subordinates as adults.

> I feel very comfortable in delegating. When I let out the reins of authority, my people respond by fulfilling my highest expectations. They are competent, motivated, and energetic workers. Above all, they learn best when I don't interfere. I learn a lot from their feedback to boot.

The democratic approach is clearly adult to adult. The motto of this type of leader, who has no qualms about sharing power, is simply: "Workers also have minds. Why not employ them? No supervisor has a monopoly on thinking."

Democratic leadership tends to mature workers. It helps nurture the adult and the free child. Through the freedom to explore options and challenges on their own, subordinates are given opportunities to develop adult capacities as well as free child creative talents. In such a climate the employee is too busy maturing and being challenged by the job to spend much time rebelling or playing games.

Yet, in spite of its marvelous advantages in bringing out the best in workers, the democratic style must be used with discretion. In some circumstances, and with some people, too much freedom can spell disaster.

The truly supportive nurturing parent leader, who over the long haul has the most productive and happiest followers, must employ a lot of adult and free child in adapting his or her style to meet the needs of his or her people as well as the needs of the job. He or she uses the adult to alertly adapt authority styles to changing conditions. Only by being dynamic in controlling the reins of authority can the truly supportive leader best create a climate of mutual trust and support. (This is discussed in chapter nine.) The supportive leader always assumes the life position of I'm OK, You're OK, but realizes that circumstances may require a more direct, autocratic approach.

> Mary is an excellent supervisor. She knows that new employees need more direction. On the other hand, she knows when to let go of the apron strings. She knows that under some circumstances there is no

time to use the participatory approach. On the other hand, she is eager to get feedback and meaningful participation from workers when time permits.

Although the truly supportive leader is trying his or her best to help workers grow and develop on the job, he or she "works" the leadership style continuum in a fashion that best meets the needs of the workers as well as the demands of the organization. If the needs of either are ignored long enough, the organization *and* the workers will suffer. Frustrate the workers and morale suffers, and with poor morale come the ills of increased absenteeism, turnover, and employee-employer conflicts. Frustrate the demands of the organization and productivity suffers, which can ultimately mean a loss of jobs and in the most severe cases, bankruptcy.

The Contingency Approach

The truly supportive boss employs what researchers in organizational behavior call the contingency approach. According to the contingency approach, the leader bases his or her style of sharing responsibilities and directing on such factors as the nature of the task, timing, and the personality of the worker.

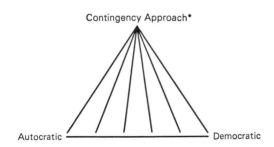

From an adult perspective, the contingency approach is the only one that makes practical sense. If a leader treats *all* individuals or

* Some call the contingency approach Theory Z, while the autocratic approach is termed Theory X and the democratic approach is termed Theory Y.

circumstances in an autocratic or a democratic fashion, he or she would be like the doctor who gives the same treatment to all patients, regardless of their condition. For some the treatment may be helpful. For others it may do harm. The effective treatment is prescribed contingent upon the individual patient's condition or illness.

The lines drawn along the continuum graphically indicate the dynamic style of the contingency approach. Contingencies, or factors that must be effectively dealt with by any successful leader, include the following.

The Nature of the Task. The structure of the task will greatly affect the impact that a given style of leadership will have on followers (4). For example, if the job is so spelled out that little deviation is possible, the democratic or participative approach is obviated. Although workers may make suggestions as to how to improve certain techniques or procedures on an assembly line, once the line is set up a novel or creative approach to the process would cause havoc. For example, as the line moves by a worker cannot be given the freedom to decide whether to attach certain parts to the frame or not. One worker put it sarcastically but aptly:

> Oh, sure, putting door handles on the cab of a car is a very mentally challenging and creative job. Sometimes a handle won't fit and you've got to move it around so it does. You have to be at least four years old to be up to the challenge.

I am not saying that assembly line jobs and other kinds of generally boring and routine jobs cannot be made more satisfying and more challenging. They can be. A number of foreign automobile manufacturers as well as a few domestic plants have demonstrated clearly how product quality and worker satisfaction are often direct results of programs that stress more employee input and job enrichment. Some manufacturers have found that morale and productivity increase when employees are allowed to work on whole sections of a car (like a carburetor) rather than simply screwing a few nuts and bolts together. On the other hand, by nature and by practicality, certain parts of any job will be routine and boring, leaving little room for creativity or challenge. Some examples of this are rotating tires, washing dishes, adding up numbers, key punching, recording scores or numbers, digging up ground, etc. Although automation has greatly reduced the drudgery in the work place, all of us still have to do some of it. During these very heavily structured and very routine tasks, the role a leader plays may be minimal. As another assembly line worker stated:

> Charlie, you aren't the foreman. The line is. It tells when, how, and what to do. For all practical purposes, Charlie, you're obsolete.

The element of task coordination will play a significant role in determining which style of leadership is preferred at any moment in time. A research director put it this way:

> People have asked me how one goes about managing a research team, which can be especially hard work, when the results may be many years off. Besides the research director being enthusiastic and supportive throughout the whole project, the research task itself demands periodic movements between the democratic and the autocratic approaches. At the outset of a given project the democratic style is essential. I have to act more like a member of the research team than a boss. At this stage I need all the feedback I can get from members of the team to questions such as: What is our research problem? How should we go about collecting data? What will be our strategy for analyzing what we have collected? If questionnaires are needed, how should they be designed? How shall we split up our subject groups if interviews are necessary? Who should call on whom? etc. At this point the adult and the free child—in terms of, say, new approaches to research designs—must be very much involved. Through this involvement my team better understands what we are about and, more importantly, they are given the opportunity to grow and to develop as researchers themselves.
>
> After research problems, goals, instruments, and territories have been set up, the research task demands an autocratic approach. Research members fully appreciate this also. If two or three researches end up calling on the same subjects or decide to alter questionnaires in midstream, there is no way to get valid or reliable measures. Additionally, unnecessary duplication of effort can turn a two-week task into ten weeks.
>
> During stage two we sample a small part of the population in order to test out our instruments and techniques. Then we shift back into the democratic approach temporarily to get input from all team members to see what changes in instruments and strategies are most important

before we firm up final instruments and approaches for our large sample of the general population.

Then, in the third stage of testing the general population, back to Theory X (the autocratic style) again. Effective leadership of any research project must be dynamic. I don't care whether we are talking about market testing a new product or surveying the chances of a political hopeful.

A very simple and clear way of viewing how task coordination demands a shift in leadership style is through team sports. For example, before a quarterback calls a play in a football game he may huddle with the other ten team members and possibly the coaches on the sidelines to get their adult feedback on what plays might work best and who can "beat" who in terms of defensive coverages. However, once the play is called the participative or democratic approach will not work. At this point all team members must execute the play called by the quarterback like well-trained adapted children. If they do not, the play will collapse. At this point there can be only one captain of the ship. If pass receivers decide to run unexpected pass routes, or a running back decides to take the ball away from the quarterback, or linemen decide not to block, the outcome is disastrous.

Any job, regardless of organizational level or sophistication, should be designed to include as much adult and free child investment on the part of personnel as possible. As I have demonstrated again and again throughout this book, when this happens workers better understand what they are about, they feel challenged, and their creative juices are free to flow. Productivity and morale are best served when adult and free child input is maximized. However, any prudent and experienced leader realizes that there are times when the task requries a parent to compliant child relationship. Less rebellion will occur during such periods if the boss carefully explains, on an adult-to-adult level, why task demands require an autocratic style. When followers have a good grasp of what is happening they can use their own adults to quell any rebellious child or critical parent uprisings within themselves.

If the bulk of the task, by its very nature, tends to be repetitive or boring—like some assembly line work—try to program in as much adult input as possible. There are always better and better ways to make "mouse traps." Some challenge and some sense of participation along the way are better than none at all. Additionally, in an atmosphere of dull work, make changes in the work environment that will at least help perk up the free child. Bright and cheery colors on the wall and piped-in music, for example, can help compensate for the lack of free child stimulation withheld by a boring job.

The Elements of Time and Timing. Time and timing are also critical ingredients in the leadership process. If little time is available in which to make a decision, then the autocratic approach may be the only feasible way. An emergency situation may arise in which a decision has to be reached in a matter of seconds or minutes. Consulting with subordinates in such a situation may be impossible.

A construction supervisor stated it aptly:

> If a piece of heavy equipment is about to fall on a worker, I obviously do not have time to consult with the group before yelling to the man to get out of the way.

Emergency situations and fly-by-the-seat-of-the-pants management can be greatly reduced through careful planning. However, even with the most careful planning, emergencies *do* arise, along with other situations that require quick thinking on the part of managers, thus precluding the participative style for the moment. Along with actual job experience, role playing has been demonstrated as an excellent technique for priming the adult for quick and alert thinking. Some organizations use assessment center exercises for testing and developing a potential leader's ability to handle emergencies and other novel situations. Through these types of evaluation centers, supervisory candidates are put in situations that simulate routine problems and crises in the work place. Assessment centers often include: in-basket exercise of typical problems faced by the supervisor during the day, handling an emergency phone call, or leading a group discussion with some irate participants. Through such simulated exercises (often videotaped for feedback purposes), employees are given opportunities to develop important leadership and decision-making skills without the expense and trauma that could easily result if they had to learn "cold turkey" on the real job (5).

Another important aspect of timing deals with the length of time a given individual has been on the job. Those new to the job require more direction and control, more of an autocratic approach. Those with a fair degree of experience require less direction. Of course, job veterans already have the know-how and confidence to function independently. For the mature jobholder, the democratic approach makes the most sense.

The effective leader periodically lets go of the reins of control as the employee gains in competence and maturity on the job. This approach of moving from a Theory X to a Theory Y style, in response to the worker's level of job maturity, is truly supportive.* A high-level executive of a service organization comments:

> When an individual first gets on the job, he or she is lost, just like a baby taking its first steps. Encouragement and direction are needed to keep the worker from falling on his or her face from any of a number of directions. Simply throwing a novice to the wolves may be democratic, but it certainly is not supportive. After experience and confidence are gained—as the worker matures—the effective leader stops leading by the hand. Less guidance at this point gives the worker room to grow and develop. A more directive style at this stage would be suffocating. Effective leaders are hung up on employee development, not on power.

The Personality of the Follower. Research, especially by the world-renowned authority on organizational behavior, Victor H. Vroom, clearly indicates that the personality of the follower is an important ingredient in determining which style of leadership will be most effective. Vroom found that individuals who had a high need for independence (which was described as the desire or need of the individual to work out problems on his or her own without help from others) and who were low in authoritarianism were more productive and more satisfied under democratic leadership, while those with reverse traits functioned better under more directive leadership (6). The term, authoritarianism, and the means of measuring this personality trait were borrowed from an earlier study by Adorno and others who basically described those high in authoritarianism as having a strong need to submit to authority (7).

In TA terminology, Vroom is simply saying that an individual

---

* For a review of specifics for helping new employees over the hump, see chapter three.

with a large adult and free child, the creative free thinker, naturally prefers a style of leadership that best permits these dominant ego states to grow and develop—that is, the democratic style. On the other hand, the individual with a large submissive adapted child prefers the direction and control provided by the autocratic parent type of leader.

My own thinking is that truly supportive leaders will try to help the more adapted followers become more independent thinkers by gradually relinquishing the reins of authority. A pointed out in chapter nine, maintaining a critical parent to submissive child relationship with followers is not conducive to developing decision makers. In the long run such a relationship may lead to overly adaptive "yes-men"—employees who are afraid of job responsibilities and who are often given to creating conflicts for others in order to cover for themselves.

THE CORRECT WAY OF CORRECTING

The ability to correct employees constructively is essential for any leader. No employee "toes the line" at all times, nor does he or she always understand the *first* time. If criticism is done constructively, things are back on track quickly, with a better understanding between the parties—and no hurt feelings. If done improperly, the corrected party may take the criticism personally and may later strike back at the correcting party or organization through a reduced effort—or even rebellion. Hurt adapted children do not make good employees. Also, improper correction may lead to a game of Uproar and no meaningful communication. Lemons can be made into lemonade. I have compiled a few tested rules for keeping employees from becoming defensive during criticism. These techniques will also work with customers or superiors if you should have to correct them concerning data on a product, a process, etc.

1. Express your own feelings—not how the other person feels. People resent others telling them how they feel.
2. Be specific when correcting someone. Vague comments lead to confusion and needless anxiety. "What is he or she talking about?" is a normal reaction to vague corrections.

3. Describe what the employee did wrong, but try not to evaluate him or her as a person. Concentrate on the job, not on the personality. People resent labels, but they want to learn how to do their jobs better.

4. Motivation for correcting an employee should come from the adult and the nurturing parent and not from the critical parent. The motive should be to help the employee become a better employee, not to try to "nail" him or her. Concentrate on finding solutions, not on finding fault.

5. Criticisms should be properly timed. If either you or the employee is upset with the other or if either of you is very tired, schedule the correction session for a later time. Let the upset or tired child in both of you subside so that the adult is free to take rational control of the discussion. Emotionally clearing the air helps free the adult.

An exercise I have used frequently with managers for changing defensive, negative stroke statements into positive ones is the lemon to lemonade exercise. For training purposes, this exercise should be done in a small group setting, with between five and twenty persons. The leader of the session should list five or six statements on a blackboard that would normally bring about negative reactions in the person being corrected. Each member of the training group then writes positive corrective statements. Before the exercise, participants should be familiarized with the five rules of constructive criticism. Allow about twenty minutes for each member to complete his or her corrective statements.

Taking one statement at a time, let various participants give their positive corrective approaches and then discuss these with the group in the light of the five rules of constructive criticism. The leader should give his or her positive corrective statements and rationale last so as not to bias the discussion of participants.

I encourage you to generate negative corrective statements and their positive counterparts that would be typical of your own operation. A sample of negative and positive corrective statements and rationale would be:

(1) *Negative Correction Statement:* "You idiot. That is truly stupid insulting a customer like that." Explanation: Directly attacks the employee. Will probably hook a critical parent in return and lead to an unproductive game of Uproar. Violates rules #1, 3, and 4.

(1A) *Positive Correction Statement:* "Isn't there something else you could have told the customer to correct the problem and still keep her patronage?" Explanation: Avoids negative fault-finding labels and gets the employee thinking about solving the problem. Questions like this tend to hook the adult rather than the adapted child or the critical parent.

(2) *Negative Statement:* "Damn! You were supposed to order two dozen!" Explanation: Gets off frustrations of the manager but nothing more. "Damn yourself" would be the natural reaction of any salesperson involved. Violates rules 3, 4, and 5.

(2A) *Positive Statement:* "We still need two dozen by Monday. You showed a lot of initiative in getting the order. I know you can straighten out the order mix-up." Explanation: Replaces negative stroke with a positive one and gets the employee involved in correcting the problem.

(3) *Negative Statement:* "Your closing argument to the jury doesn't make any sense. Explanation: Places all the blame on the party being corrected. A good way to hook an angry critical parent or an adapted child. Violates rules 3, 4, and 5.

(3A) *Positive Statement:* "I am having a hard time understanding your approach. Would you explain more fully what you mean?" Explanation: Places no blame, but immediately gets to the issue of solving the communication problem.

(4) *Negative Statement:* "Your record on getting cases completed is pitiful. Apparently, you don't give a hoot about being a social worker." Explanation: Finds fault and no solution. Is little more than a "dumping" session for the manager. Violates rules 1, 3, 4, and 5.

(4A) *Positive Statement:* "According to reports, reducing your case load has not been one of your strong points. What seems to be the difficulty? How can we correct it? Explanation: Moves straight to the solution and gets involved in solving rather than blaming.

(5) *Negative Statement:* "I guess selling is not your cup of tea." Explanation: May be trying to avoid the critical issues by not being specific. Tells the salesperson little or no useful information. Violates rule 2.

(5A) *Positive Statement:* "You give an excellent presentation, but seem to have a hard time making the close. Why don't we examine how you approach the close and see if we can uncover some ways of improving your technique." Explanation: Concentrates on specifics and gets the salesperson involved in thinking about solutions rather than failure.

NOTES

1. The concepts of Theory X and Theory Y refer to the theories described by Douglas McGregor in *The Human Side of Enterprise* (New York: McGraw-Hill Book Company, 1960).
2. Frederick W. Taylor, "Shop Management," a paper read before the American Society of Mechanical Engineers, June 1903.

3. For some excellent research and commentary on the effectiveness of different leadership styles in the face of various situational factors, see: David G. Bowers and Stanley E. Seashore, "Predicting Organizational Effectiveness with a Four-Factor Theory of Leadership," *Administrative Science Quarterly,* vol. 11, no. 2 (1966), pp. 238–63 and Robert Tannenbaum and Warren H. Schmidt, "How to Choose a Leadership Pattern," *Harvard Business Review,* May–June 1973, pp. 162–180.

4. Fred Fiedler and Martin Chemers do an excellent job of spelling out the impact the nature of the task will have on leadership style and ways of measuring task structure. For an excellent synopsis of their work, see: Fred E. Fiedler and Martin M. Chemers, *Leadership and Effective Management* (Glenview, Ill.: Scott, Foresman & Company, 1974), pp. 63–81 and 91–93.

5. For an excellent overview of the ins and outs of the assessment center as a managerial tool, see: William C. Byham, "The Assessment Center as an Aid in Management Development," Training and Development Journal, December 1971.

6. Victor H. Vroom, "Some Personality Determinants of the Effects of Participation," *Journal of Abnormal and Social Psychology,* vol. 59, 1959, pp. 322–327; Victor H. Vroom, *Some Personality Determinants of the Effects of Participation* (Englewood Cliffs, N.J.: Prentice-Hall, Inc., 1960).

7. Theodor W. Adorno and others, *The Authoritarian Personality* (New York: Harper & Row, Publishers, Inc., 1950).

THE ORGANIZATIONAL LEVEL

11

Like individuals, organizations have personalities. Some are very parent in demeanor. Decisions are made at the top and are passed down the chain of command as orders that are not to be questioned. Other organizations exude an adult philosophy. Meaningful decisions are shared at all levels throughout the organizational structure. Management has an "open door" policy toward employees. Communication flows freely upward as well as downward. Other organizations radiate a childlike climate. Decisions are made haphazardly, if at all. There is a great deal of confusion over what the policies and goals are. Often, few know who to communicate with to get things done. Everybody is either very confused or they spend a lot of time "covering their behinds" like scared children.

As in individual personality analysis, an excellent way to get a handle on an organization's personality is through script analysis. With script analysis one can get a fairly accurate and concise reading of about all there is to know about the organization from a behavioral viewpoint. The script elements are basically the same as those found in chapter four on personality analysis. A few changes have been made in substance and in wording in order to reflect the peculiarities of the organizational level.

Key organizational script elements include the following: (1) *Life Course*—the organization's plot: where it has been, where it is, and where it is going; (2) *Goals*—the ones formally stated and the real ones; (3) *Managerial Life Positions*—higher level management's feeling of okayness toward itself and others down the chain of command that ultimately characterizes managements method of sharing authority; (4) *Rules*—an organizational term for injunctions and attributions; (5) *Games*—the major ones that help construct the life course of the organization; (6) *Antithesis*—getting the organization's act together.

Before discussing a number of specific organizational scripts (which are handled in chapter twelve), I think it would be most beneficial to the reader if I first do three things: (1) clarify some of the script elements that are especially different from those discussed earlier in regard to individual scripts; (2) discuss what an ideal organizational script would look like—where it *should* be going; and (3) develop a framework for diagnosing organizational ills and ways of rectifying these or, in organizational behavior terminology, the issue of organizational development.

SOME REFLECTIONS ON THE ELEMENTS OF GOALS AND MANAGERIAL LIFE POSITIONS

Although all levels of analyses, from the individual level to the organizational level, may be discussed in terms of goals, the issue of formally stated goals versus real goals takes on particular significance at the organizational level. How often have you heard members of your own organization gripe about inconsistencies between the two?

> Well, they tell us that the primary aim of this institution is teaching. But, in actuality, this is often not the case. You try to introduce a new course and some other department jealously fights you over territorial rights to it even though they have neither the manpower nor the intention of teaching such a course in the next twenty years. Just because a course has some behavioral aspects does not necessarily mean it has to be taught in the psychology department any more than a course employing numbers

has to be taught in the mathematics department. But for some departments, global empire building is much more important than students or learning. Some universities permit empire building, and such political squabbles kill off potentially very beneficial courses.

Right, we are supposed to be in the business of generating creative ways of meeting the needs of our clients through advertising. But if you develop a strategy, copy, or visual aids that conflict with the traditional approaches dictated on high, forget it.

We should be in the banking business to serve our customers and to maximize profits. In actuality, we do neither. We are so conservative that we only make loans to those who have deposited more money in our bank than we intend to lend to them. We don't lend money here. We simply charge individuals and corporations for borrowing back their own money. No wonder that banks that were comparable in size to our bank ten years ago are now four times larger with four times as many customers and four times more profitable.

Baloney, you try to achieve something around here and you have a problem. They say they want "go-getters." What they want is mediocrity.

Look, Joe, let me set you straight. Not rocking the boat is much more important than being creative, regardless of what is written in the company manual.

The overall goals or objectives of a given organization should be stated as broad values or policies—as guideposts—for the general purposes and aims of the institution. More concrete measures of goals in terms of results should only exist for specific job areas or classifications. For example, one overall objective of a manufacturing firm may be profit maximization. This is a fairly general guideline. One concrete measure of the achievement of this guideline is for assembly line workers* to turn out so many units of a product, or *parts* of a product, per hour.**

Yet, even though overall organizational goals should serve as broad guidelines and not as specific concrete requirements or measures, they should not be "two faced" in substance either. If what people are doing

---

* Of course, a specific job classification would designate what type of product or part of the product is being assembled and would include all those performing basically the same tasks.

** For a review of specifics on setting job goals and monitoring these, see chapter three.

in an organization is radically different from what the guideposts say they should be doing, then there is a problem. Managing an organization by hypocrisy is even less palatable as an organizational level phenomenon than if it is done by a few departments or by a few individuals. Organizational level hypocrisy cuts across all departments in terms of reduced productivity and low morale. Specific examples of different types of organizational hypocrisy are discussed in the organizational scripts in chapter twelve.

There are four types of organizational climate that are maintained and reflected by four types of managerial life positions. By organizational climate I mean the psychological and philosophical atmosphere that permeates the organization. After a certain period of time in an organization an individual readily gets a "feel" for whether an organization is supportive, hostile, indifferent, strict, or easygoing. The above adjectives reflect different ways of viewing organizational climates. Transactional Analysis, through the concept of life positions, gives us specific handles for appreciating the managerial attitudes that ultimately translate into the psychological climate of the organization. It is the organizational climate that sets the overall tone for the behavior and the relationships between and among members. Of course, individual departments as well as certain individuals may deviate to a certain degree from the basic philosophical and psychological thrust of the organization. Too much resistance, however, often leads to a termination of the relationship between the organization and the individuals involved.

Following are the four basic organizational climates as dictated by managerial life positions.

I'm OK, You're OK:
Management by Self-Direction
and Commitment

This is the healthiest climate any organization can have. Relationships are characterized as truly supportive. There is mutual acceptance and respect up and down the chain of command. Communication is on a two-way street. Management is as interested in what the workers have to say as the workers are in what management has to say. There are no "axes to grind," as each party works *with* the other rather than *against* it (1). If employees need help in dealing with a certain problem, fellow workers are eager to help out. Mistakes on the part of the workers are viewed as opportunities for learning and not as opportunities to punish or "nail" as in the game of "Now I've Got You, You S.O.B." The psychological environment is free of games. The leadership style employed by organizational supervisors is predominantly Theory Z, or the contingency approach which, as discussed in chapter ten, is the truly supportive style of leadership. Although supervisors try to help the workers mature on their jobs as much as possible, they give them directions and controls when they are needed. Relationships, among all organizational members, are primarily adult to adult, with a good dose of free child creativity and humor. It's OK to be innovative and happy in this climate.

I'm OK, You're Not OK:
Management by Edict

Rather than having the theme of mutual trust and support, this type of organizational climate is characterized by one-sided respect: the respect of management for itself. This self-centered love affair permeates communications, relationships, the leadership styles that are predominantly autocratic. Management is truly its own best friend in this environment. Workers, like children in some households, are second-class citizens. They are to be seen but not heard. Employees are to do the bidding of management, whether the orders make sense or not. Communication is purely top town. Feedback from employees is not encouraged or accepted. Mistakes made by workers are treated as personal affronts to management and as opportunities to punish the culprits. As a result of this primitive, critical parent to adapted child relationship, workers either spend a lot of time rebelling (through slowdowns, strikes, or grievances) or play it safe by capitulating to the dictatorial rule. Innovation is at a minimum, as employees fear that a novel approach to a problem may not be accepted by management. A lot of energy is expended by employees in maintaining a low profile and in "covering their hindquarters," rather than in producing. Mediocrity is often the order of the day. David McClelland, the noted Harvard psychologist, points out that people who are dominated by their leaders tend to make very inefficient workers (2).

I'm Not OK, You're OK:
Management by Abdication

This type of organizational climate can be aptly expressed by the football expression "Drop back and punt." Management, afraid to take on the responsibilities assigned to them, either stays "perched on the fence" or abdicates. Buck passing goes on at all levels. As a result, when problems arise it takes a lot longer to solve them—*if* they are solved at all. In this type of climate it's difficult to figure out who is responsible for what. Because management is weak willed, it fails to back up employees when required. By not standing up for them at meetings with other, more competent bosses, this manager loses salary increases or needed office materials for his or her employees. Also, in such an environment, there is often a lot of scapegoating. By blaming others or by talking them down behind their backs, managers get a false sense of superiority and, at the same time, they are able to misdirect any criticism away from themselves. I recall the case of a large accounting firm in which a number of partners would routinely spend weeks of time on their own family accounts, which cost the firm thousands of dollars in salaries. Rather than confronting these delinquent partners or setting up some formal policy for dealing with disciplinary matters, the senior partners just complained among themselves. Morale suffered to the point that many of the most productive accountants left the firm. Many simply got tired of carrying the "dead weights," realizing that management was too gutless to do anything about it. Oh, occasionally the senior partners would discharge a helpless secretary or other office worker without even a reprimand. However, this was only a scapegoating tactic that even further emphasized their adapted child gutlessness.

If these types of organizations survive at all, they only do so at half speed. Less scrupulous employees have a field day exploiting weak-willed managers. Certainly, no one respects them.

I'm Not OK, You're Not OK:
Management by Chaos

There is little to say about this type of organizational climate except to say the obvious: It does not last long. Any organization managed like this is surely courting disaster. This type of organization has a malfunction at all ego state levels. People do not know what their responsibilities are or what they should be doing (the parent is contaminated); people do not know how to go about doing things (the adult is contaminated); and people don't care (the child is contaminated also). This type of organization might be characterized as a ship without a rudder—without even a destination. If the ship lands somewhere, it happens purely by chance. Because goals are unclear, no one knows if it was the right place to land anyway. In this type of organization people are not punished for their mistakes, but they do not learn from them either. They simply keep making the same errors over and over again. Although no organization can tolerate this chaotic state for long periods, some pass through it when they acquire other businesses they know little about or when they grow so quickly (as might happen through a merger) that they simply cannot handle the volume of business. Some brokerage houses have collapsed after mergers with other houses because of chaos in their accounting departments. After an acquisition one large brokerage house became so chaotic that to a large extent it did not know who owned what stock. In one case a woman wrote the house for a brochure. By mistake she was mailed a check for over $25,000. For a good while, the house did not realize the mistake had been made (3).

THE IDEAL ORGANIZATIONAL SCRIPT

The ideal organizational script, of course, is rooted in the supportive climate of I'm OK, You're OK. In this climate people work with each other and employee talents are developed to the fullest. People are not exploited.

Fordyce and Weil, authors of *Managing with People* and two experts in the organizational development field, view the healthy organization as being similar to the way one would view a healthy individual: responsive to change, independent, enthusiastic, and mature in handling relationships. In TA terminology, their portrait of the ideal, healthy type of organization parallels the personality of the organizational winner developed in chapter four* with the emphasis on the development

* See chapter four for portraits of the organizational winner and organizational loser.

of the adult (independent judgment and maturity), the free child (creativity and enthusiasm) and the nurturing parent (cooperation and support). On the other hand, Fordyce and Weil view the unhealthy organization as being similar to the way one would view an immature or unhealthy personality: dependent, rebellious, defensive, and overly traditional and narrow in perspective (4). This portrait is the same as that of the organizational loser developed in chapter four and characterized by the strongly predominant uses of the adapted child (dependent, rebellious, and defensive because of the lack of security in self often demonstrated by this ego state) and the critical parent (traditional, opinionated, and reluctant to change).

Fordyce and Weil give more specifics of what they consider characteristics of ideal types of healthy versus unhealthy organizations. They view the healthy characteristics as leading to a generally more effective organization both in terms of productivity and morale (5). In the following exhibit, ego states are added to their characteristics to demonstrate the flavor of the relationships from a TA perspective.

ORGANIZATIONAL WINNING AND LOSING SCRIPTS (6)
Some Characteristics of Unhealthy and Healthy Organizations[a]

	Unhealthy	Healthy[b]	
CP-AC[c]	1. Little personal investment in organizational objectives except at top levels.	1. Objectives are widely shared by the members and there is a strong and consistent flow of energy toward those objectives.	A-A
AC-AC	2. People in the organization see things going wrong and do nothing about them. Nobody volunteers. Mistakes and problems are habitually hidden or shelved. People talk about office troubles at home or in the halls, not with those involved.	2. People feel free to signal their awareness of difficulties because they expect the problems to be dealt with and because they are optimistic that they can be solved.	A-A

ORGANIZATIONAL WINNING AND LOSING SCRIPTS (6) *(continued)*

Some Characteristics of Unhealthy and Healthy Organizations[a]

	Unhealthy	Healthy[b]	
CP-AC	3. People at the top try to control as many decisions as possible. They become bottlenecks, and make decisions with inadequate information and advice. People complain about managers' irrational decisions.	3. The points of decision making are determined by such factors as ability, sense of responsibility, availability of information, work load, timing, and requirements for professional and management development. Organizational level, as such, is not considered a factor.	A-A
CP-AC	4. Personal needs and feelings are side issues.	4. The range of problems tackled includes personal needs and human relationships.	NP-FC
RC-RC	5. People compete when they need to collaborate. They are very jealous of their area of responsibility. Seeking or accepting help is felt to be a sign of weakness. Offering help is unthought of. They distrust one another's motives and speak poorly of one another; the manager tolerates this.	5. Collaboration is freely entered into. People readily request the help of others and are willing to give in turn. Ways of helping one another are highly developed. Individuals and groups compete with one another, but they do so fairly and in the direction of a shared goal.	NP-NP
CP-AC (which are gamey ego states)	6. Conflict is mostly covert and managed by office politics and other games, or there are interminable and irreconcilable arguments.	6. Conflicts are considered important to decision making and personal growth. They are dealt with effectively, in the open. People say what they want and expect others to do the same.	(any combination of NP, A, and FC or game free ego states)

221

ORGANIZATIONAL WINNING AND LOSING SCRIPTS (6) *(continued)*
Some Characteristics of Unhealthy and Healthy Organizations[a]

	Unhealthy	Healthy[b]	
RC-CP	7. Learning is difficult. People don't approach their peers to learn from them, but have to learn from their own mistakes. They reject the experience of others. They get little feedback on performance, and much of *that* is not helpful.	7. There is a great deal of on-the-job learning based on a willingness to give, seek, and use feedback and advice. People see themselves and others as capable of significant personal development and growth.	A-A
CP-AC	8. The manager is a prescribing father to the organization.	8. Leadership is flexible, shifting in style and person to suit the situation.	A-A
CP-AC	9. "One mistake and you're out."	9. "What can we learn from each mistake?"	A-A
CP-AC	10. Tradition?	10. There is a sense of order, and yet a high rate of innovation. Old methods are questioned and often give way to new ones.	A-A and FC-FC

[a] Fordyce and Weil actually list twenty-three characteristics. I have chosen ten that I think give a key summary of their analysis.
[b] The description of a healthy organization may appear millennialist. It is perhaps more a statement of direction than a state that has been achieved by any known organization.
[c] These relationships refer mainly to the relationship between boss and subordinate unless otherwise indicated by the characteristic. For example, bosses who make all the decisions for subordinates would be treating them critical parent to adapted child (or CP to AC).

ORGANIZATIONAL DEVELOPMENT

While management development and employee development are concerned with making the manager and the employee more effective, organizational development (OD) concentrates on improving the effectiveness of the organization as a whole or some large section of it. The primary focus of organizational development is behavioral change. OD asks a few basic questions such as: What is the organizational climate like in this organization and what are the relationships between and among individuals in the organization? How can we change the climate and the relationships in order to improve morale and productivity in terms of what the goals and purposes of the organization should be? One OD researcher put it rather simply: Where is the organization now? Where would organizational members like to be? How can we better help the members reach the desired outcome? (7)

Fundamentally, OD is concerned with behavioral change on a large scale. OD thus requires a long-term commitment on the part of many organizational members, especially top management. If top management is not commited to the long-range changes in values, philosophies, and relationships required by OD, the change will either not take place or it will not last. Top management, because of its power in terms of monetary and policy matters, ultimately determines the direction an organization takes. One cannot expect lower level employees to be committed to something to which their bosses only give lip service.

Usually, it is necessary to use outside consultants as the agents for change. Although in-house consultants or trainers will play a valuable role in helping to maintain the new climate and relationships, outside help is often needed to bring about the initial change. Even if in-house behavioral consultants have the expertise to bring about a successful change, other organizational members will likely view them with suspicion and distrust. Somewhat personal morale data has to be gathered in any OD effort. Members are often afraid that such data will be used against them, especially if it is collected by someone who is a member of their organization and who may be on friendly terms with higher-ups. Additionally, experts are often viewed as individuals from "out of town"—people outside the organization. Also, if morale problems are serious enough, it may take a totally dispassionate third party to resolve conflicts. In-house people may be viewed as part of the problem or as biased.

In choosing a consultant, it is essential that the individual under consideration has both behavioral and business competence. In his book, *Organization Development and Change,* Edgar Huse comments that OD is concerned with making people competent—effective and efficient—as well as happy (8).

A training director of a large sales-oriented organization tells the sad story involving a psychologist who was hired as a consultant for employee development purposes:

> In order to increase sales, we hired a psychologist as a consultant for our various agencies. If a salesperson wished to, he or she had the option of speaking to the analyst for free. No one was compelled to see the psychologist.
>
> One particular salesman, who was a top producer, began seeing the psychologist on a regular basis. The psychologist would encourage him to dig into his past to uncover any childhood conflicts which he felt might affect his current functioning. The salesperson became aware of problems he did not know existed before. In fact, he became fixated on childhood conflicts and personal problems to the extent that his sales volume substantially decreased. The salesperson got to the point where he spent most of his time drawing up lists and reports of past and current psychological data to give to the psychologist each week. All his production energy was so consumed in analytical problem searching that he had little left for prospecting and calling on customers.

Script theory is an ideal tool for organizational development. Like OD, script theory is concerned with the basic questions of: Where is the organization now? Where is it going? Where should it be going? Script theory is also concerned, like OD, with the basic values and philosophies underpinning the behavioral aspects of the organization. An understanding of management's life position provides an excellent insight into the overall philosophical position of the organization.

Any OD process, analyzing any subject or problem, requires an initial diagnosis (9). I find the following script questionnaire very helpful in any initial diagnostic work on an organization.

THE SCRIPT QUESTIONNAIRE (10)

1. Think of your organization as a person. If your organization were a person, what kind of person would he or she be? (Some organizations are so large that it may be more useful to deal only with your department, team, etc. You may wish to do both.)

2. If it's possible, recall the founding person (or persons) of your organization. What were the policies established by this person? What policies are still adhered to? Are they appropriate to meet the needs of today?

Often founding fathers were innovative in their time, but their policies have become rigid. Many times people feel "stuck" with attitudes that seem irrelevant today. If you are in an organization that still reflects a person, ask yourself: What would he or she do in the situation we have today? You may find a creative answer.

3. What would the ego state portrait of your organization look like? Would any of these fit?

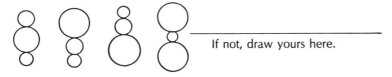

If not, draw yours here.

4. How would the above affect *your* ego state portrait as a worker? Draw yourself in relationship to your organization, using various ego state sizes.

5. How would your customers picture your organization?

6. What are the primary games played in your organization? Specifically, what can be done to eliminate or reduce these?

7. Is your organization a healthy place for people? What are the arbitrary or punitive requirements made of employees? What are the nurturing activities towards employees?

8. Does your organization have a theme (that is, staying on top, plodding along, trying hard, making it big, going downhill)?

9. What are the *stated* goals of your organization? What are the *real* goals? How do they differ?

10. If your organization continues doing what it's doing now, where will it be in five years? In ten years? Where will you be in relationship to this organization?

11. List as many of the sacred traditions of your organization as you can. Which of these are rational? Which can be changed? Which need to be changed? Is anything being done about them?

12. What did your organization fail to do this year that it should have done? What did it do that it shouldn't have done?

13. List eight characteristics of an organization that you see as *winning* characteristics.

14. List eight characteristics of an organization that are likely to be *losing* characteristics.

15. List eight major characteristics of your organization.

16. Do the organization's rules allow for freedom in decision making and creativity, or do they suggest restrictive parental dictums?

17. Have the organization's rules changed over time? What were they like when the company started? What are they like today?

18. Out of what life position do the organization's rules appear to be generated? If you could make changes in the existing rules, how would you change them?

19. How could the organization be changed to facilitate problem solving and to improve the relationships among its members?

20. What life positions does management hold toward itself and its employees (that is, I'm OK, You're OK, etc.)? How does management demonstrate these life positions?

NOTES

1. For an excellent discussion of the impact of organizational climate on member communications, see: William V. Haney, *Communication and Organizational Behavior: Text and Cases,* 3d ed. (Homewood, Ill.: Richard D. Irwin, Inc., 1973), pp. 15–16.

2. David C. McClelland, "The Two Faces of Power," *Journal of International Affairs* (1970), vol. 24, no. 1, p. 41.

3. Richard E. Rustin, *"Shades of the '60s:* Wave of Paper Work Floods Paine Webber; Back Office Is Chaotic," *Wall Street Journal,* 7 July 1980, p. 1.

4. Jack K. Fordyce and Raymond Weil, *Managing with People: A Manager's Handbook of Organization Development Methods* (Reading, Mass.: Addison-Wesley Publishing Co., Inc., 1971), pp. 8–10.

5. Forydyce and Weil, *Managing with People,* pp. 8–14.

6. Jack K. Fordyce and Raymond Weil, *Managing with People: A Manager's Handbook of Organization Development Methods,* © 1971, pp. 11–14. Reprinted with permission.

7. C. Lundberg, "Organization Development: Current Perspectives and Future Issues," paper presented to the Southeast Chapter of the American Institute for Decision Sciences, 1974, p. 1.

8. Edgar F. Huse, *Organization Development and Change* (St. Paul, Minn.: West Publishing Co., 1975), p. 14.

9. For an excellent but concise summary of typical steps in the OD process, see: Keith Davis, *Human Behavior at Work: Organizational Behavior,* 5th ed. (New York: McGraw-Hill Book Company, 1977), pp. 180–181.

10. Questions 1–5, 7–8, and 10–15 are taken from Dorothy Jongeward and others, *Everybody Wins: Transactional Analysis Applied to Organizations.* © 1973. Reprinted by permission of Addison-Wesley Publishing Co., Inc., Reading, Mass.

TYPICAL ORGANIZATIONAL SCRIPTS
Or Why Did I Have to Land in This Organization?

12

Following are some typical organizational scripts with which most of us are familiar. In fact, the scripts may be viewed as "pure" types, with most organizations possessing a number of these different script elements to one degree or another. The fundamental purpose of this analysis is to accomplish what I tried to accomplish in chapter four (on individual scripts): (1) If you can identify a number of the script elements in your own organization, I hope this chapter will help your work to restage a more successful work environment; (2) By being aware of your organization's script or the script of a competitive organization, I hope to help you better cope with political tactics and organizational manipulations (where there are people, there are politics); and (3) Additionally, I hope these scripts will help organizational consultants get a better overall feel for the types of organizational entities they may be confronting. In the end, redecisions or script changes on any level—individual, group, or organizational—*can* be made and *have* been made. However, it takes an enlightened management and the long-range commitment of all organizational members to significantly change the course of an organizational "ship." I hope this analysis will help in bringing about constructive changes.

Don't Rock the Boat, Inc.

Life Course. There are few who have not worked in or with this type of organization. Everything is fine and dandy provided nobody makes waves. Organizational members are expected to rock along like obedient, doped-up children. Even if managerial decisions do not make any rational sense in terms of the goals and the purposes of the organization, no one is to question why. Most especially, none are to challenge management on any decisions of any consequence. Even if top management establishes a hard and fast policy bent on mediocrity and the ultimate destruction of the organization, everybody is expected to sail along like schooners on a clear lake.

Villeré and Razek discuss how management often installs and maintains the don't rock the boat script:

> A "skillful" way to accomplish the "don't rock the boat" goal is to keep employees on the defensive. Immobilized through worry and fear, such employees are paralyzed into maintenance functions. As the military and a number of church organizations have demonstrated, it's hard to be innovative if you are constantly in the process of protecting yourself from a drill sergeant or an imminent prospect of Hell. Employees are kept on the defensive by lowering positive recognition to a minimum, dramatizing errors, and pushing a steady flow of "don't" memos down the line so that "no's" are the order of the day. Rarely (except occasionally by accident) is praise given or are methods and strategies set up for stimulating enthusiasm and creativity (1).

In the long run the organization loses its best talents. They head for greener, more productive organizational pastures. Mediocrity becomes the order of the day, along with organizational stagnation. In more competitive environments the "don't rock the boat" life course ends in organizational death or bankruptcy.

Goals. Formally stated: progress, achievement, and employee involvement; in reality: mediocrity and "don't do anything to disrupt the status quo."

Managerial Life Position. I'm OK, You're Not OK (Don't you ever question any of our decisions.)

Rules:
Don't make waves.
Don't succeed.
Do as you are told.
Be mediocre.

Games. "Now I've Got You, You S.O.B." (How dare you try to achieve something around here?) and "Blemish" or "Let's Sweat the Small Stuff" (If we can get them to fool around with the insignificant stuff, they may forget to accomplish anything meaningful.)

Antithesis. Management finally realizes (and in the case of many of these scripts, an outside consultant may be needed to help in the realization) that the "don't rock the boat" philosophy may ultimately mean no "boat" at all. Ways of creatively challenging employees to expand the use of their talents are actively explored and utilized. Employees are invited to participate, at least in terms of feedback, in establishing organizational priorities and policies. "Don't messages" are replaced by "do messages." Innovation is encouraged and rewarded at all organizational levels. With a devotion to this new spirit of innovation, positive motivation and employee involvement, the organization is well on its way to becoming an industry leader rather than a marginal hanger-on.

Penny Pinchers Unlimited

Life Course. This is the script of the penny-wise and pound-foolish organization. It will not spend a thousand dollars to bring in an extra one hundred thousand dollars worth of business. The total emphasis is on the cost side of the business. Organizations such as this are often run by accountants or engineer types. Obviously, it is impossible to stereotype. However, someone who has been through the Great Depression or whose training is on the cost side of the ledger might have a tendency to tunnel his or her vision on expenses. Corporations that store away a lot of cash are prime targets for acquisition. More frequently, the overemphasis on conservation will prevent them from buying the necessary equipment or paying the necessary salaries to attract top talent. Because they sow little, they reap little in revenues. The penny pincher gets what it pays for, which is not much.

Additionally, in overly tightly run organizations so much emphasis is placed on counting pennies that management does not have time to plan, to make policies, or to be on the lookout for good investments or opportunities.

> My boss doesn't have time to get this department properly organized. She is too busy checking little things—paper clips used, the cost of stationery, the use of file folders, and the okaying of any purchase over five dollars.

Needless to say, morale and productivity suffer. Employees either leave because they get fed up with pinching pennies and doing without or else they emulate management by fixating on cost and not much else.

Goals. Formally stated: profit maximization; in reality: cut costs at any cost, regardless of the effect on profits.

Managerial Life Position. I'm OK, You're Not OK (I'd better watch every little purchase, or you will steal me blind.)

Rules:
Don't spend.
Conserve, conserve, conserve.
Be frugal at all costs.

Games. "Blemish" or "Let's Sweat the Small Stuff" (I'd rather spend four hours chasing a penny down an elevator shaft than invest an hour and $10 on lunch with a customer to close a $100,000 sale.) and "Wooden Leg" or "My Excuses Are Better Than Yours" (for not spending money).

Antithesis. After losing a lot of business and top personnel to competitors, management sobers up to the fact that you have to spend money to make money. By finally concentrating on both sides of the ledger, profits increase as revenues appreciate much faster than costs. Morale and recruiting sparkle also, as salaries become competitive and employees do not feel that Scrooge is constantly looking over their shoulders. Management improves greatly, as meager cost tasks are delegated to office managers and clerks.

Red Tape, Inc.

Life Course.   In this type of organization the means become more important than the ends. Forms, protocol, formalities, rules and regulations, and procedures become more important than effectiveness. Personnel are denied easy access to information, equipment, bosses, or customers through all sorts of bottlenecks. Customers become very frustrated also:

> All I wanted to do was give them back some money. My refund was too great. Well, they told me to contact customer service, who had me fill out a complaint form even though I had no complaint. Then I was sent to financial services who told me I had to fill out a financial inquiry form. Then . . . to heck with it. Next time I'm keeping the ten dollars.

Red tape comes about for a variety of reasons. Some organizations indulge in it to avoid work. As one manager stated: "We never have any customer complaints around here. We hit them with so many forms and waiting lines that few complain."

Some organizations are very distrustful of everyone. Personnel have to fill out forms and document everything they do—even trivial things. In other cases rules set down by the prescribing fathers became sacred, even though they are cumbersome and outdated. For example, there is a large bank that requires all tellers to balance out with an adding machine because they have been doing it that way for 100 years. Tellers take hours to balance out. They also make many more mistakes than computerized teller machines which do the job almost instantaneously.

Possibly the biggest script culprit behind the red tape script is the federal government. Almost any organization of any size spends thousands of person hours and hundreds of thousands of dollars filling out government forms. It is estimated that American organizations spend around $40 billion a year filling out federal government reports and forms (2).

The following story, which I received from a reliable source, "takes the cake."

> I know of an attorney who was requested to fill out some very lengthy questionnaires for a federal agency on some heavy construction equipment. He wrote back to the agency saying that he was a lawyer and that there must be some mistake, as he did not own a construction business. The agency wrote back insisting that he fill out the forms or suffer the consequences. He spent the better part of the day filling out the forms with imaginary items—so much earth moving equipment, bulldozers, etc. He claimed that this was the only way he could get the agency out of his hair.

Ultimately, the organization becomes so tangled in its own procedures, forms, and government red tape that it almost comes to a halt.

Goals. Formally stated: efficiency through accountability; in reality: maintenance of sacred rules and forms.

Managerial Life Position. I'm OK, You're Not OK (If I don't check on you with my million forms, you will get away with murder.)

Rules (millions upon millions of them):
Don't succeed (fill out forms instead).
Be busy, not effective.
Be accountable.

Games. "Blemish" or "Let's Sweat the Small Stuff" (It is not important whether you make a profit or not. Did you fill out my forms?) and "I'm Only Trying to Help You" (by getting you to fill out all these forms).

Antithesis. An efficiency expert is called to help eliminate all the unnecessary procedures and forms. Reports and procedures are only useful when they help meet the overall goals and objectives of the organization. When they hinder the attainment of goals and objectives they should be eliminated, like any bottleneck. The personnel involved begin to support the management that is interested in furthering organizational effectiveness and not red tape.

Management Is Its Own Best Customer Corp.

Life Course. In this type of organization management preëmpts everything—including real customers, effective problem solving, and personnel—in order to glorify its own status.

Fordyce and Weil comment about another unhealthy organizational characteristic:

> Status and boxes on the organization chart are more important than solving the problem. There is an excessive concern with management as a customer, instead of the real customer (3).

Perquisites, such as a company car or an officer's washroom, should go with a manager's job. However, in "management is its own best customer," luxuries become excessive. Complaints plead for common sense.

> There are no spots for our customers to park because many managers have two parking spots.

> He's no engineer. He does not know a darn thing about structures. But because he is the boss he'll ignore our advice just to prove he's got the power. Watch the bridge collapse.

> Making profits is not important. Serving customers is not important. Improving employee relations is not important. Our job is to cater to management's every whim, even if it makes no sense at all.

I am not preaching child rebellion here. However, what I am saying is that if organizational status becomes more important than serving customers or problem resolution, the price to be paid will indeed be high.

Many a kingdom has collapsed because homage to princely whims and desires became more important than meeting the needs of the realm. Eventually the organization suffers severely from the sheer weight of its pomposity. Talent flees to competitors who put stock in expertise along with organizational position.

235

Goals. Formally stated: reward comes through selflessly serving the organization; in reality: selflessness is for everyone *but* management.

Managerial Life Position. I'm OK, You're Not OK (Management is king, and you serfs better believe it.)

Rules:
Don't be important (only management counts).
Don't question (management is unapproachable even by customers).
Be obedient.

Games. "I'm Only Trying to Help You" (by making all the decisions myself) and "Uproar" or "Who Can I Attack First" (for even thinking of questioning my infinite authority).

Antithesis. Management finally wakes up to the reality that management's main function is to serve others. If the needs of customers and personnel are not met, there will be no kingdom over which to rule. Management also realizes that true strength is built on a solid foundation of expertise and shared relationships. Management begins to spread positive strokes, particularly by listening to and learning from customers and subordinates. The dividends returned in profits and morale are many times more than commands could ever elicit.

No Rules, Just Referees, Inc.

Life Course. This is the script of an organization that is extremely political in nature. Rather than having specific criteria for promotion, for example, people are promoted because they are friends of the referees, the promotion committee. In other words, promotions, decisions, policies, and objectives are decided on the basis of political alignments. The primary objective is to keep the powers that be in office, not to do what is good for the organization or its people. Objective and rational criteria are never used, even if they exist (they rarely do). The "no rules, just referees" script demonstrates very clearly that any decision can be rationalized away to support political self-interests:

Gosh, we can't promote Dr. Jones to the associate level. He has only published twenty articles, three books, and delivered thirty papers at professional meetings. Too much of his stuff, although in top journals, is faddish in nature. On the other hand, Dr. Delaney (a friend of the senior professors) demonstrates a commitment and competence to the organization rarely equaled. (He has one book review in a second-rate journal and is not even as good a teacher as Dr. Jones.) If we don't promote Delaney to the associate level, he may leave.

Now, gentlemen, to some of you this decision to again do over the executive suites may not make sense. (It doesn't, with a capital "d".) But, how are we going to properly entertain clients in one-year-old-offices?

The "no rules, just referees" organization is run like a football game in which the visiting team (not considered to be a member of the referees' political camp) can never win. Every time the visiting team crosses the goal line, the referees either call an infraction or move the goal posts back.

"No rules, just referees" is often utilized in order to keep the incompetents in power positions. In other words, the Peter Principle (4) is maintained through the "no rules, just referees" script.

In the long run, mediocrity or conflict becomes the order of the day. The best talents, who are threats to the referees because of their competence, leave for professionally-run organizations. Employees who lack the mobility to leave or who would like to see the organization achieve something stay and fight the good fight. Grievances are filed. If minorities or women are involved, the Equal Employment Opportunity Commission is called in. The E.E.O.C. has a field day, as promotion criteria are supposed to be based on objectively tested job-related or performance data, *not* on the capricious whims of superiors (5).

Goals. Formally stated: to bring the best talent along; in reality: to keep the incompetents in office.

Managerial Life Position. I'm OK, You're Not OK (for those who are not in management's political camp).

Rules:
Whatever we want them to be at any given moment.
Anything can be rationalized.
Don't make it (for those in the wrong political camp).

Games. "Cornered" or "Heads You Lose and Tails You Lose" (for those not in my political camp); "Wooden Leg" or "My Excuses Are Better Than Yours" (I've got more ways of rationalizing decisions than anyone.); and "Smoke Screen" (Referees can always fake their incompetence.)

Antithesis. The organization receives a court judgment for millions of dollars for discriminating practices. Survival, along with government pressure, forces the powers that be to place the emphasis on pragmatics rather than on political favoritism. The most incompetent individuals retire early or are kicked upstairs into positions in which they will have minimum visibility and minimum impact on other organizational personnel. In the less dramatic case, consultants are called in to improve the performance picture. They demonstrate clearly that political alignments that impede progress and effectiveness serve no one, including the in-group. It is the competitors who reap the greatest benefits when an organization sinks into decadence and its top producers flee to other borders.

Uproar Unlimited

Life Course. In this organization management thinks that it has to constantly make "waves" in order to keep subordinates on their toes. It is basically a management by harassment philosophy.* The assumption of management is that workers have to be constantly badgered or harassed in order to be motivated.

One "uproar" manager put it this way:

> If my employees are too comfortable, they become stagnant. I've got to constantly think of ways to upset their inertia. The more I yell at them and the more I surprise them with impromptu or impossible deadlines the better.

Managers who indulge in "uproar" are often poor planners and policy makers. By keeping employees constantly in motion and in turmoil,

---

* For a review of the management by harassment approach, see chapter three.

their own incompetency is not as visible. Also, they can always say: "Who has time to plan? There are too many fires to put out."

As mentioned in chapter three, on motivation, some stimulation and anxiety improves the functioning of the adult. Too much reduces adult effectiveness and often brings out the rebellious child.

Eventually employees tire of the constant badgering. Many leave for more tranquil waters, where they are given the time and support to solve problems meaningfully. The "uproar" climate fans more fires than it puts out. Additionally, people get tired of "running around like chickens with their heads chopped off." Other employees, especially blue-collar workers, get so tired of harassment that they form unions in order to protect themselves. Others rebel through slowdowns or sabotage.

Goals.   Formally stated: to get the best from our people through stimulation; in reality: to run employees around in circles.

Managerial Life Position.   I'm Not OK, You're Not OK ("management by chaos" for those managers who are masking their own incompetence) and I'm OK, You're Not OK (for those managers who simply like to make waves).

Rules:
Jump, jump, jump.
Being in motion is more important than knowing where you are going.
Don't think—just do.

Games.   "Uproar" or "Who Can I Attack First?" and "Smoke Screen" (While everyone is running around in circles, they won't see that we don't know what we are doing.)

Antithesis.   Management begins to realize that employees learn a lot more when they are challenged than when they are harassed. Management begins to concentrate on ways to tap employees' free child creative juices and adult capacities through meaningful projects. Management also solicits employee feedback in developing plans and policies. Through a commitment to teamwork, employees and management become productive collaborators rather than enemies.

Cutthroat Enterprises

Life Course.   To a certain extent, the "cutthroat" script is an extreme version of the "uproar" script. Rather than being contented with constantly putting employees off balance through harassing tactics, the "cutthroat" manager often plays for keeps. Anyone who gets in the way is disposed of through termination. In the "cutthroat" organization, managers are often prima donnas who tolerate little or no argument or disagreement. As with the infamous British ruler of the sixteenth century, Henry VIII, "heads are lopped off" in the form of firings without notice—and with little cause.

> We (the personnel department) worked for weeks before finding a bilingual receptionist for the international department. The head of the international department comes in from Europe a week later and I happen to see him in the men's room. In a gruff voice he says, "I don't give a damn if she has resigned her other job and needs this one to support her kid. I don't like her lipstick. Get her butt out. I don't want to have to look at her tomorrow.

In the "cutthroat" organization, employees—particularly at higher levels—are pitted against one another to see who will survive. Because competition is keen and ruthless, communication between organizational members is infrequent and always guarded. It is the most vicious employees, *not* the most competent or creative ones, who usually rise to the top. Sometimes such tactics backfire.

A common tactic of an executive assassin is to get the victim out of town for a training program, a business trip, or a vacation. While the victim is gone, he or she is terminated or set up for termination by having past mistakes exposed and dramatized to superiors. While the mouse is away, the cat gets set to prey. One politically astute potential victim realized that a business trip was a setup by his boss. While out of town, he spent a lot of time circulating his boss's credentials. He landed his boss a job at another company, knowing full well that his boss was too incompetent to keep the job. When he returned from the business trip, his boss had departed for the new company and he got his boss's job. Two months later his former boss was terminated for incompetence, just as he had suspected (6).

Often, the "cutthroat" organization operates on the philosophy that the "grass is always greener" elsewhere. Thus, organizational members are constantly removed in favor of new blood. In the long run the talent well runs dry and hiring becomes a nearly impossible task as the word gets out at employment agencies and search firms.

Goals. Formally stated: we are dedicated to those who are willing to compete; in reality: one mistake and you're out.

Managerial Life Position. I'm OK, You're Not OK (Nail the bastards when you can.)

Rules:
Take no prisoners.
I'll get you before you get me.
Don't be close (or someone will nail you).

Games. "Now I've Got You, You S.O.B."; "I'm Your Friend" (just turn around so I can knife you); and "Let's You and Him Fight."

Antithesis. After the majority of the most productive people are run off or scared off, management wakes up to the fact that the cupboard is bare. A truce is finally called. Organizational members are encouraged to work *with* each other rather than *against* each other. Value is placed on bringing talent along rather than on seeing who can knock who from his or her perch. Objective criteria is set up for promotions as well as for terminations. Also, appeal procedures are established to make sure that all employees get a fair deal. Mistakes are treated as opportunities for learning, *not* for "nailing." This time the favorable word hits the labor market. Top personnel are attracted— better than the personnel ever obtained previously. The humane approach pays off in higher morale and higher productivity than the "cutthroat" approach could ever dream of.

Founder's Club, Inc.

Life Course. "To the founders go the spoils" is the motto of this organizational script. Mainly prevalent among first generation organizations, the "founder's club" relegates all authority, rank, and privilege on the basis of who joined the organization first. Even if the founding fathers are incompetent now or have become obsolete in their skills, they are still given the "divine" right to rule. "Grandfather clauses," exempting the founding guys and gals from even minimum requirements, are the order of the day in these types of organizations. Some universities, for example, have extra research demands placed on those who teach graduate courses. Sometimes, however, the earliest members of the graduate faculty are exempt from increasing research requirements placed on newer members.

Over time, overall organizational morale and productivity suffer in this hypocritical type of organizational climate. Founding members place high demands on others, but few on themselves. As one "founder's clubber" stated: "It is an organizational fact of life that some of us have to do nothing. After all, we got here first."

It is also an organizational fact of life that decadent leadership may inspire a number of things. Industry, enthusiasm, and effectiveness are not among these things, however.

The "founder's club" script often comes about from an overindulgent nurturing parent hierarchy. The rationale being:

> They helped us when we were trying to get off the ground, when the organization was founded. Few others would take a chance on a new operation. We owe them special respect and privileges for helping us to get going.

Granted, loyal founding members of an organization should be afforded some special respect. I am not suggesting that those who have given their best years to an organization should be cast aside like a worn out part or piece of equipment as was the fate of Willy Loman, the traveling salesman and central character in Arthur Miller's Pulitzer Prize winning play, *Death of a Salesman*. Willy had given his life to the company, over thirty years, and he was getting old. The son of a previous owner, Howard Wagner, would not even give him the opportunity to pursue a less strenuous inside job. To Howard, business was business, regardless of the devotion an employee had given to his company (7). Every opportunity should be explored to retrain older personnel or to employ them in less demanding jobs.

However, if the job has outgrown the man or older workers have become remiss in their duties or obsolete in their skills and are unwilling to retrain, they should not be placed in positions of leadership over far more competent and industrious new personnel. The poor example set by decadent leaders can have a devastating impact on morale.

> I had to quit that R&D firm. I came out of school excited and eager to put my inventive talents to work. I end up in a branch office with a number of older scientists who take three-hour lunch breaks and then spend the afternoon at their desks sleeping off the booze they consumed at lunch. Management said they invented some of the company's big money-making products and thus have earned the right to coast. The only inspiration I got from them was a strong desire to leave.

Goals. Formally stated: we bring the best talent along; in reality: regardless of their contribution or negative impact, to the founders go the spoils.

Managerial Life Position. I'm OK, You're Not OK (I am wonderful because I got here first. You are nothing because you did not.)

Rules:
Don't belong (only those in the "founders' club" get the special privileges).
Don't be important (you got here later and thus are not among the élite).
Pay homage to your founders.

Games. "Blemish" or "Let's Sweat the Small Stuff" (on those who got here late); "Cornered" or "Heads You Lose and Tails You Lose" (for those not in the élite group); and "Ain't I Wonderful" (I'm a founder.).

Antithesis. Management continues to give good strokes to those who have devoted their lives to the organization. Management does everything practical to retrain or relocate older members. However, management also realizes that overindulgence is a grave mistake. Newer, more competent members are also given opportunities to share their innovative ideas with the rest of the organization. Expertise and achievement, *not* seniority, become the prime criteria for promotion. The script shifts from a rendezvous with decadence to a rendezvous with prosperity.

NOTES

1. Maurice F. Villeré and Joseph R. Razek, "Organization Snafus and What to Do," *Louisiana Business Survey,* vol. 9, no. 2 (April 1978), p. 13.
2. Michael LeBoeuf, *Working Smart: How to Accomplish More in Half the Time* (New York: McGraw-Hill Book Company, 1979), p. 143.
3. Jack K. Fordyce and Raymond Weil, *Managing with People: A Manager's Handbook of Organization Development Methods* (Reading, Mass.: Addison-Wesley Publishing Co., Inc., 1971), p. 11.
4. Laurence J. Peter and Raymond Hull, *The Peter Principle: Why Things Always Go Wrong* (New York: William Morrow & Co., Inc., 1969).
5. For an excellent synopsis of the Supreme Court's rulings concerning equal employment selection devices, see: Thaddeus Holt, "Personnel Selection and the Supreme Court," in *Contemporary Problems in Personnel,* rev. ed., eds., W. Clay Hamner and Frank L. Schmidt (Chicago, Ill.: St. Clair Press, 1977), pp. 147–159.
6. For a very provocative look at executive cut throat tactics like this one, see: Lawrence Lindeman, "The Executive Stiletto," *Playboy,* vol. 16, no. 7 (July 1969), pp. 101–159.
7. Arthur Miller, *Death of a Salesman* (New York: The Viking Press, 1949), pp. 79–82.

BIBLIOGRAPHY

ORGANIZATIONAL BEHAVIOR
BOOKS AND SOURCES

ADORNO, THEODOR W.; FRENKEL-BRUNSWICK, E.; LEVINSON, D. J.; AND SANFORD, R. N. *The Authoritarian Personality.* New York: Harper & Row, Publishers, Inc., 1950.

BLAUNER, ROBERT. *Alienation and Freedom.* Chicago, Ill.: University of Chicago Press, 1964.

BLOOD, MILTON R. "Intergroup Comparisons of Intraperson Differences: Rewards from the Job," *Personnel Psychology,* vol. 26, no. 1 (1973), pp. 1–9.

BOWERS, DAVID G., AND SEASHORE, STANLEY E. "Predicting Organizational Effectiveness with a Four-Factor Theory of Leadership," *Administrative Science Quarterly,* vol. 11, no. 2 (1966), pp. 238–263.

BROWN, LELAND. *Communicating Facts and Ideas in Business.* Englewood Cliffs, N.J.: Prentice-Hall, Inc., 1961.

BUNKER, DOUGLAS R., AND DALTON, GENE W. "The Comparative Effectiveness of Groups and Individuals in Solving Problems." In *Managing Group and Intergroup Relations,* edited by Jay W. Lorsch and Paul R. Lawrence, pp. 204–208. Homewood, Ill.: Richard D. Irwin, Inc., 1972.

BYHAM, WILLIAM C. "The Assessment Center as an Aid in Management Development." *Training and Development Journal,* December 1971.

DAVIS, KEITH. *Human Behavior at Work: Organizational Behavior.* 5th ed. New York: McGraw-Hill Book Company, 1977.

FIEDLER, FRED E., AND CHEMERS, MARTIN M. *Leadership and Effective Management.* Glenview, Ill.: Scott, Foresman & Company, 1974.

FORDYCE, JACK K., AND WEIL, RAYMOND. *Managing with People: A Manager's Handbook of Organization Development Methods.* Reading, Mass.: Addison-Wesley Publishing Co., Inc., 1971.

FRENCH, WENDELL L.; BELL, JR., CECIL H.; AND ZAWACKI, ROBERT A., EDS. *Organization Development: Theory, Practice, and Research.* Dallas, Tex.: Business Publications, Inc., 1978.

GIBB, CECIL A. "Leadership." In *The Handbook of Social Psychology,* vol. 4, 2d ed., pp. 205–282. Reading, Mass.: Addison-Wesley Publishing Co., Inc., 1969.

GLUECK, WILLIAM F. *Cases and Exercises in Personnel.* Rev. ed. Dallas, Tex.: Business Publications, Inc., 1978.

GLUECK, WILLIAM F. *Personnel: A Diagnostic Approach.* Rev. ed. Dallas, Tex.: Business Publications, Inc., 1978.

GOMERSALL, EARL R., AND MYERS, M. SCOTT. "Breakthrough in On-the-Job Training." *Harvard Business Review* (July–August 1966), pp. 62–71.

GORDON, THOMAS. *Leader Effectiveness Training L.E.T.: The No-Lose Way to Release the Productive Potential of People.* New York: Wyden Books, 1977.

HAMNER, W. CLAY. "Worker Motivation Programs: The Importance of Climate, Structure, and Performance Consequences." In *Contemporary Problems in Personnel.* Rev. ed. Edited by W. Clay Hamner and Frank L. Schmidt, pp. 256–284. Chicago, Ill.: St. Clair Press, 1977.

HAMPTON, DAVID R.; SUMMER, CHARLES E.; AND WEBBER, ROSS A. *Organizational Behavior and the Practice of Management.* 3d ed. Glenview, Ill.: Scott, Foresman & Company, 1978.

HANEY, WILLIAM V. *Communication and Organizational Behavior: Text and Cases.* 3d ed. Homewood, Ill.: Richard D. Irwin, Inc., 1973.

HUSE, EDGAR F. *Organization Development and Change.* St. Paul, Minn.: West Publishing Co., 1975.

JANIS, IRVING L. *Victims of Groupthink: A Psychological Study of Foreign-Policy Decisions and Fiascos.* Boston: Houghton Mifflin Company, 1972.

KELL, CARL, AND CORTS, PAUL R. *Fundamentals of Effective Group Communication.* New York: Macmillan, Inc., 1980.

KELLY, JOE. *Organizational Behaviour.* Homewood, Ill.: Richard D. Irwin, Inc., and Dorsey Press, 1969.

KELLY, JOE. *Organizational Behaviour: An Existential-Systems Approach.* Rev. ed. Homewood, Ill.: Richard D. Irwin, Inc., 1974.

KOONTZ, HAROLD, AND O'DONNELL, CYRIL. *Principles of Management: An Analysis of Managerial Functions.* 4th ed. New York: McGraw-Hill Book Company, 1968.

LAU, JAMES B. *Behavior in Organizations: An Experiential Approach.* Rev. ed. Homewood, Ill.: Richard D. Irwin, Inc., 1979.

LEAVITT, HAROLD J. *Managerial Psychology:* An Introduction to Individuals, Pairs, and Groups in Organizations. 2d ed. Chicago, Ill.: University of Chicago Press, 1964.

LEBOEUF, MICHAEL. *Working Smart: How to Accomplish More in Half the Time.* New York: McGraw-Hill Book Company, 1979.

LIEBERMAN, MORTON A.; YALOM, IRVIN D.; AND MILES, MATTHEW B. "Encounter: The Leader Makes the Difference." *Psychology Today,* vol. 6, no. 10 (March 1973), pp. 69–76.

LIKERT, RENSIS. *New Patterns in Management.* New York: McGraw-Hill Book Company, 1961.

LINDEMAN, LAWRENCE. "The Executive Stiletto." *Playboy,* vol. 16, no. 7 (July 1969), pp. 101–159.

LUNDBERG, C. "Organization Development: Current Perspectives and Future Issues." Paper presented to the Southeast Chapter of the American Institute for Decision Sciences, 1974.

LUTHANS, FRED, AND KREITNER, ROBERT. *Organizational Behavior Modification.* Glenview, Ill.: Scott, Foresman & Company, 1975.

MASLOW, ABRAHAM H. *Motivation and Personality.* New York: Harper & Brothers, 1954.

McCLELLAND, DAVID C. "The Two Faces of Power." *Journal of International Affairs,* vol. 24, no. 1 (1970), pp. 29–47.

McGREGOR, DOUGLAS. *The Human Side of Enterprise.* New York: McGraw-Hill Book Company, 1960.

PETER, LAURENCE J., AND HULL, RAYMOND. *The Peter Principle: Why Things Always Go Wrong.* New York: William Morrow & Co., Inc., 1969.

PORTER, LAWRENCE C. "Group Norms: Some Things Can't Be Legislated." In *Readings Book for Laboratories in Human Relations Training* 1972 ed. Edited by Cyril R. Mill and Lawrence C. Porter. Washington, D.C.: NTL Institute for Applied Behavioral Science, Associated with the National Education Association, 1972, pp. 34–36.

RAZEK, JOSEPH R., AND VILLERÉ, MAURICE F. "Five Do's and Don'ts of Business Communication." *Louisiana Business Survey,* vol. 9, no. 3 (July 1978), pp. 11–12.

RUSSELL, G. HUGH, AND BLACK, JR., KENNETH. *Human Behavior in Business.* New York: Prentice-Hall, Inc., 1972.

Rustin, Richard E. *"Shades of the '60's:* Wave of Paper Work Floods Paine Webber; Back Office Is Chaotic." *Wall Street Journal,* 7 July 1980, p. 1.

Schwab, Donald P., and Cummings, Larry L. "Theories of Performance and Satisfaction: A Review." *Industrial Relations,* vol. 9, no. 4 (October 1970), pp. 408–430.

Schein, Edgar H. *Organizational Psychology.* Englewood Cliffs, N.J.: Prentice-Hall, Inc., 1965.

Sibson, Robert. "The High Cost of Hiring." *Nation's Business,* February 1975, pp. 85–88.

Steers, Richard M., and Porter, Lyman W. *Motivation and Work Behavior.* New York: McGraw-Hill Book Company, 1975.

Stogdill, Ralph M. *Handbook of Leadership.* New York: Macmillan, Inc./ Free Press, 1974.

Strauss, George, and Sayles, Leonard R. *Personnel: The Human Problems of Management.* 3d & 4th eds. Englewood Cliffs, N.J.: Prentice-Hall, Inc., 1972.

Tannenbaum, Robert, and Schmidt, Warren H. "How to Choose a Leadership Pattern." *Harvard Business Review* (May–June 1973), pp. 162–180.

Taylor, Frederick W. "Shop Management." A paper read before the American Society of Mechanical Engineers, June 1903.

Tillman, Jr., Rollie. "Problems in Review: Committees on Trial." *Harvard Business Review,* 38 (May–June 1960), pp. 6–12 and 162–172.

Trice, Harrison M. "Alcoholism and the Work World." *Sloan Management Review,* no. 2 (Fall 1970), pp. 67–75.

Villeré, Maurice F., and Stearns, G. Kent. "The Readability of Organizational Behavior Textbooks." *Academy of Management Journal,* vol. 19, no. 1 (March 1976), pp. 132–137.

Villeré, Maurice F.; Stearns, G. Kent; and Lacho, Kenneth J. "The Human Side of Performance Appraisal." *Business,* vol. 29, no. 6 (Nov.–Dec 1979), pp. 46–48.

Villeré, Maurice F., and Razek, Joseph R. "Organization Snafus and What to Do." *Louisiana Business Survey,* vol. 9, no. 2 (April 1978), pp. 13–14.

Vroom, Victor H. *Some Personality Determinants of the Effects of Participation.* Englewood Cliffs, N.J.: Prentice-Hall, Inc., 1960.

Vroom, Victor H. "Some Personality Determinants of the Effects of Participation." *Journal of Abnormal and Social Psychology,* vol. 59, 1959, pp. 322–327.

Vroom, Victor H. *Work and Motivation.* New York: John Wiley & Sons, Inc., 1964.

WILLITS, ROBIN D. "Company Performance and Interpersonal Relations." *Industrial Management Review,* vol. 8, no. 2 (Spring 1967), pp. 91–107.

TA BOOKS AND SOURCES

ACUFF, FRANK L., AND VILLERÉ, MAURICE F. "Games Negotiators Play." *Business Horizons,* vol. 19, no. 1 (February 1976), pp. 70–76.

BERNE, ERIC. *Games People Play: The Psychology of Human Relationships.* New York: Grove Press, Inc., 1964.

BERNE, ERIC. *Transactional Analysis in Psychotherapy: A Systematic Individual and Social Psychiatry.* New York: Grove Press, Inc., 1961.

"Business Tries Out Transactional Analysis." *Business Week* (12 January 1974), pp. 74–75.

DUSAY, JOHN M. *Egograms: How I See You and You See Me.* New York: Harper & Row, Publishers, Inc., 1977.

ELY, DONALD D., AND MORSE, JOHN T. "TA and Reinforcement Theory." *Personnel,* vol. 51, no. 2 (March–April 1974), pp. 38–41.

ERNST, FRANKLIN. "The OK Corral: The Grid for Get-on-With." *Transactional Analysis Journal,* vol. 1, no. 4 (October 1971), pp. 231–240.

HARRIS, THOMAS A. *I'm OK—You're OK: A Practical Guide to Transactional Analysis.* New York: Harper & Row, Publishers, Inc., 1969.

JAMES, MURIEL ET AL. *Techniques in Transactional Analysis: For Psychotherapists and Counselors.* Reading, Mass.: Addison-Wesley Publishing Co., Inc., 1977.

JAMES, MURIEL, AND JONGEWARD, DOROTHY. *Born to Win: Transactional Analysis with Gestalt Experiments.* Reading, Mass.: Addison-Wesley Publishing Co., Inc., 1971.

JAMES, MURIEL, AND JONGEWARD, DOROTHY. *The People Book: Transactional Analysis for Students.* Reading, Mass.: Addison-Wesley Publishing Co., Inc., 1975.

JONGEWARD, DOROTHY ET AL. *Everybody Wins: Transactional Analysis Applied to Organizations.* Reading, Mass.: Addison-Wesley Publishing Co., Inc., 1973.

JONGEWARD, DOROTHY, AND SEYER, PHILIP C. *Choosing Success: Transactional Analysis on the Job.* New York: John Wiley & Sons, Inc., 1978.

KARPMAN, STEPHEN B. "Fairy Tales and Script Drama Analysis." *Transactional Analysis Bulletin,* 7, no. 26 (April 1968), pp. 39–43.

"Labor Letter." *Wall Street Journal,* vol. 63, no. 6 (9 January 1979), p. 1.

LEBOEUF, M. MICHAEL, AND VILLERÉ, MAURICE F. "Tambo—Applying TA to MBO." *Atlanta Economic Review,* vol. 25, no. 2 (March–April 1975), pp. 29–35.

MILLING, EILEEN. "A New Way to Improve Effectiveness on the Job." *Nation's Business* (July 1975), pp. 65–68.

RUSH, HAROLD M. F., AND MCGRATH, PHYLLIS S. "Transactional Analysis Moves into Corporate Training: A New Theory of Interpersonal Relations Becomes a Tool for Personnel Development." *The Conference Board Record,* vol. 10, no. 7 (July 1973), pp. 38–44.

STEINER, CLAUDE M. *Scripts People Live: Transactional Analysis of Life Scripts.* New York: Grove Press, Inc., 1974.

VILLERÉ, MAURICE F. "Transactional Analysis: An Effective Management Tool." *Louisiana Business Survey,* vol. 7, no. 2 (April 1976), pp. 2–4.

VILLERÉ, MAURICE F., AND DUET, CLAUDE P. *Successful Personal Selling Through TA.* Englewood Cliffs, N.J.: Prentice-Hall, Inc., 1980.

WOOLLAMS, STAN, AND BROWN, MICHAEL. *The Total Handbook of Transactional Analysis.* Englewood Cliffs, N.J.: Prentice-Hall, Inc., 1979.

OTHER BOOKS AND SOURCES

ALBRECHT, KARL. *Brain Power: Learn to Improve Your Thinking Skills.* Englewood Cliffs, N.J.: Prentice-Hall, Inc., 1980.

BRYANT, PAUL W., AND UNDERWOOD, JOHN. *Bear: The Hard Life and Good Times of Alabama's Coach Bryant.* Boston, Mass.: Little, Brown & Company, 1974.

BUGELSKI, B. R. *The Psychology of Learning Applied to Teaching.* 2d ed. Indianapolis, Ind.: The Bobbs Merrill Co., Inc., 1971.

HOLT, THADDEUS. "Personnel Selection and the Supreme Court." In *Contemporary Problems in Personnel.* Rev. ed. Edited by W. Clay Hamner and Frank L. Schmidt. Chicago, Ill.: St. Clair Press, 1977, pp. 147–159.

MILLER, ARTHUR. *Death of a Salesman.* New York: The Viking Press, 1949.

OSBORN, ALEX F. *Applied Imagination.* Rev. ed. New York: Charles Scribner's Sons, 1957.

SHAKESPEARE, WILLIAM. *As You Like It,* act 2, scene 7.

SHAKESPEARE, WILLIAM. *Hamlet Prince of Denmark,* act 1, scene 4.

INDEX